The Uncertain Self:
Whitman's Drama of Identity

THE

UNCERTAIN SELF:

WHITMAN'S

DRAMA OF IDENTITY

by
E. FRED CARLISLE

MICHIGAN STATE UNIVERSITY PRESS

1973

FOR
BENJAMIN T. SPENCER

Acknowledgements

I have been writing this book for several years, and during that time, I have received support and advice from a number of people and agencies. I wish to thank the Department of English at Michigan State University for giving me a term free from teaching to write part of this book and the College of Arts and Letters for providing financial support for the preparation of the manuscript. I appreciate all of the criticism given by my friends and colleagues from those early suggestions by William Petrek, Walker Gilmer, and Robert K. Johnson to the more careful and detailed criticism offered by Bernard Paris, Randal Robinson, and Howard Anderson. They have all in some way helped make this a better book than it would have been otherwise. I am grateful to Russel B. Nye; his generosity and support has helped bring this book to completion. I owe considerable gratitude to Edwin H. Cady; he has been encouraging and advising me for over ten years now. And finally, I dedicate this book to Benjamin T. Spencer—a remarkably humane man, an excellent critic and scholar, and a brilliant teacher.

Contents

Preface

I charge you forever reject those who would expound me, for
    I cannot expound myself.

I give you fair warning before you *attempt me further,*
I am not what you suppose, but far different.

Even while you should think you had unquestionably caught
    me, behold!
Already you see I have escaped from you.[1] (Italics added.)

Whitman's warnings alone should caution, if not intimidate, any
critic who presumes to contain Walt Whitman in an essay or a
book; and they do, especially if one tries literally to "expound"
him—to deal with the self or identity of Walt Whitman. The volume of criticism and scholarship about Whitman and his poetry
should also caution the critic—surely Whitman's poetry has been
inspected, detected, reflected, and dissected so much that one
had better simply read and experience, rather than read and explain, again.
    I do not claim to have expounded Whitman absolutely—I am as
baffled at times by him as he was by himself; and surely I will refer
to and repeat much that critics have already thought and said. Yet
I am not just performing someone else's music or reciting another
man's ideas. I am, instead, trying to supply a new context for reading
Whitman's poetry—a context that enables a reader to deal with all
of the poetry.
    Both in his poetry and his prose Whitman speaks, time and again,
of identity or self as his central concern. In the *Preface, 1876,* for
example, he refers to *Leaves of Grass* as a "Poem of Identity": "Then
I meant *Leaves of Grass,* as published, to be the Poem of Identity,
(of *Yours,* whoever you are, now reading these lines). . . . For genius
must realize that, precious as it may be, there is something far more
precious, namely, simple Identity, One's-self."[2] Likewise, his poems
refer repeatedly to the self. In the very first poem in *Leaves of Grass*
Whitman claims to speak for the self:

One's-self I sing, a simple separate person,
Yet utter the word Democratic, the word En-Masse.

And he begins his first major poem with similar lines:

I celebrate myself, and sing myself,
And what I assume you shall assume,
For every atom belonging to me as good belongs to you.

He speaks for himself, but as I shall explain in my first chapter, he speaks of a self that emerges and exists *mainly* in relationships with others.

D. H. Lawrence was one of the first modern critics to recognize Whitman's concern with identity. Lawrence apparently thought, however, that Whitman failed to discover a meaningful self or to write a coherent poem of identity, for he taunted Whitman—"Oh, Walter, Walter, what have you done with it? What have you done with yourself? With your own individual self? For it sounds as if it had all leaked out of you, leaked into the universe."[3] And he attacked him for trying to merge with all and for sacrificing himself as a result: "He wasn't keeping to his open road. He was forcing his soul down an old rut. He wasn't leaving her free. He was forcing her into other peo-ple's circumstances."[4] I cannot accept Lawrence's diffusion theory of Whitman's identity, nor can I agree that the relationships so central to *Leaves of Grass* somehow constitute a loss of self. Nevertheless, it is clear that Lawrence discovered Whitman's major theme.

Since that time, many Whitman critics and scholars have tried to define the poetic and personal identities of Walt Whitman. Several of them, curiously enough, seem to agree with Lawrence because they argue, in effect, that Whitman sings significantly only when he speaks of the solitary, private, or lyric self whose experience consists of a series of goings out and comings in, but who never engages in any essential relation with the not-self. Whether they argue that Whitman is a humanist or a mystic, for them the meaningful reality in Whitman lies in the solitary soul—in the monologue the simple separate person speaks to the world. When Whitman claims that the self in relation to others or to the world constitutes the most mean-ingful reality, many critics no longer listen or care.[5] I disagree with them, too, because I think that Whitman discovers his essential self only when he experiences genuine dialogue with the world and with others. But that disagreement and others aside, for the moment: my

point is that regardless of their differences, critics pretty much agree
with V. K. Chari that the "whole of his [Whitman's] poetic effort was
centered in the exploration of the nature of the self."[6]

I have been concerned, primarily, in this book with describing the
complex, contradictory identity of Walt Whitman that emerges from
Leaves of Grass and with showing how problematic Whitman's identity and human situation were. "Problematic of identity" could describe the dilemma of critics—so few agree about the nature of the
self in *Leaves of Grass*. However, it more appropriately applies to
the nature of the self, its situation in the world, and its emergence
in the process of living. Identity *was*, for Whitman, a life-long endeavor. It involved contradiction and ambiguity, confusion and uncertainty, as well as clarity and confidence; in the process, Whitman
experienced failure as well as fulfillment.

The genuine doubt and occasional despair Whitman expresses in
his poetry reveal his sense of the problematic. His dramatization of
many varieties of personal experience also indicates his uncertainty
about the nature of the self and the world. Furthermore, the poetry
concentrates on the concrete, the moment, and the particular response, and thereby presents identity as a continuing experiment—
indeed as a problematic endeavor. Once more, I disagree with critics, notably V. K. Chari, who argue that Whitman's identity was
achieved, realized, and fixed by 1855 when he first published *Leaves
of Grass*,[7] nor can I agree with critics like Denis Donoghue who
argue that identity was never a problem for Whitman.[8]

By concentrating on the personality present in *Leaves of Grass*
rather than on Whitman's rhetoric, his rhythm, or his form (on the
poem as an art object), I may be thought guilty of some sort of
personalist deviation. Yet I think I am simply responding to modern
criticism's frequent failure to make poetry personal enough. Critics
have too often forgotten that a poem is a word; one spoken between
man and man; a word which embodies the voice and presence of the
poet. The reader who encounters a Whitman poem with this in mind
—who engages, actually, in a dialogue with a poet-in-the-poem—
begins to hear the voice of the poet; he begins to experience the
presence of the man who may be dead, yet who lives in the spoken
language of the poem. The reader can then no longer deal with the
poem simply as an object for analysis or classification;[9] he must,
instead, first respond to Walt Whitman—to the voice and vision embodied in the poem—with *his* whole person. Each poem differs from

every other and, therefore, the voice in one differs somewhat from the voice in every other. But when we read many poems by Walt Whitman, the voices begin to complete and confirm one another, and thus each poem becomes a moment in a continuing dialogue between the poet and his reader. From that dialogue—from the whole body of Whitman's poetry—a coherent, describable personal existence does emerge.[10] That personal existence—that identity—is what I am trying to grasp.

My study of identity in Whitman might be described as a psychological biography of Whitman's poetic persona, and in this sense it is analogous to a biography. Eliseo Vivas, for example, has said that biography involves a careful selection of the important aspects of a life, a creative apprehension of action and character, and the development of a coherent story.[11] A successful biography reveals a coherent personal existence—it determines the shape and meaning of its subject's life. A reader can discover the identity present in a body of literary work in much the same way. Instead of using the biographer's materials, however, the critic grasps the poet through a "constitutive symbol," the poem, for the presence and personality of the poetic persona are available only through the verbal action—the spoken word—of the poem.

If one thinks of a literary work as a moment in a continuing dialogue and as an art object, he implicitly identifies two types of criticisms—what Walter J. Ong designates as empathic criticism and explicatory criticism.[12] Modern critics, by and large, have practiced the second, and all know its value. Too few, however, realize that the other can deal more satisfactorily with certain key critical problems in Whitman and in poetry generally.

First, there is the problem of boundaries. As a moment in dialogue, a poem is discrete from every other moment or poem and from history (it is a unique art object), but at the same time the poem is part of the larger body of poetry—part of a continuing dialogue— that expresses a writer's literary personality and, in some way, his historical personality and world. In one sense the work does possess a certain closed quality. However, it also has an "'open' or unbounded historical potential," and in this sense it is very unlike a discrete object. Considered this way, the poem no longer need be torn apart by the autonomous-referential paradox.

The modern emphasis on the discrete, autonomous work of art has made Whitman's poetry impossible for some critics; his intrusive personality and his repeated attempts to *involve* his reader put them off. Other critics have worked to justify Whitman in the terms of objective criticism. That has been necessary and quite valuable, but explicatory criticism does not explain Walt Whitman and *Leaves of Grass*.

Second, an emphasis on dialogue and on the personal presence of the poet show that, as moments in dialogue, poems resist framing by type or genre much as they resist the boundaries objective criticism places on them. A larger unity exists to which all of a poet's poems belong than type or genre can define. "The basis for this unity is that they [the various poems] are all the utterances, the word, of one man." In Whitman's case, particularly, rhetorical or generic analysis simply does not contain him. For example, it forces one critic—in one of the best critical books on Whitman—to say at the end of his discussion of "When Lilacs Last in the Dooryard Bloom'd": "So 'Lilacs' can be said to be about an especially active kind of reading, activity at once intellectual and imaginative."[13] It seems to me something is missing—and that is Walt Whitman. The primary unity of *Leaves of Grass* is *Whitman*—not genre (not even one so large as the epic), nor rhetoric, nor even explorations in form.

Third, once one recognizes the dialogical nature of poetry, "the role of the critic becomes both cleared and more complicated." The critic understands that the poem is not just an object for analysis; it is, instead, a spoken word that engages the reader and calls on him to respond. The critic's words embody part, at least, of his response. Regarding poetry in this way helps explain and justify the critic's constant involvement in the work—an involvement he often tries to resist. Whitman, however, refuses to cooperate in that resistance, for he invites, often demands—reader engagement.

If the personal existence of Walt Whitman gives *Leaves of Grass* a certain wholeness, two conclusions follow. First, it becomes possible and necessary to treat the book as a single, unified work in which every poem exists simultaneously with every other. Chronology is not so important in this case (although it is not irrelevant) as the total dialogue which contains single poems and single moments as well as separate experiences and a variety of voices. Second, I must work with the final edition of *Leaves of Grass*, the 1891–1892 edition, for only there can one discover the complete literary personality and personal existence of Walt Whitman. Whitman's book evolved through nine separate editions. He progressively added many poems and excluded others, changing for some readers the quality of his poetry and the image of himself. But for all his revisions and exclusions, Whitman at no time disavowed any aspect of himself. He preserved the unity of his life and the integrity of his work. He preserved, in effect, the problematic of his identity.

NOTES—*Preface*

1. Walt Whitman, "Myself and Mine" and "Whoever You Are Holding Me Now in Hand," *Leaves of Grass: Comprehensive Reader's Edition* (New York, 1965). All subsequent quotations from the poetry will be from this edition.
2. "Preface, 1876," *Leaves of Grass: Comprehensive Reader's Edition* (New York, 1965), p. 750. Subsequent quotations from the prefaces will be from this edition.
3. D. H. Lawrence, "Whitman," *Whitman: A Collection of Critical Essays*, ed. Roy Harvey Pearce (Englewood Cliffs, N. J., 1962), p. 13.
4. Lawrence, p. 21.
5. Roy H. Pearce, e.g., argues in *The Continuity of American Poetry* for the ego-centric or Adamic nature of Whitman's poetry; R. W. B. Lewis says, e.g., that Whitman "was above all the poet of the self and of the self's swaying motion—outward into a teeming world where objects were 'strung like beads of glory' on his sight; backward into private communion with the 'real Me.' " (*Trials of the Word* [New Haven, 1965], p. 35) For Lewis the real Me is discovered apparently only in the private, inner self. John Kinnaird shares a similar view, see *"Leaves of Grass* and the American Paradox," in *Whitman*, ed. R. H. Pearce. Although V. K. Chari's view is quite different from the others, he defines a separate and supreme self, also.
6. V. K. Chari, *Whitman in the Light of Vedantic Mysticism* (Lincoln, Neb., 1964), p. 12.
7. V. K. Chari, p. 69: "The years from 1848 to the appearance of the first *Leaves* represented the poet's struggle for self-expression, as the years preceding it marked the struggle for self-discovery. The inner conflicts and tensions of his early life were now at rest; Whitman had achieved inner peace."
8. See his chapter on Whitman in *Connoisseurs of Chaos: Ideas of Order in Modern Poetry*.
9. Martin Buber, *I and Thou* (New York, 1965), p. 128.
10. Buber, *Between Man and Man* (New York, 1965), p. 15.
11. Eliseo Vivas, "The Self and Its Masks," *Southern Review*, I, pp. 317–336.
12. Walter J. Ong, "A Dialectic of Aural and Objective Correlatives," *The Barbarian Within* (New York, 1962), pp. 34–40. This and the next four paragraphs follow Father Ong's argument fairly closely.
13. The book is *Whitman: Explorations in Form* by Howard Waskow (Chicago, 1966). It is an excellent book; some of his interpretations of single poems are better than most other published ones. Nevertheless, I do think his scheme weakens toward the end of the book. It is very difficult to isolate, as he does, so few poems as poems of dialogue (of

"reader engagement") and, conversely, to exclude so many other poems. Waskow is right, but not entirely right. And that is my point about
rhetorical or generic criticism: it must frame individual works in a way
that they must, in turn, resist. Part of my difficulty doubtless arises from
our different purposes. Waskow's approach is primarily rhetorical or
formalist. He treats Whitman's work as a poetry primarily about poetry,
and it is. My approach treats Whitman's poetry as the presence of a
personality, and it is that, too.

PART ONE

CHAPTER ONE

Walt Whitman's Open Road

"Song of the Open Road" dramatizes Whitman's entrance onto a road that leads through the world, toward others, and eventually to a threshold of self-discovery. By entering the open road Whitman escapes "indoor complaints, libraries, querulous criticisms," and the whimpering and selfish grasping that cause people to lead lives of desperation within the petty, sterile limits of conventional society. But Whitman rejects only the creeds and schools that stifle others and threaten to suppress him. He does not seem to assert absolute freedom from limits because he still carries his old burdens with him and cannot escape them:

> (Still here I carry my old delicious burdens,
> I carry them, men and women, I carry them with me where-
>   ever I go,
> I swear it is impossible for me to get rid of them,
> I am fill'd with them, and I will fill them in return.)

Whether the burdens are the "men and women" themselves or whether Whitman is speaking to "men and women" about his burdens makes no difference, for in either case Whitman is saying that he cannot escape his past experience. In some way, he is bound to other persons or limited by the past. He is not absolutely free.

Nor is he completely free from limits in the present, for Whitman must learn the "profound lesson of reception" that the road teaches; on it "none but are accepted"—no person and no aspect of life is denied. So, at the beginning of his journey, Whitman must free himself from the limits and conventions that would prevent self-discovery, but at the same time he must unconditionally accept his past and the world as it *is*. His journey begins with a paradox: he must reject *and* accept.

From the beginning, when Whitman takes to the open road and exclaims that the earth is sufficient, until the end, when the poet extends his hand to his companion and to his reader, he insists on the actual existence and value of the road as well as on the need of accepting all he finds there. Besides that the road possesses a symbolic significance, as Whitman repeatedly says: "much unseen is also here"; the road is "latent with unseen existence." Both senses of the road persist throughout the poem, and neither yields significance to the other because they are not experientially separable—meaning and being must exist together. The freedom Whitman experiences, the acceptance he gives, and the meaning-in-being he senses are basic conditions that must prevail before Whitman's journey will carry him very far.

Section 5 begins to develop the implications of these conditions. At the beginning, Whitman finds that he is "loos'd of limits and imaginary lines" and of the "holds that would hold him." Thus, he can inhale "great draughts of space," and he finds himself better than any of the creeds, conventions, or moralities by which he has previously been limited. The road becomes a new ground of experience where the poet can discover the "soul" and "the reality and immortality of things." In effect, Whitman can find meaning and identity on the road. His new freedom and his commitment to the world of the road enable him to penetrate fact and the lived moment to discover the meaning that lies within it and that emerges from it. At the same time, he discovers "the efflux of the soul," which comes from within and which surely constitutes Whitman's potential "real me" or real self. As Whitman sees further into external reality, as he encounters more and more of the world on the road, he sees more deeply into himself. The actions are simultaneous in this poem and suggest that the meaning of the road and of the self depend absolutely on one another, if they are not one.

The imagery of section 8, which virtually fuses the fluid efflux of the soul with the sweat of love, emphasizes the fusion of the "soul" with the body and with others. From these meetings the self seems to emerge:

Here rises the fluid and attaching character,
The fluid and attaching character is the freshness and sweetness
    of man and woman,
(The herbs of the morning sprout no fresher and sweeter every
    day out of the roots of themselves, than it sprouts fresh and
    sweet continually out of itself.)

Toward the fluid and attaching character exudes the sweat of
    the love of young and old,
From it falls distill'd the charm that mocks beauty and attain-
ments,
Toward it heaves the shuddering longing ache of contact.

Although the lines imply that soul body and other are unreal entities,
or at best, partial distinctions, such a conclusion goes beyond the
evidence of "Song of the Open Road," for the poem does not quite
reveal what self or soul is, or what the meaning in the world or within
may be. It presents the conditions for discovery, and in this sense it
leads poet, companion, and reader no further than the threshold.

The second part of the poem establishes yet one more essential
condition for self-realization. Although Whitman does not say in so
many words that genuine self-discovery occurs only through a dialogue between man and man, the poem, nevertheless, suggests in
section 7 the *possibility* for dialogue first and then indicates in sections 14 and 15 the apparent necessity for any successful journey. In
earlier sections Whitman started to establish relationship with objects and people. That is, he accepted them and entered the road to
meet them, but he gave no indication that the relationship with
others was reciprocal. By the middle of the poem, however, he
speaks of a real possibility for reciprocal communication or dialogue
with others:

Why are there men and women that while they are nigh me the
    sunlight expands my blood?

What is it I *interchange* so suddenly with strangers?
What with some driver as I ride on the seat by his side? (italics
    added)

and with nature—

Why are there trees I never walk under but large and melodi-
    ous thoughts descend upon me?

In silent communication with the physical world, in a virtual touch,
in a look, or in a conversation with another person the poet experi-

ences unstated, probably momentary, yet complete dialogue.

Shortly after dialogue becomes possible, the poem moves into a third stage as Whitman challenges others to join him, and significantly he begins to speak of *we* ("Allons!—Let us go"). From this point until the end, the poet consistently refers to *we* or to *he* and *me* or to *I* and *you:*

> We will sail pathless and wild seas . . .
> He travelling with me needs the best blood, thews, endur-
>   ance . . .
> Listen! I will be honest with you.

These lines also indicate that the other will experience difficulties should he accept the challenge and join the poet. For Whitman really means that they must accept the brute facts of experience (the rude earth and rude nature). He actually intends for them to follow untrodden paths, to suffer, to be mocked, and to be constantly moving —never satisfied or complete. Indeed, he *does* not "offer the old smooth prizes"—those found indoors in the complacency, security, and desperation of inauthentic lives. He urges others to cast off the living "stale cadaver" and the lives of "secret silent loathing and despair." He insists that they seek "rough new prizes" on an endless, beginningless *open* road of rebellion and discovery where relationship is essential and where identity is a process.

The final stage of the poem confirms these points. It ends with the poet standing with another, ready to depart once more on a never ending journey of self-discovery. He has challenged both his reader and any man or woman to follow him—if they dare; and he has revealed both the hardships and the rewards of the journey. At the end, he offers his hand; in effect, he offers himself and asks that his reader and his companion in the poem offer themselves in return.

I suggested before that in "Song of the Open Road" Whitman rejects the conventions and limitations of social, political, and moral institutions, and thereby finds himself larger and better than he had thought. Yet he does not seem to reject as unreal or as escapable the existential limits of human life lived in time and history. This distinction is important, for one can assume too easily that being "loos'd of limits and imaginary lines" means total and absolute freedom from all limits—historical, psychological, or existential. But Whitman still carries the old burdens, and he discovers himself in the very world from which he is presumably free. If this distinction is valid, then key lines in "Song of the Open Road" assume more accurate and precise meanings than they otherwise have. In section one, for example, Whitman believes that the road will lead "wherever I choose," and in a sense it will. But perhaps the line means only that the road will lead as far as he chooses because it is endless and so are the possibilities for discovery. That does not require, however, a god-like poet with absolute freedom and power to transform creation or even a single road in it. Whitman accepts the road and existence unconditionally. Likewise, his realization that he is his "own master total and absolute" must be read in the context of the whole poem. He masters his own life because "what he has in him" directs it, for he has rejected the conventions that would instead master him. In other words, what he *is* will control him, and what he is is a self who finds relationship with the not-self both possible and necessary. He is not a self-sufficient, separate, subjective entity. So Whitman does find that the "great personal deed has room" and that he enjoys far greater freedom than before, but he still travels with others, on a road, in existence.

For all the sense of limits and of the emotional hells and spiritual deaths individuals experience, "Song of the Open Road" is an especially confident poem; it envisions defeat and despair only for those who fail to rebel and who persist in living

> Smartly attired, countenance smiling, form upright, death under the breast-bones, hell under the skull-bones.

Nevertheless, the traveller takes tremendous risks as he attempts to become whole—for the road demands unconditional acceptance, participation, commitment, and openness. Other Whitman poems make the hazards much clearer and much more real.[1] So although the poem asserts confidence, one cannot ignore the potential hazards of such radical action. Even for Whitman, as other poems will show, "becoming a whole" can be a "cruelly hazardous enterprise."[2] One does not move toward self-discovery through suppression, denial, or elimination. Instead he moves toward completeness only by plunging into existence and by encompassing all that he is—both in nature and in himself—and that *is* dangerous.

The conditions for becoming whole require the self to live a paradoxical "both-and" situation. That is, the self must both reject and accept. He rebels against the world as it is; yet he must establish dialogue with the world *as* it is, for only in that essential communication will he ultimately find the way to wholeness. The self also exists in an even deeper paradox, for it stands both over against the world (at a distance from it) *and* in the world (in relation to it). The logical paradox, however, simply describes the existential situation—the situation that Whitman lives, rather than thinks, in this poem.

"Song of the Open Road" suggests several hypotheses about Whitman's search for identity. (1) Whitman discovers that genuine self discovery demands freedom and unconditional acceptance. (2) He learns that meaning and identity emerge only in the lived moment through encounter. Although the real self may exist within, it is not a given, fixed entity just waiting there to be uncovered in all its wholeness. It is, instead, only potential and partial. (3) Dialogue or encounter requires the self to be open to the world and to others. Openness involves great risk—the risk of being damaged by the world and thus of failing to discover the self—but separation and withdrawal (indulgence of one's self as a simple, separate person) prevent any possibility for self-realization. (4) Finally, Whitman discovers that his goal is inseparable from the process or journey itself. That is, self-discovery is a process—a life long endeavor; it does not take place in a moment of mystic illumination, nor does one move steadily toward it as if it were the summit of a great mountain. It is, instead, a problematic journey through rugged and uneven country.

Martin Buber's conception of dialogue offers important insights into the matter of identity in Whitman. In an authentic dialogue man realizes the *I-Thou* relation so central to Buber's thinking; the individual experiences directness, mutuality, and the presentness of the other in a reciprocal relationship whose reality lies in neither of the members of the dialogue but in the meeting itself—in the sphere of the between or the interhuman. In other words, the conventional subject-object or self-world polarities cannot explain the ground on which dialogue occurs, for the relation takes place "between" the separate selves, and it involves the transcendence of each separate self. Buber suggests, in effect, that the sphere of the between lies neither in the individual nor in society; instead, one discovers it beyond the subject and this side of the object on "the narrow ridge, where *I* and *Thou* meet."[3] Buber suggests, also, that man grasps his complete humanity only in this fundamental reciprocity. He experiences his full humanity only by transcending the limits of the individual self.[4] The relationship, however, can seldom be sustained, for one normally has only momentary or transitory experiences of dialogue or of self-transcendence. One's experience, therefore, is dynamic—

it is a process. It consists of moments of dialogue and moments of separation. According to Buber, human life is lived somewhere in between the completely separate or isolated individual and the totally dialogical person.

In his book *Between Man and Man* Buber describes three realms of dialogue. Only one of them is the authentic or genuine dialogue in which one achieves a living, mutual relationship with the other. In genuine dialogue, "each of the participants really has in mind the other or others in their present and particular being and turns to them with the intention of establishing a living mutual relation between himself and them." Buber calls the second realm technical dialogue; "it is prompted solely by the need of objective understanding." Technical dialogue occurs because men must understand one another in some fashion to conduct the daily business of life. In most instances, however, a person's subjectivity is not involved, nor does the openness of genuine dialogue exist. The third realm is monologue which often masquerades as dialogue. "It is not the solitary man who lives the life of monologue, but he who is incapable of making real, in the context of being, the community in which, in the context of his destiny, he moves. . . . He who is living the life of monologue is never aware of the other as something that is absolutely not himself and at the same time something with which he nevertheless communicates."[6]

The first and third realms are the most important for my discussion of identity in *Leaves of Grass*. Monological man—the Romantic self —regards the world with which he comes in contact as contained wholly within *his* experience; he does not see the world (or others) as an independent, objective reality. For him the true meaning of earthly events does not lie in concrete experience but in some inner, subjective, or even mystic fulfillment. The Romantic self does not break through the glorification of self, feeling, and experience to any real concern about another person as an independent center of reality.[7] In other words, this monological man simply sees the world from the vantage point of his own interests, and therefore, his main purpose in any relationship is the assertion of his personal singularity. It is precisely this Romantic or monological self which Whitman must escape and transcend to discover the real, dialogical self. The simple separate person that Whitman *sometimes* dramatizes and that critics often read and admire in *Leaves of Grass* may be actually a limited monological man who seems to be self-sufficient and absolute in himself, yet who may be little more than one of the "faceless spectres" Buber describes.

Instead of being centered in the inner, subjective self—or grounded in external, objective reality, for that matter—the self revealed in dialogue, the essential self, emerges *beyond* the subject and *before* the object. One discovers this real self by entering into relation and thus by experiencing the sphere of the between. To define the nature of the self, then, one must concentrate on the relation of the self to the world—and not on self alone, on world alone, or on spirit. The dialogical approach to identity does not impoverish the self at all (either by letting it "leak into the universe" or by allowing an external limit to define the self); on the contrary, dialogue becomes the way to fuller realization of identity. One's openness to relation and his search for identity become parts of a single process: "as one finds more relatedness to other persons one discovers more of oneself; as one's sense of self becomes more complete he can more fully reach others."[8]

Besides the distinctions in the realms of dialogue, it is important to note three other points about it. (1) Buber's dialogue does not blur into a sentimentalized unity (there is, occasionally, that danger in Whitman); on the contrary, dialogue might well include conflict and opposition so long as they are personal and reciprocal. As long as each person recognizes the other as a person—so long as he recognizes the other's integrity and independence, treats him with respect and consideration, and allows himself to be genuinely open to the other —then dialogue can occur even in conflict. (2) Although dialogue yields the fullest human experience, self does not simply become an adjunct of the other or blur into the other, for the meaning of experience fulfills itself, again and again, Buber suggests, as self. The self retains its independence and subjectivity even though it enters fully into relationship. Thus it is not inconsistent to argue that dialogue and relationship constitute the meaningful reality in *Leaves of Grass* and at the same time to recognize that such a relationship is realized repeatedly through Whitman's "I"—the self. (3) The relationship need not occur only between two people, but it may be experienced with things in nature, artifacts, or art. Thus, the possibilities for experiencing genuine relationship extend to all corners of existence.

Buber indicates as much in "What Is Man?" when he explains the threefold living relationship which one must account for before he can know man and realize his essential humanity. The main relations are these: 1) the relationship between self and empirical or historical reality ("his relation to the world and to things"); 2) the relationship between the self and others ("his relation to men—both to individuals and to the many"); 3) the relationship between the self and spirit ("his relation to the mystery of being").[9] The first of these involves both a technical relation with things and an essential relation "which regards them in their essential life and is turned towards them." That is, the self can relate to a natural object or even an art object in "their wholeness, their independence, and their purposelessness," and in that way make the relationship essential. Buber includes both the individual and the many in the second relationship because man's situation obviously requires it and because he thinks it possible for man to make essential both his relation with another (the usual situation for I-Thou) and with the "we." He does recognize that man must escape "the nameless human all and nothing in which we are immersed" if he wishes to realize himself, yet Buber's distinction between the collective and the communal—the individual is absorbed into the mass in the collective, whereas the person retains his "I-ness" in a genuine community—emphasizes the possibility of a genuine relationship emerging between the self and the community. The third relationship, between the self and spirit, can be variously described—depending on one's own belief, and in Whitman, on the poem—as a relation "to God or to the Absolute or to the mystery"; it involves, as well, one's situation in regard to death. Buber introduces a fourth possible relationship—to one's self—but says that it cannot be regarded as essential in the same way as the others: first, although an individual might be divided in himself, no duality exists of the same order as the others; and second, no matter how complete or essential these three living relations become, man's relation to himself can never reach such completeness because it forces him to remain with himself.[10] Man experiences transcendence and fullfillment by living openly and by trying to make each living relationship essential.

My reasons for using this typology from Martin Buber are very simple. This approach not only explains Whitman's presentness, it also preserves his historicity, for it emphasizes that the self and its situation is open, not closed, and therefore identity is a process, not a finished condition. The typology also concentrates on relationship, and as I have suggested, the relational and communal in Whitman have far more importance than readers characteristically allow. Buber helps explain just how the Whitmanian self can exist in essential relationship without loss or diffusion of self; and Buber provides terms for dealing with, what I see, as Whitman's need to establish relationship with something outside the self. Consideration of Whitman from this point of view provides, as well, a contemporary context which includes man's relationship to God or the Absolute in any discussion of his total situation;[11] one must obviously include this dimension if he wishes to reach Whitman at all.

Not only is Buber's anthropological approach applicable to Whitman's search for identity in the world; it *avoids* a reductive psychologizing of Whitman (the translation of the meaning of the self and its experience into internal, psychic categories and dimensions)[12] and, I think, an equally reductive and divisive "mysticizing" of the Whitmanian experience.[13] Both approaches tend to subordinate what is *not* oneself to what is *within* the self, and thus, they ignore the essential nature of relationship in Whitman. The poet himself does, too, sometimes; but not often enough to make either approach a complete or even a very sound partial explanation. Whitman's poetry dramatizes *in its totality* the poet's attempt to become aware of the whole of life without reduction.[14]

Finally, I should say that although the living relationships provide a typology and thus an entrance into the self-world drama in *Leaves of Grass*, one cannot be content simply to divide Whitman's poems into loose, general categories, for the poems present many different versions of each relation—some essential, some inessential—sometimes there is no relation at all. One must account for all these differences—the failures and fulfillments—in any discussion of Whitman's poetic identity.

I shall try to do just that in the second part of this book—"Modes of Relation." Before that, however, I think it is necessary to discuss in some detail the poet's relationship to his poem and his sense of a twofold self. These topics have an important bearing on the identity I am trying to grasp, on the nature of that self, and on the self's relations with the world.

NOTES—*Chapter I*

1. Cf. "To You" and "Myself and Mine." They present concise, effective statements of the dangers encounter may bring. See, e.g., in "To You":

> Through birth, life, death, burial, the means are provided, nothing is scanted,
> Through angers, losses, ambition, ignorance, ennui, what you are picks its way.

Whitman suggests that the self picks its way as if the whole journey were loaded with dangers and required careful movement at every point to avoid destruction or to escape being overwhelmed by "pain, passion, dissolution." In "Myself and Mine" Whitman faces the threats that would prevent wholeness as frankly as he does in "To You," and he goes even further in recognizing the conflict and struggle necessary to escape an inauthentic life of mockeries— "I hold up agitation and conflict." That escape enables one merely to hold his own, but in this poem that in itself is a remarkable achievement. The self must be "gymnastic" and radical just to survive:

> Myself and mine gymnastic ever,
> To stand the cold or heat, to take good aim with a gun, to sail a boat,
>   to manage horses, to beget superb children,
> To speak readily and clearly, to feel at home among common people,
> And to hold our own in terrible positions on land and sea.

Many other poems dramatize those dangers, as well, and I discuss them in Chapter Four.

2. Martin Buber, *Good and Evil* (New York, 1952), p. 129.
3. Martin Buber, *Between Man and Man* (New York, 1965), p. 204.
4. "Human life possesses absolute meaning through transcending in practice its own conditioned nature, that is, through man's seeing that which he confronts, and with which he can enter into a real relation of being to being, as not less real than himself, and through taking it not less seriously than himself. Human life touches on absoluteness in virtue of its dialogical character." Buber, *Between Man and Man*, p. 167.

   "In being together the unlimited and the unconditioned is experienced." p. 168.
5. "No man is pure person and no man pure individuality. None is wholly real, and none wholly unreal. Every man lives in the twofold *I*. But

there are men so defined by person that they may be called persons, and men so defined by individuality that they may be called individuals. True history is decided in the field between these two poles." Martin Buber, *I and Thou* (New York, 1958), p. 65.

"The *I* of the primary word *I-Thou* is a different *I* from that of the primary word *I-It*.

The *I* of the primary word *I-It* makes its appearance as individuality and becomes conscious of itself as subject (of experiencing and using). The *I* of the primary word *I-Thou* makes its appearance as person and becomes conscious of itself as subjectivity (without a dependent genitive).

Individuality makes its appearance by being differentiated from other individualities.

A person makes his appearance by entering into relation with other persons.

The one is the spiritual form of natural detachment, the other the spiritual form of natural solidarity of connexion." *Ibid.*, p. 62.

6. Martin Buber, *Between Man and Man* (New York, 1965), p. 19-20.
7. cf. Maurice Friedman, *Problematic Rebel* (New York, 1963), pp. 45 ff.
8. Helen Merrell Lynd, quoted in Friedman, *Worlds of Existentialism* (New York, 1964), p. 402.
9. *Between Man and Man*, pp. 177 ff.
10. *Ibid.*, pp. 177-180.
11. *Ibid.*, p. 177.
12. This particular approach dominates, it seems to me, Edwin H. Miller's book—*Walt Whitman's Poetry: A Psychological Journey* (Boston, 1968).

Professor Miller's discussions of particular poems are frequently very perceptive and illuminating. The book, however, is limited by the psychological theory he employs. For all its sensitivity and intelligence, the book keeps coming back to Whitman's conflicts with his parents and his infantile fantasies. To me, Freud simply cannot contain *Leaves of Grass*, which expresses far more than the psychic tensions Miller identifies.

Professor Miller's preface suggests the radical difference between our approaches to Whitman. It would be hard to imagine two more different positions—especially from critics who occasionally agree about the meaning of individual poems. For Miller, Whitman's drama of identity has its "origins in unconscious and infantile sources"; and so, the tensions in the poems are psychic "and the external world is of little importance." In other words, the drama in Whitman's poetry is an "inner drama." For me, the drama involves an interaction between the self and the external world in which that world plays an essential role and in which the major tensions occur between self and other. I find interaction and mutuality in *Leaves of Grass;* Professor Miller finds neither.

13. James E. Miller Jr. (*Critical Guide to Leaves of Grass*) and V. K. Chari (*Whitman in the Light of Vedantic Mysticism*) both internalize, and therefore reduce, the Whitmanian experience of life.
14. cf. Alvin Rosenfeld's comments in "Whitman's Open Road Philosophy," *Walt Whitman Review*, 14 (March, 1968). See also, Buber, *Between Man and Man*, p. 166.

CHAPTER TWO

The Poet and His Poem

1. Distance and Relation

Whitman's apparent self-consciousness about himself and his poetry, as well as his continued exploitation of his book and personality, at times makes him sound like an egotistical Romantic who could not keep art and life straight. And he may have confused them pitiably. But Whitman also manifests a self-consciousness about his poetry that in many ways anticipates the modern poet's excruciating self-consciousness about where *he*, personally, stands in relation to the poem —the art object—and to the reader to whom he speaks through the poem. Although Whitman sometimes confused the man, the poet, and the poetic persona and failed, therefore, to fully and clearly define his role in relation to his poem, he nevertheless did express a clearer awareness of the highly complex relationship between a poet and his poem than critics have recognized. He was aware, yet he was also uncertain, for at one time he describes the poet as a detached and hidden artificer who communicates only indirectly with his reader, and at another he claims that the poet and his poem are one and that he and his reader enter into an intimate relation through the poem.

In "Whoever You Are Now Holding Me in Hand," Whitman warns his reader that he, the poet, is "not what you supposed, but far different." He means, in the first place, that one can encounter and know him only with great difficulty, for the demands he makes are much like those he made in "Song of the Open Road":

> The way is suspicious, the result uncertain, perhaps destructive,
> You would have to give up all else, I alone would expect to be
>   your sole and exclusive standard,
> Your novitiate would even then be long and exhausting,
> The whole past theory of your life and all conformity to the lives
>   around you would have to be abandon'd,
> Therefore release me now before troubling yourself any fur-
>   ther, let go your hand from my shoulders,
> Put me down and depart on your way.

The way is not easy, and therefore it may be far different from what one expects.

Second, Whitman warns his readers, even more significantly, about the speaker of the poem:

> But these leaves conning you con at peril,
> For these leaves and me you will not understand,
> They will elude you at first and still more afterward, I will
>   certainly elude you,
> Even while you should think you had unquestionably caught
>   me, behold!
> Already you see I have escaped from you.

He suggests that the identity or person of the poet is elusive, and that perhaps it is impossible ever to know him fully. Sometimes his identity remains completely hidden; at other times, only a part of it emerges. Moreover, the self continually changes and develops, so what may have been "genuine" in one poem or in one situation may no longer adequately represent Whitman's identity in another.

In "Are You the New Person Drawn Toward Me?" Whitman expresses open doubt about the possibility of ever knowing the person or the poet present in a poem:

> Are you the new person drawn toward me?
> To begin with take warning, I am surely far different from what
>   you suppose;
> Do you suppose you will find in me your ideal?
> Do you think it is so easy to have me become your lover?
> Do you think the friendship of me would be unalloy'd satisfac-
>   tion?
> Do you think I am trusty and faithful?

> Do you see no further than this façade, this smooth and tolerant
>   manner of me?
> Do you suppose yourself advancing on real ground toward a
>   real heroic man?
> Have you no thought O dreamer that it may be all maya, illu-
>   sion?

By expressing doubt, Whitman captures something of the mystery
and complexity of the self that is present throughout *Leaves of Grass.*

In both of these poems Whitman may be warning the reader, in
yet another sense, that the "I" who addresses him and calls him to
response and self-discovery is a supposed person—a fiction—and not
the personal, historical Walt Whitman who wrote the poems and who
then sat down to dinner. *Leaves of Grass* no doubt dramatizes images of the historical man, but the images are images and therefore
not the same as the existing man. Such an awareness may have
prompted Whitman's well-known reply to one of Mrs. Anne Gilchrist's impassioned expressions of love for him. Struck by the personal presence in his poems—"the divine soul embracing mine"!—
Mrs. Gilchrist first wrote Whitman in 1871. By the time she wrote in
January 1872, she was obviously confusing the man with his poem:

> If it seems to you there must needs be something unreal, illu-
> sive, in a love that has grown up entirely without the basis of
> personal intercourse, dear Friend, then you do not yourself
> realize your own power nor understand the full meaning of
> your own words, "whoso touches this, touches a man"—"I have
> put my Soul & Body into these Poems." Real effects imply real
> causes.[2]

And Whitman answered with a characteristic warning

> Dear Friend, let me warn you somewhat about myself—& your-
> self also. You must not construct such an unauthorized & *imagi-
> nary ideal Figure*, & call it W. W. and so devotedly invest your
> loving nature in it. The *actual W. W.* is a very plain personage,
> & entirely unworthy such devotion.[3] (Italics added.)

It is true; Whitman apparently was trying to solve the problem of
Mrs. Gilchrist (he evidently did not succeed, for she kept writing and
eventually came to America to meet and court him), so his reply may
mean no more than the situation called for: a disclaimer meaning
nothing but "go away!" It is also possible Whitman simply recognized
that in 1872 he was no longer the 1855-1860 Walt Whitman. The
poems I have been discussing and his prefaces confirm, however,

that his reply reflects a broader awareness than the immediate situation required.

Whitman wrote "Are You the New Person" in 1860, and he gave the poem its final form in 1867—well before his experience with Mrs. Gilchrist. Yet one can easily imagine that he directed some of the questions in the poem, if not to Anne Gilchrist, to someone like her. His letter warned Mrs. Gilchrist, much as his poem cautions his reader, "To begin with take warning, I am surely far different from what you suppose." What he tells her directly in the letter—that he is not her ideal, nor is he heroic—he has already suggested in the poem with the questions "Do you suppose you will find in me your ideal?" and "Do you suppose yourself advancing on real ground toward a real heroic man?" The poem implies the negative, raising real doubt about whether the "me" of the poetry (the imaginary figure) is the actual self of the poet. In the letter, Whitman explicitly says that the supposed person of the poems is *not* the ordinary, conservative Walt Whitman—"the actual Walt Whitman." Whitman's answer to Mrs. Gilchrist was inevitable, really, and not just in a personal sense. The two poems—"Whoever You Are" and "Are You the New Person"—actually anticipated and necessitated the answer to Mrs. Gilchrist, for he had apparently recognized, before he had ever heard of her, the basic distance that exists between a poet and his poem.

Unfortunately, Whitman left no extensive correspondence or criticism which painstakingly separates him from his poetry. He probably did not because his conception of the poet-poem relation did not consistently include distance. Nevertheless, his prefaces occasionally indicate that distance, as well as relationship, is a part of his poetic theory.

When Whitman refers to *Leaves of Grass* as a poem of identity, he indeed means that it "gives one man's—the author's—identity, ardors, observations, faiths, and thoughts, color'd hardly at all with any decided coloring from other faiths or other identities."[4] For Whitman, a poem *is* deeply personal; it emerges only from "beautiful blood and a beautiful brain," and it is dependent on the poet and man: "the fluency and ornaments of the finest poems. . . . are not independent but dependent."[5] Whitman also argues, however, that *Leaves of Grass* is "the song of a great composite *Democratic Individual,* male or female."[6] The self which the "poem of identity" expresses is not, then, simply a personal self. Whitman's announced national or social purpose—the epic or encyclopedic ambition he states or implies in every preface—indicates that the figure *Leaves of Grass* dramatizes is public, social, and representative. To be representative Whitman obviously had to discard elements of the personal. He still had to present himself as an individual, but also as an image or symbol of the individual American or man. The image may be related to the existing self (as one of many American individuals) or to the nation, but the images are not the *same* as the self or nation. At best these images are partial portraits and do not destroy the essential distance between the poet and his poem.

In the prefaces, Whitman does not explicitly warn his reader that such distance exists; he is probably not even conscious that he implies it. Nevertheless, he does include, as one of his major themes, a purpose that implies separation of poet and poem and that requires distance for its realization. But at the same time—and this is paradoxical—Whitman repeatedly announces the oneness of himself and his poetry. No one, therefore, can completely separate the personal, historical Whitman from the poems he wrote, from the images of himself he dramatized in *Leaves of Grass,* or from the self he advertised so boldly and, at times, so offensively in his prefaces and in contemporary publications. I shall have a good deal more to say about the connection of poet and poem later in the chapter, but at this point I might include a few details to confirm one very apparent relationship between the poet and his poem.

One need only recall the original title of "Song of Myself"—"Poem of Walt Whitman"—or read any version of it to know that someone named Whitman is the subject of the poem. Whitman names himself in section 24, as if to make sure (even after he dropped the original title) that his reader would know who the subject was: "Walt Whitman, a kosmos, of Manhattan the son." To say that Whitman merely had in mind an invented, separate personality—like a character in a novel—would deny Whitman's own statements that the poet and poem are of a piece, as well as deny one's own sense of collusion between the poet and his *persona.*

Two poems that Whitman excluded in later editions of *Leaves of Grass,* probably to make his book seem *less* personal than it was in 1856 and 1860, reveal how close the relationship between the personal existence of the poet and his poetry could be. In "Hours Continuing Long" Whitman seems to comment directly on the deep personal crisis he experienced before the publication of the 1860 *Leaves.* "Respondez!" which Whitman dropped from *Leaves of Grass* after 1876, directly states Whitman's own anger and frustration over American politics in the 1850's.

Let me bring this to a close—I pronounce openly for a new
   distribution of roles;
Let that which stood in front go behind! and let that which was
   behind advance to the front and speak;
Let murderers, bigots, fools, unclean persons, offer new propositions!
Let the old propositions be postponed!
Let faces and theories be turn'd inside out! let meanings be
   freely criminal, as well as results!

Whitman later added lines that referred to the Civil War and to
the public corruption which he described at length in "Democratic Vistas." However, the poem remained essentially the same
as it was in 1856. The bitter irony and satire expressed in "Respondez!" sound typical of Whitman the journalist and political
writer, but the tone and attitude are unusual for the *Leaves of
Grass* Walt Whitman. He may have excluded it from his book
simply because it reflected a man he no longer wished to be. But
insofar as the poem directly states Walt Whitman's disillusionment
with contemporary American politics, it is at one with the personal, historical man.

   Whitman's poetry and his prose present apparent contradictions in
his conception of the poet's relationship to his poem. One can find
evidence that Whitman recognized the distance between himself
and his poems, and in that sense *Leaves of Grass* is objective and
dramatic. Yet, time and again, Whitman claims that the connection
between man and poet is so close they cannot be separated; in fact
they are one—"Camerado, this is no book, who touches this touches
a man." Whitman did indeed contradict himself, but through his
contradictions he expresses the relationship of poet and poem, much
as he depends on contradiction in "Song of Myself" to express himself. Through contradiction he expresses his intuitive awareness that
the poet's relation to his poem involves simultaneous distance and
relation.

2. The Poet and the Reader

   As my comments about "Song of the Open Road" indicate, Whitman quite consciously thinks of his poetry as a dialogue in which the
I addresses the *you*—

Lingering a moment here and now, to you I opposite turn,
As on the road or at some crevice door by chance, or open'd
   window,

Pausing, inclining, baring my head, you specially I greet,
To draw and clinch your soul for once inseparably with mine,
Then travel travel on. ("Out from behind This Mask")

Whoever you are, now I place my hand upon you, that you be
    my poem,
I whisper with my lips close to your ear,
I have loved many women and men, but I love none better than
    you. ("To You")

In the poetry a man—a presence and voice—speaks to other men.
That may sound faintly Wordsworthian, and for that reason it may
seem sentimental or unduly personalist, therefore illegimate in an
age of neutralized, impersonal art. And Whitman may sentimental-
ize or exaggerate the poem-man equation, but in doing so, he counters the modern excess of converting poetry into some disembodied,
impersonal, self-sufficient artifact that someone has shaped, structured, or formed, but not, God forbid, spoken. In other words, Whitman's excesses do not negate his extremely important awareness of
poetry as dialogue.

Through the poetry, then, Whitman tries metaphorically and
dramatically to establish a relationship of complete openness, mutuality, and communication between himself and his reader. Although
Whitman sometimes dramatizes the response of the listener or companion in the situation presented in the poem, as in "Song of the
Open Road," dialogue is primarily a function of the poem itself, not
just of the situation, for the spoken words of the poem establish a
common ground between poet and reader. The poem, for example,
provides the basis for Whitman's claim in "Crossing Brooklyn Ferry"
that although the "I and you" may not share a common historical
existence, they nevertheless do communicate, genuinely and essentially, through the living language of the poem. Thus, the "I and you"
finally become "we," but in no way does a complete identity of the
poet and reader occur, for Whitman is aware that his reader stands
over against him and exists factually in a different time and place.
Dialogue, therefore, does not assume complete agreement or oneness. Rather, the dialogue between poet and reader resembles a
genuine conversation between two persons in which an I-Thou communication may be momentarily realized; that is, the dialogue between them involves (1) tension, (2) drama, and (3) adventure.

(1) Tension arises from the attempt of the "I and you" (Whitman
and his reader) to reach a "mutual" understanding in the meaning
of words, for words will possess, at first, somewhat different meanings

for the poet and his reader ("You will hardly know who I am or what I mean"), just as they do for two people in conversation. The reader's repeated encounter with the poem, however, calls forth new meanings—new meanings which the poet, in a sense, offers as the two attempt to reach an understanding.

> Failing to fetch me at first keep encouraged,
> Missing me one place search another,
> I stop somewhere waiting for you.

The possibility of misunderstanding results in tension which may lead, hopefully, to understanding. (2) The dialogue is dramatic both in the conflict of the poet and reader standing over against one another and in the meeting or interaction between them. (3) The sense of adventure arises from the conflict (the tension) and from the reader's discovery of new meanings in the "spoken word" each time he reads the poem or engages in dialogue with the poet.

In genuine dialogue between man and man the meeting takes place in the sphere of the between, and Whitman's poems often seek to become that "in between" by establishing a dialogue through the spoken word—that word which, according to Martin Buber, is uttered here and heard there, but which has a place "in between." "The importance of the spoken word, I think, is grounded in the fact that it does not want to remain with the speaker. It reaches out toward a hearer, it lays hold of him, it even makes the hearer into a speaker, if perhaps only a soundless one . . . The word that is spoken is found . . . in the oscillating sphere between the persons."[7] Poetry for Buber, and I think for Whitman, embodies meaning in the spoken word, and in this way it occupies the narrow ridge of the between and becomes a means for genuine dialogue to occur. Whitman's words may be solitary ("Solitary, singing in the West, I strike up for a new world"), yet they are solidary as well—solidary in an essential way, not one merely having to do with politics or sociality.[8] Whitman endures solitude for the sake of genuine dialogue through poetry—if not with those in his historical present, then with those future generations who might hear and respond to his address. The poem, then, for Whitman is spokenness to the Thou, wherever that partner might be.[9]

Although Whitman did not think or write with so specific or sophisticated an awareness of the spoken word, he nonetheless thought of his poetry as an oral medium—as spokenness.[10] For Whitman the

poem was something uttered or spoken, not written.[11] In "I Saw In
Louisiana a Live-Oak Growing," for example, Whitman explicitly
characterizes poetry as utterance: "But I wondered how it could
utter joyous leaves standing alone there without its friend near, for
I knew I could not." And he implies as well that the opposite of
poetry is silence—not a blank page. Such a poem as "I Sit and Look
Out" ends in that very silence which is no longer poetry. The poem
expresses the last words of a poet who has been overwhelmed by the
terrifying facts of the world. He has been reduced to an isolated
onlooker who sees, observes, and marks, but who does not touch or
speak; he *hears*, but only vestigially, for his participation in the world
through sound has been reduced to a minimal hearing. The visual,
in this case, *separates* him from experience and deprives him of any
sense of totality. The silence that prevails dramatically at the end
reinforces the poet's isolation by concealing meaning—meaning that
depends for Whitman on words, voice, and relation.

Even when vision and sound work together to constitute Whitman's primary mode of perception and expression, vision is helpless
without the intelligence and intelligibility provided by voice or
words:

> My voice goes after what my eyes cannot reach,
> With the twirl of my tongue I encompass worlds and volumes
>   of worlds.
>
> Speech is the twin of my vision . . . ("Song of Myself")

Voice penetrates and encompasses experience in a way the eye
cannot. For through voice Whitman engages and translates experience. The poet may be a seer, as Whitman says in the 1855 *Preface*,
but without the spoken word to embody and communicate meaning,
there *is* no meaning for Whitman—only silence. Meaning may exist
unformed in experience, but without speech—without Whitman's
"prophetical screams"—it remains "Waiting in gloom, protected by
frost":

> Come now I will not be tantalized, you conceive too much of
>   articulation,
> Do you not know O speech how the buds beneath you are
>   folded?
> Waiting in gloom, protected by frost,
> The dirt receding before my prophetical screams,
> I underlying causes to balance them at last,

My knowledge my live parts, it keeping tally with the meaning
of all things. (25)

Unless Whitman speaks the password—"I speak the pass-word
primeval"—he cannot "indicate the path between reality and their
souls."

Whitman's interest in oratory and rhetoric partly explains his emphasis on voice,[12] and quite possibly his bardic pretensions to be a
singer of tales also explain his concern with the spoken word. Such
explanations, however, are really quite inadequate, for Whitman's
association of language with sound and presence goes well beyond
mere analogy, as his comments in *An American Primer* confirm.

Throughout his essay, Whitman thinks of language as a spoken
medium. From the beginning, he associates words and speech: "The
Americans are going to be the most fluent and melodious voiced
people in the world—and the most perfect users of words." "What
beauty there is in words! What a lurking curious charm in the sound
of some words! Then voices!"[13] Then, he goes on to talk about the
meaning and magic embodied in the human voice. Whitman knows
that language, a fundamentally oral-aural medium, achieves its full
power and meaning only through speaking and listening. Much of
that power results, not only from the sound of the voice, but from the
personal presence revealed in the voice and through the word. Whitman indicates such an awareness in these remarks:

> To all thoughts of your or any one's mind—to all yearnings,
> passions, love, hate, ennui, madness, desperation of men for
> women and of women for men,—to all charging and surcharg-
> ing—that head which poises itself on your neck and is electric
> in the body beneath your head, or runs with the blood through
> your veins—or in those curious incredible miracles you call
> eyesight and hearing—to all these, and the like of these, have
> been made words.—Such are the words that are never new and
> never old.
>   What a history is folded, folded inward and inward again, in
> the single word I. (pp. 3–4)

When Whitman says that words "have a sound of presence"
("words of Behaviour," specifically) he implies more than personal
presence. He seems to claim, for example, that words virtually possess a being or life of their own: "I put my arms around them—touch
my lips to theirs" (p. 12). But he avoids any extreme exaggeration or
excessive emphasis on the magical quality of words when he associates, a few pages later, the being he discovers in words with the

voice and presence of a speaker: "A perfect writer would make words sing, dance, kiss, do the male and female act, bear children, weep, bleed, rage, stab, steal, fire cannon, steer ships, sack cities" (p. 16). For Whitman words are also invested with the presence of things and actions; words somehow partake of the actuality they make intelligible. But here again, it is the writer or user (the speaker, really) who invests words with such presence through his own voice and person. "A perfect user of words uses things—they exude in power and beauty from him—miracles from his hands—miracles from his mouth—lilies, clouds, sunshine, woman, poured copiously—things, whirled like chainshot rocks" (p. 14).

The voice that speaks meaning in words also speaks *to* a reader—both directly, as in "I whisper with my lips close to your ear" ("To You") and indirectly in "I sound my barbaric yawp . . ." ("Song of Myself," Section 52). The word embodies the presence of the poet, and it is that person who addresses and engages the reader. In this sense Whitman does not exaggerate when he claims that he and his book are one:

> Camerado, this is no book,
> Who touches this touches a man.

The spoken word situates the listener (or reader) in the midst of actuality and relates him to a presence: word and thing become inseparable.

Whitman's insight into language and presence reveal, I think, an unformed sense of what Martin Buber means by "actual occurence" and, perhaps, what Walter Ong means by the sense of simultaneity conveyed through the spoken word. Several comments in *An American Primer* support this possibility more explicitly than Whitman's remarks about presence do. Whitman says, for example, that the spoken language—for him the living, existing language—is not recorded in any dictionary, nor is it even in print: "The words continually used among the people are . . . not the words used in writing, or recorded in the dictionaries by authority." He is referring here, of course, to the vernacular and to the new words required by a new nation; however, he is also saying that the language which actually occurs among people is spoken and unrecorded. "The Real Dictionary [the one that would truly record the language] will give all words that exist in use"—the "living speech in the real world." The perfect user of words draws on that language, and he invests it with meaning,

power, and presence by speaking it. In this sense Whitman is thinking of the whole English language—not just of the American vernacular.

Although Whitman does not quite say that words have no existence
or meaning unless they are sounded, he does indicate that the spoken
word possesses greater meaning than either the unspoken or the
written word: "All words, spoken from these, have deeper, sweeter
sounds, new meanings, impossible on any less terms.—Such meanings, such sounds, continually wait in every word that exists—in these
words—perhaps slumbering through years, closed from all tympans
of temples, lips, brains, until that comes which has the quality pa-
tiently waiting in the words" (p. 20).

Whitman occasionally speaks of the communal nature of language in the *Primer,* and he also seems aware of the reciprocal
quality of speech or the spoken word. However, he says virtually
nothing about dialogue. Nevertheless, when one relates Whitman's obvious concern with the spoken word as the embodiment
of intelligence and intelligibility to his deep concern in the poetry
with encounter and dialogue, one must recognize that voice, presence, and dialogue figure prominently in Whitman's poetry and
in his ideas about words.

I am not trying to make Whitman into some sort of hero or prophet
of communion, nor do I think that all his poetry achieves or dramatizes the genuine dialogue I am trying to define. I am saying, however, that the address of *I* to *you*—Whitman to his reader—is not
simply the inauthentic address, disguised as dialogue, of a lyric poet
who wishes to claim the world's attention for his monologue. Whitman's poetry, rather, is a genuine attempt to communicate what he
means—an attempt to be true as a man and a poet. And in that
quality one can find a basis for defining what it is Whitman communicates—what kind of truth his poetry speaks.

Whitman sometimes claims a truth well beyond the personal, existential truth I mean by his attempt to be true as a person:

> Passage to you, your shores, ye aged fierce enigmas!
> Passage to you, to mastership of you, ye strangling problems!
> You strew'd with the wrecks of skeletons, that, living, never
>   reach'd you.   ("Passage to India")

For all his pretentions about *the* truth in "Passage to India" and other
similar poems, most of Whitman's significant poems concentrate on

his attempt to communicate the encounter of the concrete, personal
self with the reality standing over against him. It is true—the prefaces comment more often on the function of the poet to speak *for*
the people rather than to speak *with* them. But even though the
prefaces say very little about dialogue, communication is implicit in
the poet's primary function "to indicate the path between reality and
their [the readers'] souls." The poet, in a sense, points the way, but
most of the poems show that he points through communication between man and man.

So, I think it is legitimate and necessary to interpret the basic
truth of Whitman's poetry as the truth of the human word spoken
between man and man about man-in-the-world. The poet speaks
the truth insofar as he means what he means and says what he
means. This relation between meaning and saying—their oneness
or unity—is absolutely essential to genuine dialogue, to the truth
spoken between poet and reader. The truth of a poem, from this
point of view, involves three different elements or relationships.[14]
First, the poet must be true to a reality he perceives and knows—

> Ever the hard unsunk ground,
> Ever the eaters and drinkers, ever the upward and downward
>   sun, ever the air and the ceaseless tides,
> Ever myself and my neighbors, refreshing, wicked, real,
> Ever the old inexplicable query, ever that thorn'd thumb, that
>   breath of itches and thirsts,
> Ever the vexer's *hoot! hoot!* till we find where the sly one hides
>   and bring him forth,
> Ever love, ever the sobbing liquid of life,
> Ever the bandage under the chin, ever the trestles of death.
>   ("Song of Myself," section 42)

> Whoever you are, I fear you are walking the walks of dreams,
> I fear these supposed realities are to melt from under your feet
>   and hands . . .

> The mockeries are not you,
> Underneath them and within them I see you lurk.
>   ("To You," 3)

Second, he must try to be true to the person he addresses as a man
and whom he wishes to respond as a man:

> Listen! I will be honest with you,
> I do not offer the old smooth prizes, but offer rough new prizes.
>   ("Song of the Open Road")

Whoever you are, I now place my hand upon you, that you be
    my poem,
I whisper with my lips close to your ear,
I have loved many women and men, but I love none better than
    you.

The poet, finally, must be true to the word he speaks—the word that
is spoken.

> He swears to his art, I will not be meddlesome, I will not have
> in my writing any elegance or effect or originality to hang in the
> way between me and the rest like curtains. I will have nothing
> hang in the way, not the richest curtains. What I tell I tell for
> precisely what it is.[15]

The reader, then, does not respond to an absolute truth, an idea,
or a set of values—he does not even respond, primarily, to a version
of experience or a perspective on truth. He responds, instead, to the
presence of Walt Whitman in the poem. He silently answers a poet
and man who may say something worthwhile and who may establish
genuine communication with the reader. This kind of poetic truth
has its ground in the sense of communion with other persons. It
emerges in the spoken word which actualizes the language of being-
with-one-another. Although one perceives that presence through the
many masks Whitman assumes in *Leaves of Grass*, the masks basically reveal rather than hide the person who is there. The poet, in
effect, believes in his reader, and therefore, he addresses him; he calls
him to intimate response and to a reciprocal belief in the poet.[16]

I have suggested that the poet exists in a complex distance and
relation situation in regard to his poem. He stands apart from it, and
thus the "I" of a particular poem is a persona, not the historical poet
at all. Yet, the poem as dialogue indicates that the poet somehow
speaks through his poem to the reader. So the problem remains: how
does Whitman speak to his reader in his poems of dialogue? The
poem is not simply a reader-poet dialogue; instead, it involves, first,
a dialogue between the author and the poet-persona, or character,
in the poem, and second, it involves a dialogue between the persona
and the reader. The author presents an image of himself, or of man,
as the persona, and he engages in dialogue with that character in
order to develop the complete dramatic situation in the work. In
poetry such as Whitman's, the author and his persona stand in a much
closer apparent relationship than, say, a novelist and his characters
do. Nonetheless, the persona *is* an imaginary figure. This image of

the poet, then, is not simply a direct expression of the author, nor is the image wholly detached from him; rather it emerges as a genuine product of the dialogue between author and character. An awareness of distance and relation is essential here, for the poet does not simply talk to himself in another monologue that appears as dialogue. He has, in fact, invented or developed a concrete image of a person (an extension of himself, true) that possesses a reality outside himself, and thus a kind of dialogue between the author and his persona is possible.

The persona or poet that speaks in each poem (or the Walt Whitman that emerges in *Leaves of Grass* as a whole) retains something of the open, unfinished, quality of a concrete person in living dialogue. This is particularly apparent in Whitman's poetry; the "real me" he would discover and that seeks expression remains open and unfinished because something of it emerges in each encounter and in each new role dramatized in the poetry. The persona remains open, also, because it is only completed through the dialogue of reader and character; the reality of that persona continually emerges as each new reader encounters the poem and creates it anew. The author-persona dialogue makes the reader-character dialogue possible; that is, the interaction of poet and persona *produces* the image of man presented in the poem. But only through the reader-character communication is the dialogue of the poem completed because the "imaginary figure" cannot become the man or person speaking in the poem without the personal response of the reader.[17] There is, then, quite clearly a dialogue between the poet and his reader, but it is not so direct as the phrase indicates.

3. The Man, His Poems, and the World

By concentrating now on Whitman's personal and poetic response to four decisive periods in his life I can clarify his different and sometimes contradictory conceptions of the poet-poem relationship and I can begin to describe the actual relation between poet and poem.

The four periods focus and intensify the various private and public stresses working on Whitman throughout his life, and therefore these periods are particularly helpful in showing that identity for Whitman was deeply problematic and that the poem became, for him, a mode of personal discovery and communication. Two of the situations resulted largely from public pressures—the social and political situation in America around 1850 and the Civil War in the 1860's. The other two decisive times issued from mainly personal dilemmas having to do with Whitman's psychological and sexual nature—the famous, mysterious crisis of 1858–59 and the equally vague and obscure one of the early 1870's. I say "mainly personal" or "largely public" for good reasons; it is impossible to separate these spheres completely in the life of a man like Whitman. The deep personal crisis of the late 1850's, for example, resulted in a sense of depression and disruption that closely paralleled the national situation in those tense years, so perhaps even this crisis, presumably the most serious personal one biographers know about, issued from a complex interaction of Whitman's personal and public situations.

A.

Around 1850 Whitman apparently reached a crisis in his political and journalistic life. For years he had worked on newspapers as a type setter, reporter, and editor, and during this time he was deeply engaged in the social and political controversies of his age. He had gone to New York first in 1841 to take a job with the New York *Aurora*, and he soon became involved with party politics. By 1846, he had become the editor of a metropolitan daily—the Brooklyn *Eagle*. As a typical editor, he participated throughout his career in the scurrilous journalism characteristic of his day; he wrote features about the city; and, naturally, he asserted editorial opinions on numerous matters and issues—local ones concerning the city and working conditions for women, and such national ones as the Oregon dispute, the Mexican War, slavery, and the free soil movements. The slavery and free soil issues brought on the immediate crisis. Whitman's support of and his participation in the free soil movement led him, finally, to give up journalism and politics in disgust.

He had hoped, along with the other New York Democrats, that the party would take a stand on free soil in 1848 and perhaps even nominate an anti-slavery candidate. It did not, but even before the outcome the New York Democrats had walked out of the convention. Probably as a result of the free soil controversy, Whitman lost his job with the *Eagle*, left the Democratic party for the Free-Soil party, and was on the verge of being disillusioned with all party politics. By 1850 he was completely so. He believed that the politicians had betrayed the cause and him, so he blasted them with passionate sarcasm in a poem called "The House of Friends."[18] With that he virtually withdrew from the field, and then *Leaves of Grass* really started simmering as Whitman thought, wrote, worked as a carpenter, and loafed. He kept in touch, however, writing an occasional newspaper article and enjoying the city, but he was no longer a public man. The 1852 election seemed to reinforce his decision— the Democrats were still dominated by slaveholders, and they went on to win the election much to "Whitman's intense disgust."[19]

Whitman renewed his journalistic career and his interests in politics in 1856, but he did so for only a short time. He published an article on the slave trade, and he wrote but did not publish *The Eighteenth Presidency*, a harsh, contemptuous criticism of Buchanan, Fillmore, and the political system that elected them. Whitman even became an editor again, of the Brooklyn *Daily Times*, and renewed his close concern for municipal problems. His return, however, did not last long, for he lost the *Times* job in 1859. It is as if he were testing and confirming his earlier choice to be a *poet* engaged in American life rather than a journalist of involvement. Whitman did not entirely repudiate politics or social commentary at any time —he wrote a good deal for the newspapers during the war, and he wrote "Democratic Vistas" in the late sixties. Nevertheless, by the late 1850's the new Walt Whitman (Walt instead of Walter) had been invented and born, and now he was maturing.

B.

But he was maturing into another crisis—this time a deeply personal one. There is very little for biographers or critics to go on in describing the nature of Whitman's turmoil and depression during 1858–59, but most Whitmanians agree that Whitman experienced a tremendous emotional and intellectual upheaval during those years and that the 1860 edition reflects that conflict. (They do not concur, of course, about the degrees of intensity, morbidity, and depression in the book). Whether it resulted from Whitman's dilemma over his sexuality, from the loss of a close friend or lover, from both, or from some other unknown cause, the crisis seems to be a fact of the poetic and personal life of Walt Whitman. The *Calamus* poems, many of Whitman's revisions as he was preparing his third edition, and some of the poems later included in *Sea-Drift* provide sound evidence for a biographical connection, but the most important and revealing poem seems to be "Hours Continuing Long, Sore and Heavy Hearted"—the poem I referred to at the beginning of this chapter.

Although Whitman dropped it from *Leaves of Grass* after 1860, it is so important that I should quote it completely here:

> Hours continuing long, sore and heavy-hearted,
> Hours of the dusk, when I withdraw to a lonesome and unfre-
> quented spot, seating myself, leaning my face in my hands;
> Hours sleepless, deep in the night, when I go forth, speeding
> swiftly the country roads, or through the city streets, or
> pacing miles and miles, stifling plaintive cries;
> Hours discouraged, distracted—for the one I cannot content
> myself without, soon I saw him content himself without me;
> Hours when I am forgotten, (0 weeks and months are passing,
> but I believe I am never to forget?)
> Sullen and suffering hours! (I am ashamed—but it is useless—I
> am what I am;)
> Hours of my torment—I wonder if other men ever have the
> like, out of the like feelings?
> Is there even one other like me—distracted—his friend, his
> lover, lost to him?
> Is he too as I am now? Does he still rise in the morning, de-
> jected, thinking who is lost to him? and at night, awaking,
> think who is lost?
> Does he too harbor his friendship silent and endless? harbor his
> anguish and passion?
> Does some stray reminder, or the casual mention of a name,
> bring the fit back upon him, taciturn and deprest?
> Does he see himself reflected in me? In these hours, does he see
> the face of his hours reflected?

The poem does not appear as a controlled, artistic rendering of loss, pain, and death such as Whitman achieved in "Out of the Cradle Endlessly Rocking" and in the beautifully uttered expression of alienation and despair of "As I Ebb'd." Whitman distanced and tran-scended his anguish and depression in those poems by giving them dramatic and aesthetic reality, but in "Hours Continuing" he did not. Presumably, then, one hears the direct voice of the actual man ex-pressing emotions that he has not yet elaborated and shaped into a dramatic expression rather than the voice of the poetic persona. Whitman's exclusion of the poem in all his editions after 1860 sug-gests that he suppressed it because it exposed too much.

Gay Wilson Allen argues convincingly[20] that "Hours Long" and other poems in that edition have considerable personal significance; he concentrates on the series of "blue paper" revisions that seem to reveal a period of real torment during the time the poet prepared his 1860 edition. Allen claims that the different versions of the poems not only indicate conflicting themes or poetic attitudes; they reveal

a poet at war with himself. The confident poet of America battled
with the *Calamus* poet who had ventured into untrodden paths and
who was virtually overwhelmed by the lonely distraction he experienced as a result.

Besides the personal dimension, one can discern a kind of public-
private interaction here—as if the crisis were somewhat related to
Whitman's earlier disillusionment about American politics. As an
editor this time (1857–59), Whitman had not been any more successful and effective in realizing his social ideals than he had been before;
he finally lost this editorship in June 1859; and no doubt he was
driven back, once again, on himself—this time without the inner
strength and confidence of 1850. Disillusioned with public conditions, threatened by personal disruption (maybe even derangement),
Whitman's depression probably intensified. The public pressures, in
this case, were a prelude to personal confusion.

It is quite possible that the one poem and the 1860 edition as a
whole reveal as much about the man as I say—surely the poetry
dramatizes intense stresses that Whitman had apparently never un-
dergone before. Nevertheless, nothing confirms beyond all doubt
that "Hours Continuing Long" is a direct, diary-like expression of
personal despair; it may simply be a bad poem or the product of a
mood not nearly so deep and pervasive as some argue. This period
in Whitman's life is a confusing and obscure one; for example, no
letters at all are available for the time between July 1857 and January
1860, and only two exist for 1857, neither of much use or interest.[21]
Knowing little as one does, it would be easy to exaggerate Whitman's
suffering and his distraction. Asselineau says as much when he argues
that Frederick Schyberg exaggerated "the morbid character of the
1860 edition."[22] Besides Asselineau's argument, two biographical
facts support not only Whitman's successful emergence from his
despair; they provide grounds to question, tentatively, the actuality
of any deep, extended mental depression. During these crucial years,
Whitman seemed to function fairly normally. That is, he worked as
steadily and competently in his editorship of the *Times* as he ever
had, and he functioned well enough to bring a new edition—a considerably expanded and revised edition—of his poetry to press. The
point is that no one will ever know what really happened or what
Whitman's actual state of mind was. Doubtless, something happened
during those years (something readers keep hearing in the poetry,
and quite rightly, I think); something happened that deeply affected
the man, the poet, and the poems. And this obscure, complex experi-

ence reveals (although inexactly) that the man, poet, and poems are of a piece.

C.

In contrast to the late 1850's, readers know far more about Whitman's experiences in the Civil War than about any earlier part of his life. *Drum Taps* reflects many details of that experience, and Whitman wrote numerous sketches, letters, and other prose pieces about the war and his part in it. Rather than summarize those activities, however, I will concentrate simply on the points I am developing through this discussion of the major crisis periods in Whitman's life and poetry.

First, the Civil War experience repeats the movement from crisis or despair to equilibrium that Asselineau emphasizes in Whitman's life and poetry.[23] The last two stages of *Drum Taps*, for example, give clear, effective articulation to this rhythm. After Whitman's initial bellicosity and vigorous celebration of the northern cause (the first stage), he soon recognizes how incredibly destructive and mutilating the War is. Not only has the Union been disrupted and threatened with destruction, but each man in the war must face that ultimate personal limit—his own immediate and violent death. Although the crisis for Whitman does not involve such an imminent threat—he was a wound-dresser, a visitor at the hospitals, not a soldier at the front—the poet shows in *Drum Taps* what an intense personal awakening real war causes. The poetic persona never seems threatened by despair over the war, but he recognizes it for what it is, and that recognition—expressed in the poems—makes him virtually repudiate the cause which had originally moved him to enthusiastic support of the North against the South. In the poems Whitman passes through the crisis (the second stage) and seeks stability and equilibrium (stage three) through both personal and public resolutions, emphasizing once again how closely related those two spheres of experience were for him. He listens for a prophetic national voice calling for union and love, but he also looks to a deep personal relationship with another person. The last part of *Drum Taps*, then, includes poems of reconstruction, and these correspond to the last phase in the progression from crisis to equilibrium.

Second, the war experience and the poetry reveal an apparent interaction of the historical man's experience with the poems. Indeed, the relationship is far more apparent in *Drum Taps* than in most of Whitman's poetry. The poems trace Whitman's own personal change from an aggressive, bellicose patriot to a saddened, fatigued realist who had learned the horrible cost of war. And, as I suggested, the poems concentrate, intensify, and shape this experience for the poet. This progression is not limited to the life and poetry separately (although it is evident in each separately), but it takes shape more importantly between the life and the poetry. The political disillusionment of 1850, for example, fundamentally affected Whitman's decision to turn to poetry for personal realization. In 1855 he invented and announced a new self—a vigorous, confident, yet even then, essentially realistic self. In "Song of Myself," particularly, Whitman dramatized, through the experiences of the new self, his transcendence of the disillusioning political experiences. After the personal crisis of 1858–59, Whitman achieved a certain equilibrium in the escape from depression which the 1860 *Leaves of Grass* represents and dramatizes. *Drum Taps* obviously draws on Whitman's personal experience, but, more than that, the shaping and intensification in the poems of Whitman's personal experiences expresses him (*realizes* or *fulfills* him) in a way the historical experience does not. In a real way, Whitman does translate himself as he translates history. I *am* oversimplifying the poet-poem relationship here, but I do so to make a point.

Whitman's experiences in the war (1) actualized some of the qualities of the self and some of the conditions the self must face which he had dramatized earlier in "Song of Myself" (as if to anticipate and prepare for the crisis); it provided a situation in which the new Whitman could be tested, proven, and realized. The war (2) also influenced the poetry, for in *Drum Taps* Whitman concentrated, enlarged, and resolved his own experiences in it. So in a very basic way the experience of the historical man interacts with the poetry.

Needless to say the relationship of the poet and poem that one can infer from *Drum Taps* does not explain Whitman's life and poetry definitively; for the Civil War was not the last crisis in the poet's life. I am not suggesting, therefore, that Whitman resolved all his tensions or problems by going through the war crisis or that he successfully sublimated his so-called "dangerous" sexual impulses through "healthy" man-to-man relationships in the hospitals. The repetition of the crisis pattern, the continuing struggle throughout Whitman's life for wholeness, the Tom Sawyer letters of the 1860's (which Allen refers to), and numerous other details underscore the problematic of self and experience Whitman lived as a man and dramatized in his poetry. The fourth major crisis in the life and poetry confirms, I think, this problematic of identity. The particular experience seems to have deeply personal origins, similar in nature to the agitation and torment he had experienced some ten years before. A brief look at it will be enough to make my point about the poet and his poem.

D.

Knowledge of this crisis is based on a personal manuscript notebook in which Whitman alludes to a deep personal disturbance. It includes such distressed comments as these:

> cheating, childish abandonment of myself, fancying what does not really exist in another, but is all the time in myself alone— utterly deluded & cheated by *myself*, & my own weakness— REMEMBER WHERE I AM MOST WEAK, & most lacking. Yet always preserve a kind spirit & demeanor to 16. But PURSUE HER NO MORE.

> *It is* IMPERATIVE, that I obviate & remove myself (& my orbit) *at all hazards* [away from] from this *incessant enormous* & [enormous] PERTURBATION

> TO GIVE UP ABSOLUTELY & *for good, from this present hour,* [all] this FEVERISH, FLUCTUATING, *useless undignified pursuit of 164—too long, (much too long)* persevered in, —so humiliating—*It must come at last* & had better come now —(It cannot possibly be a success) LET THERE FROM THIS HOUR BE NO FALTERING, or NO GETTING—*at all henceforth,* (NOT ONCE, *under any circumstances)—avoid seeing her, or meeting her, or any talk or explanations—*OR ANY MEETING WHATEVER, FROM *THIS HOUR FORTH, FOR LIFE.*

> *Depress the adhesive nature.*

> ---

> *It is in excess—making life a torment.*

> ---

> *All this diseased, feverish disproportionate adhesiveness*[24]

With such passages available, this period of personal emotional torment seems somewhat better documented than the earlier one. Yet biographers and critics have only the notebook as evidence, and it seems to be limited to a brief period in the summer of 1870. Therefore, this time in Whitman's life remains almost as obscure and confusing as the earlier crisis in the late 1850's. Biographers do not even

know *positively* if the passion and anguish Whitman expresses here
results from an affair with a man or a woman. It seems probable that
the shame, guilt, and the self doubts Whitman felt resulted from his
intense desire for another man and from his fear of rebuke by him.
Asselineau vigorously argues:

> But what was the danger that menaced him and that he must
> at all costs escape? A close examination of the manuscript of this
> resolution reveals it. The cause of these troubles was not a
> woman, but a man. All the masculine pronouns of the text have
> been erased and replaced by their feminine equivalents, but
> under the superscription they can still be very clearly seen.
> There can be no doubt: Whitman deliberately camouflaged his
> private notes. Moreover, one of the pages is missing , and it was
> probably Whitman himself who tore it out, finding his admis-
> sion too compromising. If he feared the judgment of posterity
> to this extent, how much more he must have feared the scandal
> that would have broken out if anyone had known the true
> nature of his passion. This would explain the panic that seems
> to have seized him and his frantic efforts to smother such dan-
> gerous tendencies.[25]

The available evidence and the persistent and repeated problematic
in Whitman's personal and poetic experience tend to confirm the
argument. Nevertheless, the notebook provides very slim evidence.
It exposes a troubled man, surely, but the pervasiveness and the
duration of that trouble seem impossible to know.

Whitman's letters reveal very little (they seldom do), but one of the
Peter Doyle letters, written July 30, 1870, may say something about
the source of Whitman's self doubts and may indicate the object of
his perturbation.

> Pete, there was something in that hour from 10–11 oclock (part-
> ing though it was) that has left me pleasure & comfort for good
> —I never dreamed that you made so much of having me with
> you, nor that you could feel so downcast at losing me. I foolishly
> thought it was all on the other side. But all I will say further on
> the subject is, I now see clearly, that was all wrong.[26]

The night of parting must have been July 26, 1870, just eleven days
after Whitman had noted his agitation and need to break off a relationship. If one can legitimately connect the letter with the notebook
(and I am not sure one can), then the source of Whitman's disturbance becomes clearer; it is based on his ambiguous, disturbing sexuality and, perhaps specifically on his relation with Peter Doyle. The

connection, however, is only *possible,* at best; there is simply not enough evidence to be sure.[27]

Very little in Whitman's action or in his poetry at this time reveals the inner turmoil the notebook expresses. The poetry of the late sixties and early seventies even suggests that Whitman is beginning to solve the problematic of himself by denying it and that he is beginning to obscure the relationship between the personal man and the poetry. Several of his poems in the 1871–72 edition, as well as some earlier revisions, support this point. Whitman had written in 1865, at the end of the war, that he wanted the dreadful spirit of war to remain part of him and of his poetry, so that (it appears) no one would ever forget the horror and terror experienced by all men in war:

> Spirit of hours I knew, all hectic red one day, but pale as death
>   next day,
> Touch my mouth ere you depart, press my lips close,
> Leave me your pulses of rage—bequeath them to me—fill me
>   with currents convulsive,
> Let them scorch and blister out of my chants when you are
>   gone,
> Let them identify you to the future in these songs. ("Spirit
>   Whose Work Is Done")

By the time he revised "By Blue Ontario's Shore" for the 1867 edition, however, he seemed to have forgotten the concrete conditions of war and remembered only the abstract (and here disembodied) principle of union and the great northern cause:

> (Lo, high toward heaven, this day,
> Libertad, from the conqueress' field return'd,
> I mark the new aureola around your head,
> No more of soft astral, but dazzling and fierce,
> With war's flames and the lambent lightnings playing,
> And your port immovable where you stand,
> With still the inextinguishable glance and the clinch'd and lifted
>   fist,
> And your foot on the neck of the menacing one, the scorner
>   utterly crush'd beneath you . . .

Out of context, it is difficult to tell the difference between this poet and the poet of "Beat! Beat! Drums!" He has virtually dissolved all conflict and complexity into an abstraction. He has blamed the real disruption and permanent blight of the war on the South and thus has purified Democracy.

One finds a similar level of abstraction in "The Base of All Metaphysics" (it entered *Leaves of Grass* in 1871). If one reads it in context (in *Calamus)*, then it states a legitimate generalization or "making public" of a primarily personal relationship; in context the personal and the public exist simultaneously. But when one thinks of the poem separately from the others (and one must to understand the kind of poem Whitman was writing around 1870), he recognizes that Whitman clearly subordinates (virtually denies?) the concrete, personal relationship essential to *Calamus* by committing himself to abstraction. "The Base of All Metaphysics" entered Leaves of Grass in 1871, and if the 1870 notebook *does* reveal a man deeply disturbed by his homosexuality, then the poem provides evidence that Whitman is denying and abstracting his personal experience in order to sublimate it.

"Passage to India" is the classic poem which shows Whitman's turning from a situation in-the-world toward commitment to abstract universals and to a spirit virtually out of space and out of time. The personal, relational (except insofar as God exists in relation to his true son, the poet), the communal, and all the strangling problems of human life find very little expression in this poem. To some extent the poem indicates (as the Prefaces in 1872 and 1876 do) that the poet is turning toward death, immortality, and spirit as the most meaningful sphere of experience and that his poetry is, too. But as he expanded his consciousness to meet the God of "Passage to India," Whitman *narrowed* the image of himself, and he began, as well, to omit from the poetry more and more of the historical man. These later poems seem less personal than either the Civil War or the 1860 poems, and they seem to have solved many strangling problems. Yet the relationship of the poet and poem had changed more in appearance than in essentials. Likewise, the problematic in Whitman's personal and poetic experience has not completely disappeared.

Whitman seems to achieve fulfillment around 1870 by announcing success and by denying crisis. He apparently wishes to transcend crisis and disruption so thoroughly that he virtually dissovles them in abstract universals. Instead of confrontation, he chooses exclusion or sublimation as his means of achieving transcendence. Nevertheless, such poems remain an extension of the man—a man for whom the problematic of identity was still very real, in spite of the poetic experiences and the accompanying image of the self. This problematic persists in three distinct ways. (1) The notebook passages I quoted reveal both deep personal agitation and agonizing self-doubt; they were written, presumably, after much of "Passage to India" had been composed. The "Passage to India" state of mind, then, did not permanently exclude or overcome others. (2) Whitman's age and illnesses began to affect him physically and psychologically in 1870 and later; sometimes he achieved serenity but he also suffered from depression. Just a few years after he wrote "Passage to India" Whitman published "Prayer of Columbus" (1874), and in it he doubtless articulated the depression and debility that he frequently experienced. The poem reveals a tremendously diminished sense of self for whom neither the union of "Passage to India" nor the self-sufficiency of "Song of Myself" is possible. The poem calls everything into doubt.[28] (3) During this period, Whitman's disillusionment with democracy in America continued. Although he had written and published part of "Democratic Vistas" in 1868 and 1869, he did not publish the entire essay until 1871. Even though it was written before, the essay probably reflects Whitman's ideas well into the 1870's. If anything, American society and politics of the Gilded Age were worse than they were in the fifties, and in his essay Whitman exposed contemporary corruption and failures. He indicates that he is aware of America's problematic and perhaps of his own as an American. The man, then, remains the object of public and private stresses, as he had always been. These pressures show that the inner war in Whitman and his struggle for wholeness continued. Although the poems have become a less apparent battleground for the turmoil, they nonetheless speak for the man—a man who would now rather sublimate than confront.

4. The Poet and His Poems

Once again the reader finds himself confronted by a complex relation between poet and poem: they seem inseparable (the poem is an extension of the poet), but the poet is, after all, the maker of an "imaginary figure," a persona, who exists as a unique entity separate from the poet. Not only is the situation complex; it changes, too. That is, distance and relation vary in degree from one poem to another; surely, there is less distance between the poet and his poem in "Hours Long" than in, say, "When Lilacs Last in the Dooryard Bloom'd" or in "Passage to India." Not only that: the image of the self changes from poem to poem (many different persona appear), and it changes fundamentally over a period of years as the historical Whitman did (he gets older, less bold and more conservative, less concrete and more abstract). The situation is indeed complicated; it is seldom the same in one poem as in another. Nevertheless, such changes and differences do not affect the essential situation of the poet's relationship to his poem and to his poetic persona, Walt Whitman.

In 1855 Whitman invented and introduced "Walt Whitman, an American," and during the rest of his life, he went on to articulate, define, develop, and revise that new self. In many ways he even tried to live the life of that personality, for, as I have indicated, poet influences poem and poem influences poet. But the essential relationship remains the same for all the specific differences one finds. Based on what I have developed in this chapter, I think the relationship of the imaginary figure to the man (the *function* of the persona *for* the man) can be explained in six ways. (1) The persona represents a *reorganization* of Walter Whitman's life from a public or politically oriented one to a life devoted to poetry. (2) The imaginary figure is quite clearly an *extension* of the man; Whitman's war experience and the poems based on them provide one obvious example of extension. (3) The "I" of Whitman's poetry becomes a means of *enlarging* and *fulfilling* the self; through the second self Whitman could seek the "real Me" and thus, when successful, achieve a self-realization not available to him in his earlier political and journalistic life. (4) The poetic persona, then, provides a way of *confronting* experience; it is not simply a means of escape or a compensation. (5) By confronting experience through the imaginary figure, Whitman could achieve personal *transcendence.* Not only could he emerge from himself through the experiences dramatized in the poems; he could (6) *reach out* to others and establish dialogue with them through his poetry.[29]

During the early 1850's, just before the first *Leaves of Grass* appeared in 1855, Whitman reshaped his whole personal life. Disillusioned with politics and released from his editorship of the *Eagle,* Whitman left the public world almost completely. He became a sometime carpenter and worked with his father building houses; he also spent a good deal of his time apparently loafing, but actually thinking and writing. His dress, manner, and whole style of life changed as he began elaborating and shaping the figure he had roughly described in his earliest extant notebook, sometime in 1847.[30] The really significant reorganization, however, took place in Whitman's inner life; the dress and manner were simply manifestations of a deep, essential change. The new man had been waiting for several years, as the notebook indicates; now he had his chance to emerge as Whitman devoted virtually all of his attention and energy in the early 1850's to the creation of his book and to the invention

of the imaginary figure, Walt Whitman. Whitman had written poems
and stories before, all uniformly conventional, sentimental, and unrealistic; but he had also recognized America for what it was, and he
had written about it as such. The "Poet" and the man had existed,
really, as two separate men. The reorganization of Whitman's life
achieved a consolidation of the two, as Whitman moved from politician to poet—from Walter Whitman to Walt Whitman. The dropping
of "er"—slight as it appears—required a radical action (perhaps the
most radical of Whitman's life), for Whitman had to reach into himself and discover a potentially whole man (for whom the problematic
of self was very real) and a poet buried beneath the politician, journalist, and conventional author.

Whitman, in effect, dramatized the reorganization of his life in the
new man who was born, to all intents, on July 4, 1855. That new man
was an extension or continuation of the historical man who had
significantly reshaped *his* own life. Much that I have already said
about the interaction of poet and poem substantiates this point about
extension. First, one finds an extension of Whitman's political interests in a few of the poems from the fifties.[31] But the poet's genius and
wholeness did not lie in satire or social commentary; he discovered
himself, instead, in the further extension and enlargement of his
political interests into a concern with the personal, relational, and
communal. Second, the uncertainties, doubts, despair, and division
characteristic of the author's personal and public life find expression
in the poems, particularly in the alienation or isolation to transcendence pattern that informs both the life and the poetry. Finally, the
dialogical principle argues for extension, too, for if the dialogue of the
poet and reader is to be genuine, then the man must be involved in
some way. The imaginary figure in the poem must be an extension
of the man, not *just* a fictional second self. Whitman frequently tried
to convince his audience and himself that he and the imaginary
figure were one—and in some important ways they were. Yet complete fusion or oneness simply did not occur; both man and persona
(a poet in each case) retain their separate identities, for all they may
share.

The extension of the self into the poetry involves structuring, concentration, and transformation of the self into the new man, the
imaginary figure of Walt Whitman. In this way an enlargement of the
self takes place. Whitman finds himself, for example, in "Song of the
Open Road" larger and better than he thought:

I am larger, better than I thought,
I did not know I held so much goodness.

In "Song of Myself" his new awareness gives him a remarkably expansive vision:

Space and Time! now I see it is true, what I guess'd at,
What I guess'd when I loaf'd on the grass,
What I guess'd while I lay alone in my bed,
And again as I walk'd the beach under the paling stars of the
    morning.

My ties and ballasts leave me, my elbows rest in sea-gaps,
I skirt sierras, my palms cover continents,
I am afoot with my vision.

The expanded self encounters vast ranges of experience and meets innumerable individuals. He would—and in some ways does—encompass all experience. But enlargement does not just refer to an expansive self or vision, for the persona's failures receive the same concentration and enlargement, as he unsuccessfully confronts mystery and recognizes his own failures. Enlargement in this case occurs through the shaping and intensification of experience, not so much through an expanded consciousness.

Through extension and enlargement Whitman discovers and fulfills himself, achieving a kind of wholeness he had not known before. The separation between the public man, who confronted the brutality of New York and the division and uncertainty in American life, and the private writer, who wrote sentimental, conventional poetry and fiction, effectively disappears as Whitman integrates them into his new life as a poet.[32] *Leaves of Grass* functions as a fulfillment because it brings a divided man together without completely repudiating any aspect of the self. Whitman becomes a private poet insofar as he keeps his integrity and independence and writes as he must, yet he is a poet who says "This is the city and I am one of the citizens." *Leaves of Grass,* then, represents an initial and continuing movement toward psychological wholeness for Whitman; it becomes part of his constant inner struggle to achieve stability and wholeness. Whitman's expansive drives, the extension and enlargement of himself in the poetry, reflect, for the most part, normal tensions and healthy expansive behavior, not simply a neurotic self-doubt and inner malaise for which Whitman attempted to compensate.

The other three elements which describe the poet's relationship to his poem are means to and features of fulfillment. That is, Whitman discovers and fulfills himself through confrontation, encounter, and dialogue, and in this way he experiences transcendence. His own sense of his poetry as dialogue—as a means of reaching out to others to overcome solitude and to complete himself—confirms my point. Although Whitman made many friends and acquaintances through his newspaper work, during the Civil War and, as a poet, throughout his life he remained a very lonely man. He recognized that he had many friends: he appreciated them, he loved them, and they contributed a great deal to him. Nevertheless, he was continually haunted by loneliness and fear as his notebooks, the letter to Peter Doyle, and above all, the poetry indicate. Late in his life he sensed that he had wandered all of his life with few comrades, and he recognized how essential his poetry had been to whatever fulfillment he had experienced. Sometime in 1882, he indicated in a small notebook his desire to write a "Poemet embodying the idea I wander along my life hardly ever meeting comrades . . . For I have not met them[.] Therefore I have put my passionate love of comrades in my poems."[33] To some extent then, Whitman transcended solitude through the encounter of his poetic identity with others and through the dialogue of the poet with his readers. Whitman knew that he needed more than mankind, the world, or the universe; he needed others—even if they came to him in imaginative or fictional form through art; he needed them if he was to become a real person and achieve personal unity.

The articulation and definition of an imaginary ideal self in the poetry also prepared Whitman to face realities in his own life he had no way of predicting. The poetic identity actually influenced the real man in a substantive way. James M. Cox argues, for example, that in the poetry Whitman wrote during the pre-Civil War years, he anticipated and prepared himself for the action demanded of him in the war.[34] By creating himself as poet in "Song of Myself", by defining his relation to the future in "Crossing Brooklyn Ferry", and by confronting personal loss and individual death in "Out of the Cradle", Whitman armed himself for the horror of war. He was able to "confront the experiences," indeed "experience the confrontations" in the Civil War because he had anticipated them in language. During and just after the war, the poetry resumed its function of the translation and fulfillment of history; in *Drum Taps* Whitman translates the meaning of war and death, and in "Lilacs" he triumphs over war by completely recognizing and grasping the present in which he lived.

I have been arguing, on the one hand, that the poet and his poem are of a piece. One must not forget, however, that the poet and his poem—the man and the imaginary figure—exist quite separately from one another, as well. They differ so much that one must distinguish very clearly between biography and literary biography if he wishes to understand the identity problem in Whitman and if he desires to interpret the poems accurately. I have tried so far both to separate *and* relate them. However, the primary purpose of my book is to concentrate on literary biography and the problematic of identity emerging there. In other words, I shall devote the remainder of the book to a study of the poetic identity of Walt Whitman. I shall not ignore the biographical; nevertheless, the priority must go to the imaginary figure because his is the identity one cares about and can know.

NOTES—*Chapter II*

1. Walt Whitman, *The Correspondence, 1868–1875*, ed. Edwin Haviland Miller (New York, 1961), p. 135.
2. Quoted in Gay Wilson Allen, *The Solitary Singer* (New York, 1955), p. 440.
3. Whitman, *Correspondence, 1868–1875*, p. 170.
4. "A Backward Glance," *Leaves of Grass: Comprehensive Reader's Edition* (New York, 1965), p. 563.
5. "Preface, 1855," *Leaves of Grass*, p. 714.
6. "Preface to as a Strong Bird," *Leaves of Grass*, p. 743.
7. Martin Buber, *The Knowledge of Man* (New York, 1965), p. 112.
8. Cf. Maurice Friedman, *To Deny Our Nothingness* (New York, 1967), p. 287.
9. *The Knowledge of Man*, p. 118. Buber distinguished "three modes-of-being" of language—present continuance, potential possession, and actual occurence. The first is a language of the "being-with-one-another of living men in whose personal texture of speech the present continuance becomes actualized." Buber means by present continuance "the totality of that which can be spoken in a particular realm of language in a particular segment of time" (p. 110). The second mode refers to language that is historically possessed—"the totality of what has ever been uttered in a certain realm of language" (p. 110). "The third mode-of-being of language is that of its actual occurrence—its spokenness, or rather being spoken—the word that is spoken" (p. 111). This mode is the realization of man's will to turn to someone in communication. Language in this sense is not a historical acquisition; it is language being spoken. Buber goes on to explain that "the genuine author and genuine dialogue—both draw from the present continuance of language." They draw on the language of the being-with-one-another of living men, and they embody that language in the language of "actual occurence." The genuine author does not draw "from the dammed-up basin of possession, but from the gushing and streaming waters"—the word that is spoken (p. 111). By giving a language of community actual occurence, the poet overcomes the distance between himself and the other. He addresses the other standing at a distance (both temporarily, spatially, and personally), but "in addressing it, he enters into relationship" (p. 117).
10. Except for one essay, "Voice as Summons for Belief," I did not read any of Walter J. Ong's work until after my ideas were formulated. Nevertheless, his work has confirmed my ideas and considerably extended my awareness of the spoken word, poetry, and dialogue. See esp. "The Dialectic of Aural and Objective Correlatives," "Voice as Summons for Belief," "Personalism and the Wilderness," in *The Barbarian Within*

(New York, 1962) and *The Presence of the Word* (New Haven and London, 1967).

11. F. O. Matthiessen was one of the first modern critics to recognize the oral quality of Whitman's poetry—see *American Renaissance* (New York, 1941), p. 559.

12. Matthiessen also first emphasized oratory in Whitman's poetry, pp. 549 ff. Whitman describes his own sense of the power and presence the spoken word can embody in "Father Taylor and Oratory," *Prose Works*, II, p. 551–552.

"For when Father Taylor preach'd or pray'd, the rhetoric and art, the mere words, (which usually play such a big part) seem'd altogether to disappear, and the *live feeling* advanced upon you and seiz'd you with a power before unknown. Everybody felt this marvelous and awful influence.

"I repeat, and would dwell upon it . . . among all the brilliant lights of bar or stage I have heard in my time . . . though I recall marvelous effects from one or other of them, I never had anything in the way of vocal utterance to shake me through and through, and become fix'd, with its accompaniments, in my memory, like those prayers and sermons—like Father Taylor's personal electricity."

13. *An American Primer* (Boston, 1904), pp. 2–3.

14. Cf. Buber, *The Knowledge of Man*, p. 120.

15. "Preface, 1855," p. 717.

16. Cf. Walter Ong, "Voice as Summons for Belief," p. 66.

17. Cf. Friedman, *To Deny Our Nothingness*, p. 27.

18. Cf. G. W. Allen, *The Solitary Singer*, pp. 103 ff. and Roger Asselineau, *The Evolution of Walt Whitman* (Cambridge, 1960), pp. 40–41.

19. Allen, p. 191.

20. Allen, pp. 221–228.

21. See E. H. Miller, *The Correspondence, 1842–1867.*

22. Asselineau, p. 113.

23. Cf. Asselineau, p. 114.

24. *Uncollected Poetry and Prose of Walt Whitman*, vol. II, ed. Emory Holloway (New York, 1932), pp. 95–96.

25. Asselineau, p. 187.

26. *The Correspondence, 1868–1875*, p. 101.

27. Edwin H. Miller points out the possible connection between the notebook and the letter, and he indicates, along with others, that " '164' was undoubtedly intended to conceal Doyle's initials, P (16) D (4)," p. 101n. (See the third Notebook passage quoted above.)

28. See pp. 143–147 for a fuller discussion of "Prayer of Columbus."

29. I have drawn in James M. Cox's discussion of Samuel Clemens and Mark Twain—see *Mark Twain: The Fate of Humor* (Princeton, 1967)—for my sense of Whitman's relation to his persona. Cox suggested as much for Whitman in his article, "Walt Whitman, Mark Twain, and the Civil War." *Sewanee Review* (1961).

30. See *Uncollected Poetry and Prose*, II, pp. 66–67, 69.

31. "A Boston Ballad" and "Respondez," e.g. (esp. p. 206).

32. Allen implies at several points that the political and public self was inessential to Whitman; apparently the real Whitman lay within, behind the mask of Walter. But it seems to me that the public man is essential; he is transformed and enlarged, but not repudiated. The interaction of public and private spheres continues throughout Whitman's life. Whitman changes from Walter to Walt, he does not change his name altogether.
33. Quoted in Allen, p. 504.
34. Pp. 187–193.

CHAPTER THREE

The Self, Space, and Time: the "Soul and I"

On his title page Whitman introduces the basic duality of the self which he felt through most of his life, both as man and poet:

Come, said my Soul,
Such verses for my Body let us write, (for we are one,)
That should I after death invisibly return,
Or, long, long hence, in other spheres,
There to some group of mates the chants resuming,
(Tallying Earth's soil, trees, winds, tumultuous waves,)
Ever with pleas'd smile I may keep on,
Ever and ever yet the verses owning—as, first, I here and now,
Signing for Soul and Body, set to them my name.

Although Whitman did not include the poem as an epigraph until 1874, it does express his initial—and continuing—awareness of the mystery of the self—its twofold or dual nature as soul and body. They are two—engaged apparently in a dialogue with one another; yet they are one, as well. At the same time, Whitman also speaks of communicating with a reader and of "tallying" the things of the world, and in doing so, he implies a second basic division which pervades *Leaves of Grass:* the separation between the me and the not-me. In *Specimen Days* he calls this separation "the most profound theme that can occupy the mind of man."[1]

Interesting as it is, the epigraph poem, however, raises rather than answers questions: what *is* the soul for Whitman? the body?

how are they one? *how* does the poet tally things? in what *kind* of dialogue do the soul and body engage? the self and the world? Even at this abstract level, one finds difference, change, and contradiction; he finds, once again, the *essential* problematic of identity Whitman dramatizes in *Leaves of Grass.* And the basis of that is the mystery of the twofold self.

In his 1847 Notebook Whitman said this about the mystery and miracle of the self:

> My life is a miracle and my body which lives is a miracle; but of what I can nibble at the edges of the limitless and delicious wonder I know that I cannot separate them, and call one superior and the other inferior, any more than I can say my sight is greater than my eyes . . . I cannot understand the mystery, but I am always conscious of myself as two—as my soul and I: and I reckon it is the same with all men and women.[2]

During his formative years as a poet and as a person, Whitman was clearly puzzled and awed by the problem of identity. He found no easy solution then or in the early 1850's when the tensions between public and private realms became acute for him. Nor did he at any time discover a single, definitive sense of himself. For all his later complacency and prosaic assertions about spirit, the self remained, particularly in the context of his whole book, largely a mystery—a problem.

In this chapter, I shall begin answering the questions the epigraph raises and begin confirming some of the suggestions made in the first two chapters. Whitman himself speaks of "soul and I," and provides thereby an appropriate phrase for discussing the twofold self and the relation of the self to the world.

1.

Although no one perspective is definitive, the self's temporal and spatial context provides an initial understanding of the *Soul* and *I.* The *Soul* is limited by neither time or space, whereas the *I* is limited by both. As one identity of the Whitman persona, the *Soul* transcends temporal and spatial limits and expresses or perceives, as Professor Allen has said about Whitman, the "oneness of time, nature, and of soul and body."[3] Once again Whitman's Notebook provides a helpful explanation. His sense of the *Soul's* capacity to imaginatively identify itself with others and to *be* others and other things as well is expressed in this passage from the Notebook:

> The soul or spirit transmits itself into all matter—into rocks, and can live the life of a rock—into the sea, and can feel itself the sea—into an oak, or other tree—into an animal, and feel itself a horse, a fish, or bird—into the earth—into the motions of the suns and stars.[4]

This same sense of identity and the Soul's freedom from physical or spatial limitation carries over into the poetry in such lines from "Song of Myself" as

> My ties and ballasts leave me, my elbows rest in sea-gaps,
> I skirt sierras, my palms cover continents,
> I am afoot with my vision. (33)

> I ascend from the moon, I ascend from the night,
> I perceive that the ghastly glimmer is noonday sunbeams reflected,
> And debouch to the steady and central from the offspring great or small. (49)

Through the image of a dream Whitman breaks through spatial limitations in "The Sleepers":

> Now I pierce the darkness, new beings appear,
> The earth recedes from me into the night,
> I saw that it was beautiful, and I see that what is not the earth is beautiful.

> I go from bedside to bedside, I sleep close with the other sleepers each in turn,
> I dream in my dream all the dreams of the other dreamers,
> And I become the other dreamers. (1)

The *Soul* also escapes the limits of finite time. Another Notebook passage describes Whitman's early conception of the insignificance of time for the *Soul:*

> My right hand is time, and my left hand is space—both are ample—a few quintillions of cycles, a few sextillions of cubic leagues, are not of importance to me—what I shall attain to I can never tell, for there is something that underlies me, of whom I am a part and instrument.

With this basic idea Whitman identified a *Soul* freed of temporal limitations. He expresses the idea in "Song of Myself" in Section 44 beginning with the line "I am an acme of things accomplish'd, and I an encloser of things to be," and in Section 46:

> I know I have the best of time and space, and was never mea-
>   sured and never will be measured.
>
> I tramp a perpetual journey.

As Whitman comes to an end of his long poem, he explicitly indicates that his "I" (the "I" as the *Soul*) spans all time:

> The past and present wilt—I have fill'd them, emptied them,
> And proceed to fill my next fold of the future. (51)

The *I*, conversely, is limited by both time and space; it lacks the capacity to perceive or express the transcendent vision available to the *Soul*. It is an oversimplification to define the *I* as being repre- sented whenever the *Soul* is not; nevertheless, this is partially true. If the vision or awareness of the narrative I does not extend beyond time and space limitations, then it is confined by them and is no longer the *Soul;* it is the *I*. In "Drum Taps," for example, the speaker sings of all America and envisions himself traveling through all the states. But actual time and space circumscribe the vision, or point of view, in the poems. The journey does not compare to the *Soul's* voyage in a poem like "Passage to India." The "Children of Adam" poems celebrate the body through the main theme of procreation and physical love. Necessarily, then, the subject limits the awareness in the poems to finite time and space. Even though Whitman refers to the abstract importance of procreation, he dramatizes no tran- scendent vision or awareness of it in the poems.

This initial distinction between the *Soul* and *I* is based on the degree of awareness or consciousness evident in the two aspects of identity. The awareness of the *Soul* transcends time, space, and ordinary human limitations, and thus the *Soul* perceives unity where division previously existed. The *I*, of course, does not share this ex- panded consciousness; rather it is limited by time and space—in short by conventional human perceptions. In the last analysis, the *Soul* subsumes the point of view and identity of the *I* without negating the level of existence and perception represented by it.

Necessary as this distinction may be, it is clearly inadequate, for the explanation leaves one with an elementary separation and with a statement merely *that* the *Soul* encompasses the *I*. But the particular quality of the experience, the meaning of freedom and limitation, the actual conditions under which the poet experiences his expansive vision, and the exact nature of the self remain open. To make the explanation of the dual self clearer and more precise, I should like to explore two major Whitman poems: "To Think of Time" and "Crossing Brooklyn Ferry."

2.

In "To Think of Time" Whitman presents a series of ideas which define, essentially, a Transcendentalist conception of the unity of the temporal and the eternal. Although he uses concrete images and experiences to develop the poem, he does not actually *dramatize* an experience—as he does, for example, in "Song of the Open Road"— so much as he *illustrates* a conception of time with specific examples. Whitman makes a good deal of the concrete and historical before he commits himself to the eternal; nevertheless, the final section clearly places the poem within a Transcendental metaphysic.

In the first seven sections, Whitman concentrates on time as process and on the facts of existence, especially on the reality of death. Time passes and carries an individual eventually to his death. During his life, that individual lives with the everyday facts of existence and with the constant presence and threat of death—"the burial lines." There are occasional hints in these sections that "you and I" will no longer care about "these wonders of city and country" after "we" die because "we" will "lie beyond"—in eternity, perhaps. Whitman also implies an unseen, ultimate reality when he refers to the difference between the vision of the living and the vision of "a different living":

> The living look upon the corpse with their eyesight,
> But without eyesight lingers a different living and looks curiously on the corpse.

For the most part, however, Whitman ignores and obscures the possibility of the unseen or the eternal by emphasizing the temporal and the concrete.

As a matter of fact, he virtually says that once one dies he will no longer care about life—"we make little or no account"—because "we" will simply be out of it; "we" will be dead:

> To think the thought of death merged in the thought of materi-
>   als,
> To think of all these wonders of city and country, and others
>   taking great interest in them, and we taking no interest in
>   them.
>
>   . . . .
> Slow-moving and black lines creep over the whole earth—they
>   never cease—they are the burial lines,
> He that was President was buried, and he that is now President
>   shall surely be buried.

Whitman reinforces this impression of the actuality and finality of
death by focussing on physical dying and on the condition of the
corpse. And in the fourth section he dwells at some length on the
funeral procession of "an old Broadway stage-driver." He does ask
the question "is there anything more?" Perhaps in the context of the
whole poem that question implies an exuberant, confident *yes*, but
as the poem unfolds the question *is* a question; the answer remains
doubtful. The tone of the first seven sections also confirms the poet's
immersion in the concrete and his uncertainty (at least his lack of
concern) about the unseen. But he experiences little if any doubt
because he is simply not concerned about it. He is, however, certain
of the concrete; he accepts death and human limits; he is apparently
resigned to his fate. The muted tone—the cold, December depression of Section 4—expresses that apparent resignation.

If one has any doubts about Whitman's acceptance of the concrete
and his insistence on the reality of good and evil, section 6 should
remove them:

> The domestic joys, the daily housework or business, the build-
>   ing of houses, are not phantasms, they have weight, form,
>   location,
> Farms, profits, crops, markets, wages, government, are none of
>   them phantasms,
> The difference between sin and goodness is no delusion,
> The earth is not an echo, man and his life and all the things of
>   his life are well-consider'd.

Whitman states as directly as one can that "this world" is real, important, and meaningful—not merely a sign for another or an unreal
shadow that gives way to some Transcendental spiritual dimension;
it "is no delusion."

Through this concrete-temporal world, an individual receives his
"identity"—his own "weight, form, location" (Section 7). Whitman

obviously has in mind a conventional Transcendental idea (similar to the one he develops in "Eidolons"), but at this point in the poem he simply says that one realizes his identity and achieves personal meaning in the lived moment. In the context of the whole poem, however, the lines mean exactly the opposite: even though one receives identity through his body, that body or the individual's particular moment in time exists in the Absolute and must finally give way to it. Nevertheless, in section 7, the poet is still confined to the concrete, the historical, and the temporal.

The eighth section of "To Think of Time" places the poem in a much different perspective from the one that unfolds with the poem. In this final part, one discovers that laws do exist beyond those laws of time, place, and man mentioned in section 7; that death does not mean annihilation; and that the known life, for all its apparent concreteness, is after all transient and perhaps even a kind of "phantasm." Although Whitman possesses no exact sense of immortality, he nevertheless, commits himself to it with supreme confidence, knowing that death will lead somewhere and that "it is good." This same confidence "that every thing without exception has an eternal soul!" resolves all the contradictions and strangling problems of the temporal-historical world, so that "sin and goodness" in themselves no longer really mean anything. They may not be delusions, but they are not absolute, either, for they have their place in the "exquisite scheme" which gives them, finally, a Transcendental rather than a human significance. So in the final analysis all that Whitman so carefully specified and affirmed in sections 1–7 becomes merely a function of immortality:

> I swear I think there is nothing but immortality!
> That the exquisite scheme is for it, and the nebulous float is for
>   it, and the cohering is for it!
> And all preparation is for it—and identity is for it—and life and
>   materials are altogether for it!

"To Think of Time" is indeed a Transcendentalist poem that proclaims the fusion of the temporal and the eternal. In it Whitman presents a typical Transcendental Enthusiast[5] metaphysic. That is, Whitman—the Transcendentalist for the moment—perceives no separation between time and eternity; all time is "for" eternity and the eternal informs and gives meaning to time. Experience involves a reciprocal relation between time and eternity as well as a recognition that the two, actually, are fused from the start.[6]

Whitman resolves the paradox of the simultaneous existence of process or change and permanence by an apparent acceptance of the principle of "nonradical development."[7] That is, development and change occur within a cycle or pattern that repeats itself endlessly in, for example, a birth, growth, death, and rebirth pattern. The cycle is finite because it never goes beyond certain limits; yet it is infinite because it constantly returns on itself.[8] Within the large pattern (Whitman's "exquisite scheme") things do change, yet they remain the same because they are informed and fused by the eternal spirit. Change, in this sense, is teleological because all development is inevitable and moves toward ultimate realization of Being, yet each moment, each thing, already is part of Being.

Whitman further resolves the paradox by equating Being and God. (He does not refer to "god" in "To Think of Time," but he does refer to the Absolute and in other poems he speaks of "God" in an Enthusiast sense). This God is both immanent and transcendent. The temporal-eternal world *is* God's life expressed in the real; for him all things exist in God and are a part of his life. It is apparent, then, that the moment can pass away, yet remain forever as part of Being or of God. Since the real is an expression of God's life, then obviously the Transcendentalist discovers in sensory experience types and symbols of eternal process, just as Emerson discovers that natural facts are signs of spiritual facts. Whitman seems to say the same thing in the poem when he asserts that everything has an eternal soul and that all is for immortality.

The attempt to achieve balance between the temporal and eternal and to maintain both worlds simultaneously—in short, the attempt to "live" the fusion—usually fails, for the Transcendentalist more often realizes his metaphysic in abstract principle than in his moment-by-moment existence. Surely this is the case in "To Think of Time." Whitman simply *says* that everything is for immortality; he does not discover it as part of the action or dramatic situation in the poem. He presents the temporal-historical world at length; then, he simply states "there is nothing but immortality." That provides the necessary intellectual perspective; one understands what he means, but Whitman has not dramatized the realization of fusion in a lived moment in time. The unity he holds out as the underlying principle of the temporal-eternal world exists only intellectually or abstractly, and therefore it results, ironically, in incompleteness rather than in the totality Whitman seeks. Moreover, throughout the poem Whitman stands outside the temporal; he stands as an observer and does not immerse himself in it as a participant. He sees, thinks, and dreams it all, but he does not "live" it as he does in "Crossing Brooklyn Ferry." Dramatically, then, he is incomplete, for the concrete is never really present to him.

The problem is not simply one of realization, either, for the ideas Whitman works with argue that the finite assumes meaning only in the infinite or the eternal: the moment exists in the Absolute. Ultimately, then, the concrete, finite self is absorbed into the infinite or subordinated to it as a mere transient moment in an exquisite scheme. The value of its concreteness (its beautiful blood and brain, its heave of impulse) is diminished because the concrete and the present have no meaning *for* themselves.

The value of "To Think of Time" in my discussion of the *Soul* and *I* is probably obvious, for the situation of the twofold self in some cases directly parallels the situation of the temporal-eternal world. Time is the key to identification of the *Soul* and *I* and to distinguishing between them, but time, as I have indicated, simply helps describe the different capacities for awareness or consciousness the *Soul* and *I* possess. The *I* is historical, temporal, and transient, even if it is not an echo or a phantasm. The *I* participates in becoming— in the change and development of the concrete world. It may seek always to realize the condition and awareness of the *Soul,* yet its action and efforts assume meaning in time, in the life cycle, much as the natural or temporal world does. In "To Think of Time" Whitman develops the realm, so to speak, of the *I* when he describes the temporal-historical world of process, limits, and death, but he does not successfully dramatize a point of view or awareness of the *I* as he does, for instance, in "Drum Taps" or "Calamus."

The *Soul,* on the other hand, informs and gives meaning to the self; it relates the self to the eternal—to Being or God. In other words, the *Soul* is that aspect of God or of the Absolute that every man possesses. Whitman typifies the knowledge and awareness of the *Soul* in the final sections of "To Think of Time" when he declares that the eternal, after all, constitutes the significant reality. The *Soul* receives identity by its "body" (the *I,* in this case), yet the *I* exists significantly only in and for the *Soul* (the moment-in-the-Absolute). Therefore, the real "me," the essential self, is identical with the *Soul,* and no matter how vigorously the Whitmanian Transcendentalist might celebrate bodies and the historical, the *I* remains part of the non-essential self. Since the twofold self is basically an image or a microcosm of the temporal-eternal world, the fusion of *Soul* and *I* occurs on the same ground the fusion of temporal and eternal takes place.

These two conceptions of time—the temporal and eternal—both involve duration, yet they represent different forms of duration. Human time (the temporal) appears as duration if one finds a way of establishing the continuity from moment to moment—if he, in other words, discovers the significance or pattern of the temporal. The Transcendentalist recognizes pattern, first, in the natural or human cycle of change and return. But ultimately each moment and the pattern as a whole achieve real meaning in the context of cosmic time, which has, of course, eternal rather than historical or natural duration. Since the eternal can be concentrated in a particular moment of human time, then the eternal gives the moment all the profundity, all the infinity of duration, a man can experience.[9] Ideally, the Transcendentalist—Walt Whitman in "To Think of Time"—experiences each moment and his whole life in the Absolute: the moment-in-the-Absolute. In this way, the two times merge and fuse, yet in man's experience they retain their difference, as well. In fusion the self knows the fullness of experience and becomes the Soul-I, yet he remains aware that he is also Soul *and* I.

3.

Time explained this way does indeed inform "To Think of Time" and a number of other Whitman poems. Yet I find this particular distinction between times and between the *Soul* and *I* inadequate to explain the essential experience Whitman dramatizes in most of his major poems. Whitman's emphasis on concreteness, on dialogue, on the uncertain nature or mystery of the Absolute, his concentration on the self-in-the-world, and his underlying assumption that the self and experience are open—that life is an open road—force me to seek a different explanation for time and, finally, for the self.[10]

Whitman's theme in "Crossing Brooklyn Ferry" is obviously communication or dialogue between himself and others. The communication takes place through the shared experience he dramatizes in the poem and realizes through the language of the poem. In the first section Whitman refers to the experience itself, crossing the Brooklyn ferry, and to meditation. These become the basis for the communication realized in and through the poem. First, as others cross the East River, they will share their situation and their responses with the poet and, thereby, all will achieve a measure of identity. Second, the poet's meditation as he writes and his dramatized meditation as he stands on the ferry thinking about the experience should also stimulate the reader's response. The poem, then, concentrates on "shared experience" in two ways: it presents the common experience of the dramatized action, the dialogue of the poet and others as New Yorkers and human beings, and it establishes a dialogue between the poet and reader, so it is a shared experience in itself.

The second section expresses Whitman's conviction that there *is* meaning in experience. It also introduces his sense of place, action, and other persons as he asserts his confidence in the response of others and as he begins to describe the concrete situation:

> The glories strung like beads on my smallest sights and hear-
>   ings, on the walk in the street and the passage over the
>   river,
> The current rushing so swiftly and swimming with me far away,
> The others that are to follow me, the ties between me and them,
> The certainty of others, the life, love, sight, hearing of others.

This reference to "the glories strung like beads" is crucial. For with it Whitman fixes the basis for communication in a particular time and place, and, for all the depth and timelessness the shared experience reaches, Whitman never discards the concrete, historical ground. He discovers what it is, finally, that "fuses" him to others and that "pours" his meaning into them only *in* the world—in the lived, human moment.

Communication in the poem occurs on three levels of experience. First, the poet and others simply share an actual experience of crossing the river. Second, they share a common humanity which is not limited to the ferry or the city. Finally, they communicate through an inner sphere; they engage in a dialogue of souls which enables them to transcend certain human limits. Although the poem moves structurally from one level to another (following the structure of the experience), Whitman does not reduce the value of any level of experience, for he encompasses all three, in the end, as parts of the totality he discovers through communication.

At the first level of experience, each individual is limited to the span of his own life.

> These and all else were to me the same as they are to you,
> I loved well those cities, loved well the stately and rapid river,
> The men and women I saw were all near to me,
> Others the same—others who look back on me because I look'd
>   forward to them,

(The time will come, *though I stop here to-day and to-night.*)
    (Italics added.)

Whitman specifically recognizes that even he will "stop here," for as
a man and poet he too is limited to a particular time and place. And
he retains this sense of limitation throughout the poem. Nevertheless, the situation and the responses to it link the poet with those who
live in a later time. Although the experience connects the living with
the dead, it does not do so in any supernatural or spiritualistic way,
for at this point only the objective place and the concrete experience
provide the basis for communication:

> It avails not, time nor place—distance avails not,
> I am with you, you men and women of a generation, or ever so
>   many generations hence,
> Just as you feel when you look on the river and sky, so I felt,
> Just as any of you is one of a living crowd, I was one of a crowd,
> Just as you are refresh'd by the gladness of the river and the
>   bright flow, I was refresh'd,
> Just as you stand and lean on the rail, yet hurry with the swift
>   current, I stood yet was hurried,
> Just as you look on the numberless masts of ships and the thick-
>   stemm'd pipes of steamboats, I look'd.

Whitman begins the fifth section by asking "What is it then between us?" His answer leads him to a deeper sense of the experience,
for now he realizes that he shares more than the actual crossing with
the others. He shares a common humanity with them, and that
becomes the basis for dialogue between man and man. The experience remains grounded, however, in the concrete and historical as
Whitman accepts his body and his human limitations:

> What is it then between us?
> What is the count of the scores or hundreds of years between
>   us?
>
> Whatever it is, it avails not—distance avails not, and place avails
>   not,
> I too lived, Brooklyn of ample hills was mine,
> I too walk'd the streets of Manhattan island, and bathed in the
>   waters around it,
> I too felt the curious abrupt questionings stir within me,
> In the day among crowds of people sometimes they came upon
>   me,
> In my walks home late at night or as I lay in my bed they came
>   upon me,
> I too had been struck from the float forever held in solution,

> I too had receiv'd identity by my body,
> That I was I knew was of my body, and what I should be I knew
>   I should be of my body.

Whitman recognizes that his "identity" emerges and assumes meaning only in time—in Brooklyn and in Manhattan.

In section six Whitman clearly accepts his humanity by recounting
the desperate, despairing, guilty, lonely life that he has shared with
all men:

> It is not upon you alone the dark patches fall,
> The dark threw its patches down upon me also,
> The best I had done seem'd to me blank and suspicious,
> My great thoughts as I supposed them, were they not in reality
>   meagre?
> Nor is it you alone who know what it is to be evil,
> I am he who knew what it was to be evil,
> I too knitted the old knot of contrariety,
> Blabb'd, blush'd, resented, lied, stole, grudg'd,
> Had guile, anger, lust, hot wishes I dared not speak,
> Was wayward, vail, greedy, shallow, sly, cowardly, malignant.

But he is not overwhelmed by all that. He sees, also, that men share
the joys of living, as well, both in moment by moment experiences
(like crossing a Brooklyn Ferry) and in genuine communication with
others. The discovery of the interhuman—yet to come in all its fullness—transforms those dark experiences, but it does not negate
them. Whitman accepts their reality unconditionally, and then transcends them through the mutuality of the "essential We."[11]

In this essential relationship, Whitman overcomes the limits of
time and place, the dark patches of his being, and his own conditioned nature as he experiences the unlimited and unconditioned
through his discovery of the interhuman—the dialogical center of
human life. By exposing his own evil in section 6, Whitman casts
aside his mask and the remaining barriers between himself and others, and he prepares himself for the transformation—the transcendence—that openness achieves. For just after that, in sections 7 and
8, Whitman dramatizes the completion of dialogue. He moves still
closer to his reader:

> Closer yet I approach you,
> What thought you have of me now, I had as much of you—I laid
>   in my stores in advance,
> I consider'd long and seriously of you before you were born.

Following that challenge to meet him in dialogue—to respond to his look and voice—he goes on to explore the subtle inner sphere that "fuses" the "you and I" into "we." Although he can only grasp that inner, timeless, shared existence through indirection, the experience of it does transform the poet and others into the "We."

It is, surely, a spiritual experience that ties men's souls together. The link is a "subtle" one that flows through human time, giving the tie a meaning and direction beyond itself. And it connects Whitman and those to whom he speaks with the source of life—the "eternal float of solution." But Whitman finds the spiritual only through his experience of the human community—the "essential We" that the poem both establishes and dramatizes. Whitman confirms this in the final section when he re-establishes the concrete situation in which his meditation and the action of the poem began. He never really let go of it, for practically every section in the poem expresses it; yet his explicit return at the end of the poem firmly establishes the ground of communication and the modes of dialogue the poem presents. Whitman reaffirms the place:

> Flow on, river! flow with the flood-tide, and ebb with the ebb-
>   tide!
> Frolic on, crested and scallop-edg'd waves!
> Gorgeous clouds of the sunset! drench with your splendor me,
>   or the men and women generations after me!
> Cross from shore to shore, countless crowds of passengers!
> Stand up, tall masts of Mannahatta! stand up,
> beautiful hills of Brooklyn!

He refers, again, to man's evil and malignancy: "Throb, baffled and curious brain! throw out questions and answers!" The questions are presumably those same baffling ones he raised in section 5 and answered in 6. He remembers, also, the masks one wears and the roles he plays to hide his inner reality from others:

> Live, old life! play the part that looks back on actor or actress!
> Play the old role, the role that is great or small according as one
>   makes it!

Whitman reaffirms, as well, the essential I and you dialogue: "Consider, you who peruse me, whether I may not in unknown ways be looking upon you." He even relates all these parts of the experience to the flow of life—to the real reality. The vision that emerges encom-

passes the past and present and future, too, the poet's inner and outer
experiences, the good and evil in him and all men; and it includes
both himself and others.

A basic transformation has taken place. Whitman's participation in
the essential We, for example, has transformed the divisive, destructive impulses he dramatizes in section 6. He sees those impulses now
as only parts (very real parts, however) of the totality he has discovered. He and the others must nevertheless still live those lives, but
now they can consciously share them—live one another's malignancy
—through the mutuality of the interhuman. They do not just live
common experiences of evil and despair, either. The joy and exuberance that possess Whitman in the final sections indicate they share
far more. This new perspective, then, enables Whitman to possess all
he has been and all he speaks of in the poem, but he transforms it
all as well.

The recognition occurs within time and space, yet at the same
time, Whitman transcends their limits. The experience assumes
meaning only at the moment Whitman lives it; yet past, present, and
future are all made present in that concrete experience—just as
those persons Whitman addresses are made present to him and,
perhaps, to the reader in the dialogue of the essential We. The poem
itself has substance and meaning only in its concreteness, yet it, too,
transcends Whitman and history by repeatedly making both present
to its readers. I am suggesting, then, that in "Crossing Brooklyn
Ferry" Whitman discovers the absolute or the spiritual in the moment—a quite different condition for discovery of the "soul," the
"eternal," or the "spiritual" than Whitman presents in "To Think of
Time."

In "Crossing Brooklyn Ferry," Whitman discovers meaning-in-
being in the lived moment through his encounters with objective
reality and through communication with others. He confirms his
discovery of personal meaning in things when he says, near the end
of the poem, that he (now "we") "receives" the objects and their
meaning.

> We receive you with free sense at last, and are insatiate hence-
>   forward,
> Not you any more shall be able to foil us, or withhold yourselves
>   from us,
> We use you, and do not cast you aside—we plant you perma-
>   nently within us.

Each object and each moment contributes to Whitman's discovery of his genuine self, and as the final lines indicate, place and things also lead to Whitman's discovery of the spiritual bond linking all men:

> You furnish your parts toward eternity,
> Great or small, you furnish your parts toward the soul.

Since the entire experience is essentially a spiritual one and because the objects become essential parts of that experience, they are thus informed by its spiritual quality—"being than which none else is perhaps more spiritual." Cities and rivers become spiritual because they are the ground of discovery. That is what the objects "are," but they are permanent or spiritual only in the context of the experience and the poem. They possess no intrinsic spirituality.

Whitman refers to the objects as appearances, but they are reality, too. They achieve their permanence ("objects than which none else is more lasting") as part of a man's total experience. Whitman does not, however, make those objects simple projections of his own subjectivity. On the contrary, he insists on their independent, other reality. He receives them; he plants them permanently within him; yet he does not penetrate them fully or understand them completely:

> You have waited, you always wait, you dumb, beautiful minis-
>   ters,
> We receive you with free sense at last, and are insatiate hence-
>   forward,
> Not you any more shall be able to foil us, or withhold yourselves
>   from us,
> We use you, and do not cast you aside—we plant you perma-
>   nently within us,
> We fathom you not. . . .

In a similar manner, Whitman insists that he is not wholly the other; for experience of the essential we does not destroy the reality of the simple separate person. Whitman's body, for example, remains his, and the "other's" body remains *his*. Whitman experiences full communication, finally, as a separate self, even though such realization becomes possible only through dialogue.

I am saying simply that in "Crossing Brooklyn Ferry" Whitman realizes a common identity within human experience and not initially or ultimately beyond it. Therefore, the end of the poem does not mean that natural facts are signs of spiritual ones; it suggests, instead, that the meaning of experience is not imposed either by the self or by some external objective reality or power. Meaning arises only in the lived moment—in the sphere of the interhuman where the poet discovers the essential "we" unfolding in existence and in the poem. The self that emerges is not then a fixed principle or a complete entity that simply finds expression in some body or moment in time. The self does *emerge;* it is discovered and, in a real sense, created in the lifelong endeavor of living. In "Crossing Brooklyn Ferry" Whitman dramatizes *living*—not life nor some fixed, eternal state, not a world that is for immortality alone.

Although these two poems are roughly contemporary,[12] "Crossing Brooklyn Ferry" is nevertheless a radically different poem from "To Think of Time." The lines that one might quote together to show parallel ideas—

> I swear I think there is nothing but immortality!
> That the exquisite scheme is for it, and the nebulous float is for
>   it, and the cohering is for it!
> And all preparation is for it—and identity is for it—and life and
>   materials are altogether for it!
>   ("To Think of Time")

> Suspend here and everywhere, eternal float of solution!

> You furnish your parts toward eternity,
> Great or small, you furnish your parts toward the soul.
>   ("Crossing Brooklyn Ferry")

> It is not to diffuse you that you were born of your mother and
>   father, it is to identify you,
> It is not that you should be undecided, but that you should be
>   decided,
> Something long preparing and formless is arrived and form'd in
>   you,
> You are henceforth secure, whatever comes or goes.
>   ("To Think of Time")

> Appearances, now or henceforth, indicate what you are,
> You necessary film, continue to envelop the soul,
> About my body for me, and your body for you, be hung our
>   divinest aromas.   ("Crossing Brooklyn Ferry")

—mean quite different things, actually. For I am suggesting that in "To Think of Time" Whitman *asserts* that the moment exists in the absolute; for all his efforts to value the concrete, he finally discards it as the self breaks through to spirit; whereas, in "Crossing Brooklyn Ferry" Whitman *presents* a situation in which the Absolute exists only in the moment. There are three basic reasons for this radical difference. (1) In the Ferry poem, experience is much more concrete and personal in the non-historical mode of time than it is in "To Think of Time." (2) The real self is discovered in contact and communication in "Crossing Brooklyn Ferry" rather than through the abstract-intellectual statement Whitman relies on in "To Think of Time." (3) Whitman actually participates in history and the human in "Crossing Brooklyn Ferry"; whereas in "To Think of Time" he discounts the concrete by holding himself from it and by committing everything to an abstract immortality—to the "nebulous float." This remarkable dissimilarity suggests that early in his poetic career Whitman regarded the self and time as highly problematic—so much so that he embodied quite different conceptions of them in two roughly contemporary poems.

"Crossing Brooklyn Ferry" dramatizes a situation in which chronometric and mythic times figure significantly. I have tried to describe the experiential difference between the two. The distinction, however, needs some explicit comment to indicate how mythic time illuminates "Crossing Brooklyn Ferry" and to show the relevance of mythic time to the question of the twofold self, the *Soul* and *I,* and to its relationship to the world.

Chronometric time refers to time that is spatialized, quantitative, and successive. It divides and dichotomizes experience. It makes existence into a series of discrete moments, into historical sequence, or into a cause and effect chain of events. Chronometric time is, in short, clock time—experience regulated by an order that ignores, to some extent, the essential rhythms of human life. The conception of space related to this is, of course, inseparable from the conception of time. Space, too, acts as a severe limit; distance and separation characterize man's spatial situation in relation to others and to the world. The individual knows only the realm, so to speak, that he can see, the particular *place* in which he passes time. Limited wholly to this time man lives divided, deprived, and isolated. He is merely a function of time or history. He cannot experience intuitive perception, an I-Thou relation, discovery of his genuine self, or totality. In this situation man becomes completely immersed in the instant—the historical situation. He may even be overwhelmed by it. His life, in other words, is defined by the clock, by the historical moment, and by space as a limit and measurement.

Chronometric time, to some extent, defines the world of the "I" —the physical, historical man who lives as a simple, separate person without meaningful contact and without transcendence. He experiences the dark patches, for example, but without communication. He lives the desperate life—"smartly attired, countenance smiling, form upright, death under the breast-bones, hell under the skull-bones"— of the man absorbed in the instant, in progress, or in achievement. But I must caution against mistaking these forms of inauthenticity as definitive of Whitman's "I"; they are not, but they do figure importantly in that aspect of the dual self.

For Whitman to discover the fullness and totality of himself and his experience, he must move from an exclusive sense of successive time to an awareness of time as an unbroken continuum. He must discover mythic time and recover a kind of mythic consciousness. Whitman transcends conventional time (chronometric) in part through memory; that is, memory—or his discovery of myth—associates him with the past, tradition, and the continuing human community. He transcends time, also, by joining, past, present, and future in the lived present moment. That is, he *lives* or *experiences* the continuity of life from the past into the future, and he makes that flow present in the moment.

Mythic time, then, refers to that dimension of life in which one experiences the community mind and the wholeness of living. It is, in the words of Octavio Paz, as long as an eternity and as short as a breath.[13] In this dimension of existence, life and time coalesce into a single whole—into a perpetual or continuous present. One can experience in that sphere, for example, an I-Thou presentness in which chronometric time is suspended, and in which man experiences totality in presentness.

Man's conception of spatiality assumes similar qualities. Instead, for example, of being locked in his narrow realm, man, in Martin Buber's words, experiences a "world."[14] He perceives wholeness in his experience because he can see beyond his realm to a world he shares with others; he experiences, actually, the spatiality of each other—of I-Thou. Therefore, space which localizes and separates and chronometric time avail not, as Whitman would say in "Crossing Brooklyn Ferry." Through this mode of perception man experiences space as situation, context, or totality. He understands it in terms of relation rather than just in terms of the objective, physical space that natural science measures and defines. This transcendence of space and time corresponds to the awareness or experience of the *Soul* in the twofold Whitmanian self.

It is important to recognize, however, that Whitman *recovers* the mythic—the essential we or the communal. He does not regress or return to the original, primordial mythical thinking or consciousness about which Cassirer speaks, for example—a perception in which man experiences time and space without rationalizing them or without forming constructs of them. Instead, mythic time involves a recovery which occurs only after the emergence of individuation, differentiation, history, and philosophy.[15] This time perspective provides for Whitman's actual condition of distance and relation. Distance provides the human situation—individuation and history, for example. Relation provides for man's transcendence *in* that situation —for his experience of I-Thou or of mythic time. Mythic time, in this sense, is a dimension of experience which cuts across the empirical, historical dimension, and thus it is both inseparable from history and independent of it.

When Whitman achieves some sense of mythic time, he becomes aware that his experience is both historic and prophetic, timely and timeless, historical and creative. In "Crossing Brooklyn Ferry" he discovers the mythic only in the lived, concrete, immediate present. In that moment where history and myth intersect *Soul* and *I* become *Soul-I* (one word, no longer two) or the complete, whole self.

I can clarify this point about intersection and totality by borrowing and slightly modifying a diagram from Philip Wheelwright,[16] which should help clarify, as well, the relation of chronometric and mythic time and the relationship of the *Soul* to the *I:*

The horizontal line represents the relation of the individual to external phenomena—to empirical and historical experience or, as Wheelwright calls it, to "secular experience": "that trafficking with things, relations and ideas that makes up our everyday commonsense world"[17] and, I might add, that is structured and regulated by chronometric time and space. The vertical line represents mythic experience, "a dimension of experience cutting across the empirical dimension as an independent variable." Man knows it as a partici-

pant in the community mind which is, Wheelwright says, "darkly
aware" of mystery. That is, through "the profound sense of together-
ness,"[18] characteristic of mythic awareness, man comes to glimpse or
to know something of the infinite.

My modification involves, first, an emphasis on the intersection of
the two dimensions and, second, some change in the terms. For me
the E-P horizontal line represents historical experience and the
realm of the *I*, and the vertical C-M line represents mythic experience and the world of the *Soul*.[19]

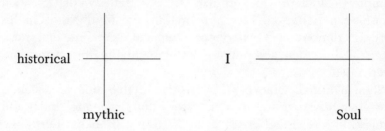

historical   I

        mythic   Soul

The diagram, then, illustrates the twofold nature of the self in "Crossing Brooklyn Ferry" and, I think, through much of *Leaves of Grass*.
It shows, as well, how the mystery of the dual self in Whitman might
be resolved.

The *Soul* and *I*, the mythic and historical selves, are quite distinct,
yet they are existentially one if the self becomes essential. The Whitmanian self becomes essential only as he fully experiences the three
basic relations implied in my discussion: the self in relation to empiri-
cal-historical reality, the self as part of the community, and the self
in relation to mystery of the infinite. That complete self emerges at
the point of intersection in the lived, concrete, immediate moment.
The moment or point of intersection represents the narrow ridge of
the between where man's life becomes essential—where Whitman,
in "Crossing Brooklyn Ferry," becomes *Soul-I*.

NOTES— *Chapter III*

1. *Prose Works 1892*, ed. Floyd Stovall (New York, 1963), I, 258.
2. *Uncollected Poetry and Prose*, ed. Emory Holloway (new York, 1932), II, p. 66.
3. Gay Wilson Allen, *The Solitary Singer* (New York, 1955), p. 155.
4. *Uncollected Poetry and Prose*, II, p. 64.
5. The term is used by E. D. Hirsch, *Wordsworth and Schelling* (New Haven, 1960).
6. Hirsch, p. 62.
7. Hirsch, p. 75.
8. Hirsch, p. 70.
9. Georges Poulet, *Studies in Human Time* (Baltimore, 1956), p. 26.
10. Poulet indicates a related view when he argues that the movement or journey in Whitman's poetry "is not oriented towards a transcendent reality . . . Whitman's procession has nothing terminal or sacramental about it. It simply advances, and in advancing unfolds itself; it occupies the worlds and the times; but never, in contrast with Emerson, does it transcend worlds and times. For it is in the world and in time that the pulse of life beats" (pp. 344–45).
11. Martin Buber, *The Knowledge of Man*, p. 106.
12. "To Think of Time" first appeared in *Leaves of Grass* in 1855; "Crossing Brooklyn Ferry" appeared in 1856.
13. Octavio Paz, "The Dialectic of Solitude," *The Labyrinthe of Solitude* (New York, 1961), p. 209.
14. See Martin Buber's distinction between realm and world, *The Knowledge of Man*, pp. 60–61.
15. Whitman's poetry does not always make a clear distinction—either consciously or experientially. Sometimes, Whitman obviously seeks the primordial, the original unity of existence, with no concern for the historical. He does this, e.g., in "Starting from Paumanok": "A world primal again, vistas of glory incessant and branching," section 17. Even here, however, he is aware of continuity with the past and would concentrate in the present the totality of man's experience. In "Crossing Brooklyn Ferry" Whitman dramatizes mythic time precisely as I am using it, and even though he would return to the original source of life and time in "Passage to India," he attempts, at least, to preserve some connection with the historical present.
16. Philip Wheelwright, "Poetry, Myth, and Reality," *The Modern Critical Spectrum*, ed. Gerald and Nancy Goldberg (Englewood Cliffs, N. J., 1962), p. 307.
17. Wheelwright, p. 307.
18. Wheelwright, p. 310.

19. The angle of intersection, by the way, is relatively unimportant. Although it does imply a certain spatial orientation, the point of intersection is what is important—whatever shape diagram or graph one might use to illustrate it.

PART TWO

Modes of Relation

To understand the poetic identity of Walt Whitman one must carefully examine the essential relationships of the self Whitman dramatizes and the various images of the self which emerge in those relations. If the vast difference between my approach and V. K. Chari's and Edwin H. Miller's approaches to the question of identity in Whitman has not been clear before, it surely will become clear now. For I am arguing that through the personal, the relational, the communal, and finally the spiritual, Whitman moves toward fulfillment and wholeness. He does not achieve real or essential existence in terms of the self alone; instead he realizes it through the drama of the self and the world—through the meaning he attains by giving himself, in relation, to the not-self. Whitman overcomes and withstands the problematic of self and world only through encounter and dialogue.

V. K. Chari, however, argues that the self cannot relate to another without losing its identity, for the individual who engages the other or posits the other as a condition of its own existence ceases to be an individual.[1] For him, then, the Whitmanian self is not "torn by an inner differentiation [there is no problematic] and caught in an endless web of relationship. It is supra relational, indeterminate . . ."[2] There is a radical difference here between our views, and I think a similar distinction exists between James E. Miller, Jr. and myself. For all his inversion of mysticism as a way of preserving Whitman's commitment to concreteness, Miller sees the meaningful reality in Whitman as basically internal or subjective. He says, for example, at the end of a discussion of the self and others: "As the earth is but the projection of the senses of an individual, so that earth reflects the internal condition of the individual. Selfhood remains supreme in an external world of the self's own creation"[3]—where objects or other persons, apparently, have no independent, other reality. Therefore, essential relationships (such as I shall elaborate here), seem either illusory or nonessential in Miller's version of the Whitman identity. Although he writes from a basically Freudian and therefore very different point of view, Edwin H. Miller would also argue that the significant reality in Whitman is internal or "psychic." To him, *Leaves of Grass* expresses an "inner drama."

In *Leaves of Grass* Whitman attempts to encompass a vast amount of personal, American, and human experience; he does so by dramatizing numerous encounters of the self with the not-self and by assuming many different masks or roles. In effect, Whitman is asking *What is man?*

> Who goes there? hankering, gross, mystical, nude;
> How is it I extract strength from the beef I eat?
>
> What is a man anyhow? what am I? what are you?
> ("Song of Myself," 20)

And he tries to answer that question as fully as he can. One needs, therefore, a context for discussing those relationships that accounts for the extensiveness Whitman attempts. The threefold living relationship Martin Buber elaborates in "What Is Man?" provides that context of essential relations which I have explained in my first chapter. My use of Buber, by the way, does not imply that Whitman's experiences are necessarily of the same order or quality as Buber's or that Buber's philosophy is definitive for Whitman. I am confronting the Whitmanian self in its whole or total situation, and Buber provides an entrance into that situation.

CHAPTER FOUR

The Simple Separated Person

This chapter deals with the poems that dramatize different versions of the isolated self. Although the self is sometimes painfully lonely, isolation and alienation in Whitman are hardly identical because Whitman often celebrates the joy of being a detached, single one. Isolation has at least two sides—one Whitman laments, the other he celebrates. In either case the self is incomplete; it does not live a fulfilled life because it has established no real relationships with anything or anyone beyond itself. The "simple separate person" refers in Whitman to a negative situation rather than to the ultimate condition for which every individual strives. If one takes the phrase literally and simplistically—without defining it in terms of the individual person that emerges aware of and part of his total situation—it refers to an incomplete limited self.

Whitman dramatizes three images of the isolated self. The first two correspond to the versions of isolation just mentioned, and the third reflects a self involved in potentially destructive psychological and physical experiences. (1) In celebrating the simple separate person, Whitman idealizes the monological, complacent, self-sufficient man who ignores certain realities and diminishes the importance of relationship. He stands supremely and triumphantly apart from things, others, and perhaps even from the Absolute. (2) The negative of this magisterial self is the alienated and despairing man whose agony results from the failure or loss of all that previously made him confident. He feels his aloneness as a terrible burden and curse rather than as a supreme achievement and pleasure. (3) Whitman also

dramatizes the self in situations (such as war) which interrupt, destroy, or prevent essential relationships that already exist or are at
least potential. The self in this case stands in the midst of suffering
and death and is not simply locked up in its own sensibility. The
possibility of alienation or despair results primarily from his encounter with the facts or convulsions of history and may issue in both
psychic and physical damage, whereas the agony of the Romantic self
results largely from his inability to escape the torment of his own
soul.

Whitman's sense of evil (or his lack of one) inevitably comes up
whenever one discusses despair, suffering, or death in his poetry.
Predictably, readers have disagreed over the quality and significance
of Whitman's experiences of "evil." Few argue that Whitman's sense
of evil is as intense, pervasive, and irrevocable as Melville's. Nevertheless, Stephen Whicher did argue a few years ago, and I think quite
soundly, that Whitman achieved a tragic awareness and vision at
least in "Out of the Cradle" and in the other crisis poems of that
period.[1] There are certain facts and situations that Whitman encounters which are incontrovertible and which he accepts unconditionally as such; he does not always try to account for them
with abstract universals or transfigure them into something
spiritual. Yet critics persistently argue that "evil" has no significance or reality for Whitman. Throughout his life he maintained a
"perfect internal harmony" and "fulness of spirit" which enabled
him to resolve all dilemmas or appearances of evil in terms of the
real, transcendent, supranatural spiritual reality.[2] Many non-mys-
tic critics argue a similar view: Denis Donoghue argues that even
though Whitman could sympathize with suffering, he could translate the pain of others too easily by assimilating it "to the genial
law of his own equation."[3]

Since I am not trying to resolve the question here or survey the
various opinions of others, I would prefer simply to discard the term
"evil" and use words like suffering, despair, pain, death, violence,
destruction, loneliness, etc. that refer more specifically to the situation in the poems, and I would prefer to let the poems speak for
themselves. One finds extensive and persistent awareness in Whitman of physically and psychologically disruptive experiences. Besides personal suffering and public crises which caused Whitman
deep personal distress, one finds in the poems an expression of the
historical insecurity, tension, and conflict characteristic of nine-

teenth century America.[4] Moreover, Whitman's radical action of
repudiating all objective determinants and his unconditional acceptance of existence expose him to all the dangers and oppressive
loneliness isolation can bring.

When I spoke in Chapter Two of the apparent psychological crisis
Whitman experienced in 1870, I quoted passages from his notebook
that indicated great distress or "perturbation." Whitman also included there an "outline sketch of a superb calm character":

> his emotions &c are complete in himself irrespective (indiffer-
>   ent) of whether his love, friendship, &c are returned, or not
> He grows, blooms, like some perfect tree or flower, in Nature,
>   whether viewed by admiring eyes, or in some wild or wood
>   entirely unknown
> His analogy the earth complete in itself enfolding in itself all
>   processes of growth effusing life and power for hidden pur-
>   poses.[5]

In the poem "Me Imperturbe" he also describes the self-sufficient
and self-contained individual:

> Me imperturbe, standing at ease in Nature,
> Master of all or mistress of all, aplomb in the midst of irrational
>   things.

The two describe the monological or Romantic self that constitutes
the first major image of the isolated man in Whitman. For him nothing is problematic. He is "complete in himself." Evidently, he recognizes neither the need or essentiality of relationship, and he possesses
such self-assurance that nothing seems to challenge or threaten him.
The wholeness he presumably achieves (both passages claim completion or fulfillment) results from exclusion and withdrawal rather than
from a realistic encounter and participation in the complexities of
life.

In "Song of Joys" Whitman emerges, in the end, as the kind of
simple separate person to whom I am referring. Whitman presents
the egocentric self first, then he seems to present that self as actually
encountering others in a relation that transcends the individual, but
finally he confirms the initial impression.

At the beginning, the poet apparently desires to possess every
conceivable occasion for joy; he cannot be satisfied even by the experiences this world gives him:

> It is not enough to have this globe or a certain time,
> I will have thousands of globes and all time.

The longing for possession is the key, for it indicates that he sees
these joys as reflections or mirrors of his own feelings. He does not
so much project or create the world in his own joyous image; instead,
he would remove the world into himself by selecting, possessing, and
coloring it in terms of his own sensibility and desires. He would
absorb it into himself without encountering it or without recognizing
it as an independent other.

The "vast elemental sympathy" Whitman speaks of in line 23
confirms this initial image of the self. "O the joy of that vast elemental
sympathy which only the human soul is capable of generating and
emitting in steady and limitless floods." Presumably, Whitman refers
to the sympathy that enables him to feel the joys of all those other
people; and he also finds the sympathy itself an occasion for joy. The
sympathy he "emits" for others, however, does not involve any reciprocal or essential relationship with them; nor does it lead to any
significant self-transcendence. Sympathy, in this case, is a feeling for
another, but still largely in terms of one's own sensibility. It does not
involve a recognition and understanding of that other person in
terms of his sensibility and being.

Later, Whitman seems to qualify and revise this initial image in
two ways. (1) He begins to imaginatively identify himself with other
individuals and thus recognize their concreteness and independence
—the actuality of their situations.

> Another time in warm weather out in a boat, to lift the lobster-
> pots where they are sunk with heavy stones, (I know the
> buoys,)
> O the sweetness of the Fifth-month morning upon the water as
> I row just before sunrise toward the buoys,
> I pull the wicker pots up slantingly, the dark green lobsters are
> desperate with their claws as I take them out, I insert
> wooden pegs in the joints of their pincers,
> I go to all the places one after another, and then row back to
> the shore,
> There in a huge kettle of boiling water the lobsters shall be
> boil'd till their color becomes scarlet.

(2) He also speaks of a basic interaction between himself and
the world—an interaction upon which his identity depends and
through which he comes to know the essential inner reality of himself.

> O the joy of my soul leaning pois'd on itself, receiving identity
> through materials and loving them, observing characters
> and absorbing them,
> My soul vibrated back to me from them, from sight, hearing,
> touch, reason, articulation, comparison, memory, and the
> like,
> The real life of my senses and flesh transcending my senses and
> flesh,
> My body done with materials, my sight done with my material
> eyes,
> Proved to me this day beyond cavil that it is not my material
> eyes which finally see,
> Nor my material body which finally loves, walks, laughs, shouts,
> embraces, procreates.

Whitman appears to value concrete reality and intuitive identification with others as essential parts of his experience: the poem, in
other words, shifts, apparently, to the dialogical. But one soon recognizes that relationship is simply an occasion for Whitman's joy and
not an essential aspect of his experience. The poem turns out, in fact,
to be a monologue, and the self emerges as primarily egocentric.

The address by the poet to himself excludes the essential living
relations, even the one between the self and God. The dramatized
dialogue with others proves to be incomplete and not genuine. The
relationship of the self to the external world is simply irrelevant to
the poet's experience of God-likeness, for Whitman asserts a su-
premacy for himself and his soul that makes the "exterior" or the
"proud laws" of concrete reality ultimately powerless and meaningless:

> O to struggle against great odds, to meet enemies undaunted!
> To be entirely alone with them, to find how much one can
> stand!
> To look strife, torture, prison, popular odium, face to face!
> To mount the scaffold, to advance to the muzzles of guns with
> perfect nonchalance!
> To be indeed a God!

Not only that—he finally asserts that this world (the land and the city
and other persons) is tiresome and unendurable:

> O to sail to sea in a ship!
> To leave this steady unendurable land,
> To leave the tiresome sameness of the streets, the sidewalks and
> the houses,
> To leave you O you solid motionless land, and entering a ship,
> To sail and sail and sail!

Whitman's cry not only reveals his longing for greater, more intense, purer joys than he has known—ultimately a transcendental, other worldly joy; it obscures, as well, his awareness of the continuing threats in this world of "something pernicious and dread"—"something" he would deny and escape through the "jubilant song" of the self-sufficient and self-contained Romantic self. Finally, the relationship of the poet and reader is neither dramatically nor functionally present in the poem. One has no sense here of a presence or voice addressing or speaking with his reader. One becomes aware of a man —of Walt Whitman—but he neither "touches" him or encounters him in dialogue; instead, one simply hears the poet declaiming "A Song of Joys."

The poem also engages in a conscious exclusion of those realities which would question and even threaten the aplomb and the presumed completeness of Walt Whitman, and this evasion helps clarify, in yet another way, the image of the self the poem presents. Whitman's description of "the whaleman's joys" is a particularly revealing example of what I mean, especially if one compares Whitman's brief description of the quickest *joys* of the chase with Melville's sense of the quickest *perils* of the chase. Whitman focuses on a concrete situation; he indicates that one can know the whaleman's joys only by participating in the chase—imaginatively if in no other way, and he does momentarily become the other. Yet he ignores the potential total situation: he excludes the dangers (the perils), and he sees none of the savagery and violence involved. I am not saying Whitman *should* have shown a Melvillean sense of whaling; he simply did not, and that is the point. The self in this poem can convert complex, ambiguous—even painful—situations into simple, joyful ones. He insures his detachment and wholeness (his aplomb in the midst of irrational things) by making joyful noises and by painting everything with a joyous brush.

In short, he evades all the discoveries Walt Whitman had made by 1860 in his awkward, perhaps even desperate, attempt "to make the most jubilant song!" My point about evasion—and *conscious* evasion —seems to be confirmed by those four ambiguous, provocative, difficult lines near the middle of the poem:

(O something pernicious and dread!
Something far away from a puny and pious life!
Something unproved! something in a trance!
Something escaped from the anchorage and driving free.)

These are the only parenthetical lines in the poem, and that fact draws attention to the way the lines interrupt the sequence of joys Whitman presents. The lines are also the only ones that remotely suggest a vague, pernicious something that could undermine and destroy the poet's joyous state of mind. Although they are unclear and possess no substantive content, they do represent a threat which surfaces momentarily in the vast ocean of joy and frees one to think of other poems in the 1860 edition.[6] That threatening something, below the surface, eating away the joys, might be the despair and overwhelming sense of failure dramatized in "As I Ebb'd"—or the torment and guilt of the *Calamus* poems. One also inevitably thinks of Whitman's own personal crisis; the "something" might be the "pernicious" perturbation that repeatedly upset him during his life. No one of these possibilities need to be taken literally as the meaning for "Song of Joys"; the possible meanings and the lines do indicate, however, that the Whitman persona knows he is excluding a significant dimension of experience so that the joys will appear to be total.

This poem differs radically from "Song of the Open Road" and so the self emerging from it differs from the Walt Whitman who entered "onto" the road. In that poem, Whitman's experiences take place in-the-world—in relation to the concrete, within the limits of the "exterior," and in relation to other persons. His discovery that he is better than he thought and his experience of the possibility of genuine dialogue actually depend on the essential relationships Whitman establishes in the poem; whereas in "A Song of Joys" the joy and freedom Whitman would achieve depend on his extricating himself from relationships. The version of the self Whitman dramatizes in "A Song of Joys" corresponds to the Whitman of the first part of "Song of Myself" who stands apart from all the pulling and hauling and who finds that the everyday realities confronting him are not part of his real self.

But the self in "A Song of Joys" neither values nor experiences the essential relationships which Whitman expresses and realizes in "Song of Myself." Whitman's ability to imagine himself momentarily as another in "A Song of Joys" may indicate a potential for the kind of relationship Whitman concentrates in a line such as "I am the man, I suffer'd, and was there," but the Joy poem moves in another direction: toward the God-like monological man, away from the man who —for all of his expansiveness and enlargement of himself—participates in the world with others. In "Crossing Brooklyn Ferry" Whitman achieves a real relation between the poet and reader and

dramatizes, as well, a genuine dialogue of the essential We. Neither
relation is even potential in "A Song of Joys."

For all the difficulty one might have in reconciling "A Song of Joys"
with his general impression of the 1860 edition and with the period
in Whitman's life that edition supposedly represents, it is absolutely
necessary to think of it in relation to the most depressed poems of
that third edition. For the existence of these extremes—the apparent
peak-joys of "A Song of Joys" and the hopeless despair of "As I Ebb'd"
—underscore the problematic of identity in Whitman. The larger
image of the self emerging from the 1860 edition reveals the poet's
uncertainty about himself and the nature of experience as "Leaflet"
suggests:

> Who is now reading this?
>
> May-be one is now reading this who knows some wrong-doing
>   of my past life,
> Or may-be a stranger is reading this who has secretly loved me,
> Or may-be one who meets all my grand assumptions and ego-
>   tisms with derision,
> Or may-be one who is puzzled at me.
>
> As if I were not puzzled at myself!
> Or as if I never deride myself! (O conscience-struck! O self-
>   convicted!)
> Or as if I do not secretly love strangers! (O tenderly, a long time,
>   and never avow it;)
> Or as if I did not see, perfectly well, interior in myself, the stuff
>   of wrong-doing,
> Or as if it could cease transpiring from me until it must cease.[7]

The negative of the simple separate person who rejoices in his
extraordinary individuality is that man who has fallen into deep
despair because he has lost confidence in himself and in the reality
he thought he knew and could conquer. "As I Ebb'd with the Ocean
of Life" is Whitman's classic expression of alienation and despair. It
is so well known that I need not quote it at length except to confirm
my placement of it in this section. In the poem Whitman discovers
his personal insignificance as a man and a poet; he identifies himself
with the meaningless "little wash'd-up drift" along the shore, and
ends the poem virtually as he began it—oppressed by his insignificance and by the mystery of nature and death. Although the "I"
knows that something exists beyond the shore—beyond his limited

perceptions, it remains a mystery. For him only the finite self exists in a world of human fallibility and depression.

Whitman develops this sense of inadequacy and insignificance, first, by drawing a contrast in sections 1 and 2 between that which the poet knows and the vast spheres of experience he does not know. As the poet walks along familiar shores, he is fascinated by the things he sees, and nothing disrupts his mood or his sense of security. In such a contented, contemplative mood, the Transcendental doctrine of correspondence even seems possible—"the old thought of like-nesses." When the poet thinks of himself in a knowable time and space situation, he possesses a clear sense of location. But when he confronts all that he does not know, he begins to feel a severe sense of dislocation and disconnection.

In the second part, Whitman confronts the mystery of the universe, represented by the vast, unknown ocean, and through that encounter he realizes his own personal insignificance and the tremendous inadequacy of his knowledge:

> As I wend to the shores I know not,
> As I list to the dirge, the voices of men and women wreck'd,
> As I inhale the impalpable breezes that set in upon me,
> As the ocean so mysterious rolls toward me closer and closer,
> I too but signify at the utmost a little wash'd-up drift,
> A few sands and dead leaves to gather,
> Gather, and merge myself as part of the sands and drift.

He now sees that what fascinated him and seemed so important before (the scum, the scales, and the leaves that had suggested "the old thought of likenesses") have become disconnected, meaningless bits and pieces along the beach. In his lonely situation the poet also confronts the mystery of himself. He once thought he knew who he really was, but now he recognizes that he has not understood anything, even about himself:

> Aware now that amid all that blab whose echoes recoil upon me
>   I have not once had the least idea who or what I am,
> But that before all my arrogant poems the real Me stands yet
>   untouch'd, untold, altogether unreach'd,
> Withdrawn far, mocking me with mock-congratulatory signs
>   and bows,
> With peals of distant ironical laughter at every word I have
>   written,
> Pointing in silence to these songs, and then to the sand beneath.

His apparent failure to understand both the world and himself baffles and balks him—bends him "to the very earth":

> I perceive I have not really understood any thing, not a single
>   object, and that no man ever can,
> Nature here in sight of the sea taking advantage of me to dart
>   upon me and sting me,
> Because I have dared to open my mouth to sing at all.

In this poem Whitman is completely alienated from himself, from empirical reality, from others, and from spirit. His real self mocks him from an unbridgeable distance; nature is hostile to him; there is no other person anywhere; and he does not even know the name of the Absolute he calls to, but who does not respond: ("You up there walking or sitting/Whoever you are . . ."). The only relation possible for him identifies him with the "wash'd-up" drifts—"a few sands and dead leaves." And for a moment, he thinks of himself and all of nature as mere meaningless noise and motion:

> You oceans both, I close with you,
> We murmur alike reproachfully rolling sands and drift, know-
>   ing not why,
> These little shreds indeed standing for you and me and all.

Such a relation simply intensifies his awareness of his insignificance and isolation.

The remaining two parts elaborate and intensify the basic condition of alienation and despair. After facing the unknown both in himself and beyond—an encounter which calls everything into question—Whitman turns back to that which he does know.

> You friable shore with trails of debris,
> You fish-shaped island, I take what is underfoot,
> What is yours is mine my father.

He accepts objective, physical reality and sees himself as part of it. He even gives himself to it, but his own commitment is not enough:

> I throw myself upon your breast my father,
> I cling to you so that you cannot unloose me,
> I hold you so firm till you answer me something.

He seeks a response from what he once knew. He looks for some confirmation that he does have a real connection with the concrete and with the source of life. He calls to the father, seeking the touch of love and the breath of life as response. But Whitman hears only the moaning of the fierce old mother—nothing from the father. Even that which was home, relation, and meaning (Paumanok—"the shores I know"—the knowable in life), now has become remote and mysterious. The poet's recognition of his separation from both himself and the world shows him that his previous confidence and contentment were illusory: he is in fact homeless.

He turns outward again and calls to the ocean and mystery, hoping for some final response that would restore confidence and meaning for him—"deny not me." Nothing, however, points the way out of his hopeless isolation; the sea moans and rustles "hoarse and angry," but it gives no word, no sign, as the "fierce old mother" does in "Out of the Cradle."

Failing, then, to discover the real me in the world or in himself and finding no significant response or relation anywhere, Whitman is overwhelmed by what is not himself; he is lost in the confusing flux of a hostile, remote nature. His failure results in dislocation, grief, anxiety, and emptiness. He accepts limitations as definitive, and this leads to frustration and despair, for in his world everything is relative, finite, and fragmented; he finds chance and death everywhere.

Whitman clearly stands at the edge of mystery or even at the edge of an abyss; his incapacity to know or relate to anything calls everything about himself and life into question; by the end of the poem the self is virtually shattered. Yet Whitman does not stand at the edge of nothingness or of total obliteration of personality. He stands alone —alienated and despairing (one cannot soften that fact)—but he insists that something or someone exists beyond the limits which have overwhelmed him, even if he is completely cut off from whatever or whomever it may be:

> We, capricious, brought hither we know not whence, spread
>   out before you,
> You up there walking or sitting,
> Whoever you are, we too lie in drifts at your feet.

In other words he keeps listening for the word that never arises in "As I Ebb'd" but which does come later.[8]

Two other poems—among the many one might choose—suggest the different emotional responses of the poet to alienation and despair. In "I Sit and Look Out" Whitman simply "looks" upon "all the sorrows of the world, and upon all oppression and shame." The poem dramatizes his encounter with the disillusioning, terrifying, depressing, and confusing brute facts of life. These conditions appear to be endless: "All these—all the meanness and agony without end I sitting look out upon." Such a stark confrontation with meanness and agony leaves him empty—beyond all sorrow and emotion. He stands apart, completely separated from the world. Unable to act, he merely sees and hears, and at the end of the poem he has nothing more to say.

"Tears" possesses almost the opposite emotional quality; the poem seems very much like the work of Poe in its expression of extreme sadness and emotional frenzy. Whitman's use of *tears* twelve times in the poem sufficiently indicates its emotional pitch. It simply describes an emotional storm of confusion, desperation, fear, and despair that has overwhelmed the speaker. The poem establishes a day-night contrast in which nighttime, the hidden, personal reality, exposes the real turmoil and torment behind the "sedate and decorous" daytime mask. The real me seems to be a tormented self. In "A Hand Mirror," to extend this idea, the real me (at least the self within, behind the mask) is physically, psychologically, and morally rotten.

> Hold it up sternly—see this it sends back, (who is it? is it you?)
> Outside fair costume, within ashes and filth. . . .

If one compares these four poems—"As I Ebb'd," "I Sit and Look Out," "Tears," and "A Hand Mirror"—with Whitman's more positive expressions, he discovers one of the major tensions contributing to the problematic of identity in Whitman. The poems not only reveal an awareness of tension and uncertainty in the total work, but they also show—more intensely in this case—that Whitman's sense of the problematic persisted throughout the development of the poet and his book. Whitman published both "As I Ebb'd" and "I Sit and Look Out" in 1860. But "I Sit and Look Out" ("A Hand Mirror," too) was written during that earlier period (1856-57) in which the exuberance and confidence of 1856 presumably dominated Whitman's state of mind.[9] "As I Ebb'd," of course, emerged from the "dark period" of 1859. "Tears" first appeared in *Leaves of Grass* in 1867, but it is not clear when Whitman wrote it. Now, short poems do not necessarily displace the impact of larger more positive ones, but they do indicate that the threat of alienation and despair, in some form, persisted in Whitman's awareness and poetry throughout his most creative years.

One can follow this awareness well into the 1870's: "Prayer of

Columbus" provides the evidence. Just as "As I Ebb'd" dramatizes complete alienation and the failure to achieve the transcendence of "Out of the Cradle," so "Prayer of Columbus" presents the complete failure of both the "Song of Myself" and "Passage to India" visions. Most readers quickly recognize the sickness unto death Whitman describes in the poem, but most seem convinced that Columbus receives compensation for his physical and psychological debility through his conviction that he knows and can depend on God. Actually, instead of discovering a "sustaining knowledge of God,[10] Columbus becomes completely confused in the end and must question the possibility of any communion or relation with God at all.[11]

The man in this poem is overwhelmed by an even deeper despair than that of the persona in "As I Ebb'd." He is weakened physically, "sicken'd and nigh to death," and mentally—"I am too full of woe." He has given up completely on himself and the world: the exuberant, confident self Whitman dramatized in the early years has disappeared; even the strength of the figure in "As I Ebb'd" has deteriorated; and of course, the true son of God Whitman celebrates in "Passage to India" cannot be found in "The Prayer of Columbus" anywhere. As a result, he must depend on God, for he has nothing else—even his achievements mean nothing unless they have come from God. Thus his last gesture toward God results as much from the speaker's despair and desperation as from his faith. The God Columbus seeks differs greatly from the immanent God in "Song of Myself" and the available God in "Passage to India." This one does not seem to exist in time at all; he is remote and silent.

The distance between man and God becomes evident in a series of comparisons Whitman makes in the poem. (1) Columbus says several times "Thou knowest . . . Thou knowest," and indeed he assumes that God does know all. But Columbus himself can merely pray and accept: "Accepting all from Thee, as duly come from Thee." He possesses no real knowledge:

> The end I know not, it is all in Thee,
> Or small or great I know not. . . .

(2) The poem sets up a here-there rhythm as well; that is, weak, limited man is here, and God is *there*, where all life will be transfigured. Columbus speaks of his knowledge of "the brutish measureless human undergrowth," and he feels certain that it will be transfigured after death in God—

> Haply the brutish measureless human undergrowth I know,
> Transplanted *there* [the end—which "is all in Thee"] may rise
>   to stature, knowledge worthy Thee. . . . (Italics mine)

(3) The light (whether it be God, life, the imagination, knowledge, or whatever) that once came, in part at least, from within, now exists only in God:

> That Thou O God my life hast lighted,
> With ray of light, steady, ineffable, vouchsafed of Thee. . . .

(4) The contrasts indicate, finally, the vast gulf which stands between man and God—between the temporal and eternal—which Columbus would bridge by his submission and his weak call. "One effort more . . . Old, poor, and paralyzed, I thank Thee. . . . I yield my ships to Thee."

One finds Columbus, then, poured out, exhausted, lost, and paralyzed. Everything in this world has collapsed and failed for him, and as a result he has no confidence in any part of life. He has no choice, therefore, but to turn to the remote, supreme God who is both the source and the end of "all." At *least*, Columbus has confidence in God.

At this point he suddenly becomes aware that his faith may be madness instead of truth—"Is it the prophet's thought I speak, or am I raving?" The question is not answered; instead, Columbus goes on to question what he knows of himself and his whole life:

> What do I know of life? what of myself?
> I know not even my own work past or present,
> Dim ever-shifting guesses of it spread before me,
> Of newer better worlds, their mighty parturition,
> Mocking, perplexing me.

He discovers, through the doubts his questions express, that the direction of his whole life and his convictions have been guesses and, therefore, unreliable and dubious. Even the new world he envisions —like everything else he thought he knew—mocks and perplexes him now. The next-to-last stanza, thus, casts everything into doubt and confusion, and as a result Columbus seems to lose confidence even in the God he thought he knew. With that he has lost everything. The lines do not *repudiate* the possibility of future fame for Columbus or the existence of the God he addressed, but the questions and doubts effectively destroy his confidence. As far as he is concerned, God may be an illusion and "newer better worlds" the hope of a madman.

The last stanza does nothing to restore the validity of his vision. The question—"Is it the prophet's thought I speak, or am I raving?" —has broken into the experience and destroyed any chance of absolute assurance. It colors the meaning of the poem from the question to the end. Therefore, the vision Columbus sees and the anthems he hears (as he implicitly recognizes) may be hallucinatory. He says, in effect, that he is uncertain of their meaning, and the explanation he offers begins with "As if":

> And these things I see suddenly, what mean they?
> *As if* some miracle, some hand divine unseal'd my eyes. (Italics
>   mine)

In the end, Columbus does *not* know. He is alone. He has not been saved.

In the middle poems in "Drum Taps," Whitman dramatizes his encounter with one of the major facts and convulsions of American history. He recognizes that he and the men fighting the war are in a situation which interrupts, destroys, and prevents essential relationships. In Whitman's perspective, the war becomes a human version of all the brutal, violent, mutilating facts of existence which one cannot escape. If this experience does not *destroy* a man, it fragments his life, it isolates him, and it might damage him physically or psychically. On the other hand, the dangers and horrors of war can also bring men into closer relationships with one another than they might have experienced under normal conditions, and such relationships constitute an important part of Whitman's experience in "Drum Taps" and in the war. They will figure, however, in another part of my discussion. It is important, for now, that war also takes away the comrades or friends it may give; and it, likewise, threatens to destroy the very union it would preserve.

"The Centenarian's Story" signals the change from Whitman's super-patriot attitude about war to a more realistic understanding of the real war. The change and the difference between the two attitudes emerges in the poem, first, through the old man's response to the spectacle of the troops drilling before a smiling audience:

> Why what comes over you now old man?
> Why do you tremble and clutch my hand so convulsively?
> The troops are but drilling, they are yet surrounded with smiles,

Around them at hand the well-drest friends and the women,
While splendid and warm the afternoon sun shines down,
Green the midsummer verdure and fresh blows the dallying
    breeze,
O'er proud and peaceful cities and arm of the sea between.

The speaker and the audience seem to glorify war, but the old man
has experienced its reality and, therefore, he shudders when he sees
America again going to war. Through the old man's story the poet
begins to see that war is a sickening slaughter.

Several of the poems following "The Centenarian's Story" present
a series of brief, realistic descriptions of war scenes—"Cavalry Crossing a Ford," "Bivouac on a Mountainside," and "An Army Corps on
the March." These in turn develop into a series of poems that concentrate on the loneliness, loss, waste, destruction, and death caused by
war. In his initial bellicose state of mind Whitman clamored for his
countrymen to give up everything for the war—all the normal activities of life—home, work, religion, relations with others. He celebrated these interruptions not only as necessary but as exciting and
heroic as well. Later on, he assumes the perspective of the lonely
soldier who feels his separation as a loss. There is no drum beating,
no call to arms, no heroism in "By the Bivouac's Fitful Flame"—

While wind in procession thoughts, O tender and wondrous
    thoughts,
Of life and death, of home and the past and loved, and of those
    that are far away;
A solemn and slow procession there as I sit on the ground,
By the bivouac's fitful flame.

War cuts men off from their homes, their past, and their loved ones.
It leaves them isolated in a weary world of violence; it may even kill
them. In short, war interrupts and destroys the flow of life and it
brings violent premature death. Whitman indicates this in "Come
Up from the Fields Father" where he contrasts the fertility of the
farm and the fulfillment of autumn with the deprivation war brings
by killing the son; the death makes the natural fertility of the land
meaningless for the family and imposes a burden of sorrow on the
mother which she will carry for a long time. The war not only destroys soldiers; it deprives others of meaningful life.

In "A March in the Ranks Hard-Prest, and the Road Unknown" the
constant threat of violent, unjust death makes the soldier's "road" in
war dark and unknown. The individual soldier has no sense of the

total war; he does not know where he marches or what he will find in or beyond the woods. He marches along a midnight road, deep in the woods, that leads him to a lurid, shadowy, ominous building:

> We come to an open space in the woods, and halt by the dim-
>   lighted building,
> 'Tis a large old church at the crossing roads, now an impromptu
>   hospital. . . .

It is more like a House of Death than a place where lives are saved. The soldier who speaks in the poem finds there "a mere lad, in danger of bleeding to death" and a "crowd of . . . bloody forms"; he passes "some in the death-spasm sweating"; he hears "an occasional scream or cry"; and he smells "the odor of blood." The road to war leads into a frightening, demonic underworld—a nightmare. More-over, the road is also unknown and ominous because it may lead a man to his own death.

The soldier's way remains unknown as he marches toward no goal at the end; he does not even contemplate the peace that may follow the war because there may be no peace, no goal or end for the individual soldier except death. If this poem does not implicitly ques-tion the value of the cause (can it be worth the cost?), it shows that one forgets the cause when he is immersed in suffering and death.

In "A Sight in Camp in the Daybreak Gray and Dim" Whitman dramatizes another dimension of his awareness of war's destructive-ness and irrationality. The poet describes himself lifting the blankets from the faces of three corpses lying on stretchers outside his tent. The greatest impact of the poem is in the last three lines:

> Then to the third—a face nor child nor old, very calm, as of
>   beautiful yellow-white ivory;
> Young man I think I know you—I think this face is the face of
>   the Christ himself,
> Dead and divine and brother of all, and here again he lies.

They convert the poem into a moving comment on man's repeated destruction of virtue and value in his existence. Man, irrevocably and obviously, becomes his own destroyer in the midst of a war intended to save and preserve. Whitman does not quite say it; nonetheless, the poem does call the ideal or cause into question once more, for the war to save the Union leads to the destruction of another "Christ."

"The Wound-Dresser" climaxes the series of poems in which Whit-man dramatizes his stark confrontation with violence, mutilation,

and death. The poem describes the speaker's own evolution from the
"arous'd and angry" man who would "urge relentless war" to the
saddened, weary man who resigned himself "To sit by the wounded
and soothe them, or silently watch the dead." The radical difference
in the two attitudes also emerges in the contrast between the youths,
who urge the old man to tell them stories of the excitement and
heroism of war, and the wound-dresser;

> Now be witness again, paint the mightiest armies of earth,
> Of those armies so rapid so wondrous what saw you to tell us?
> What stays with you latest and deepest? of curious panics,
> Of hard-fought engagements or sieges tremendous what deep-
> est remains?

The young people no doubt sound very much like the wound-dresser
did when he beat the drums and called for relentless war. But now
his deepest memories dwell on "many of the hardships, few [of] the
joys." Thus, his story returns him to a hospital where the wounded
and dying lie suffering. In a sense the old man must sit and look out
on all the suffering and dying, which he cannot control, much as the
poet does in "I Sit and Look Out." But there is a difference between
the two situations—and this no doubt saves Whitman from falling
into complete mental and emotional paralysis in the war poems: as
a wound-dresser he *can* offer some assistance and comfort even
though he can do nothing to change the conditions of life and death.

Each of the three main images of the "separated" man present
versions of the limited, isolated *I*, for each is trapped, primarily
within himself or in time. The "positive" image of the Romantic self
(the Romantic egotist) is locked in his own sensibility, which he thinks
is the world. The Romantic agonist (the negative image) is devastated
by his discovery that he is not the world, nor is it him; thus his own
limits and failures overwhelm him. The third image of the self is
isolated (and potentially alienated) by conditions over which he has
no control; he is limited by the human situation and history. His
situation, then, is quite different from those of the other two (for he
at least has confronted that independent other). Although each
figure differs from the others, they do share a general condition. They
live divided, deprived, or isolated lives; they experience no meaningful contact or relation; they possess no authentic or even relatively
complete sense of themselves. In other words, in their pure or abstract forms, they experience no movement toward completeness or
toward the condition of the *Soul*.

NOTES—*Preface to Part II*

1. V. K. Chari, *Whitman in the Light of Vedantic Mysticism* (Lincoln, Nebraska, 1964), p. 35.
2. Chari, p. 81.
3. James E. Miller, Jr., *Critical Guide to Leaves of Grass* (Chicago, 1957), p. 209.

NOTES—*Chapter IV*

1. "Whitman's Awakening to Death," in *The Presence of Walt Whitman*, ed. R. W. B. Lewis (New York, 1962).
2. Chari, pp. 154 ff.
3. See Donoghue's essay on Whitman in *Connoisseurs of Chaos* (New York, 1965).
4. See, e.g., Perry Miller, "The Shaping of the American Character" and Richard Chase, "Walt Whitman as American Spokesman," both in *Whitman: A Collection of Critical Essays*, ed. Roy H. Pearce; Marius Bewley develops this sense of division in broad terms in *The Eccentric Design.* It is not an uncommon view of the American experience.
5. *Uncollected Poetry and Prose*, II p. 96.
6. These lines are much more difficult than they seem at first. I am reading them as a revelation of a buried fear of some vague threat to Whitman's psychological well-being—perhaps an early indication of the torment his sexual ambiguity caused him. My reading is admittedly open to question. The crucial line which establishes the way one reads the other three (syntax and parentheses make the lines a unit) originally read, according to Bowers' *Whitman's Manuscripts: Leaves of Grass (1860)* (Chicago, 1955): "O something wild and untamed!" It is not clear, however, if both words were changed at the same time—they are written in different inks on the ms—or when Whitman made the change. Whitman altered the line to read "O something pernicious and dread!" The revisions change the meaning radically; for "wild" and "untamed" could refer to the kind of freedom and joy Whitman seeks and has been describing before and after these lines, but "pernicious" and "dread" simply cannot. Perhaps Whitman means that ordinary, conventional people might regard the freedoms and joys as pernicious and dreadful because they would be shocked; such a reading is dubious, however, because Whitman has not been speaking of that kind of "wild" or "untamed"—neither of spontaneous sexuality nor of untrodden paths of manly love. The revisions and the later addition of paren-

theses point to the possibility I have chosen; that is, Whitman allows a counter-theme and threat to surface momentarily. The fact that another poem ("Leaflet") expresses self doubt and personal guilt even in 1856–1857 tends to support my reading.

7. The poem is "Leaflet" ("Calamus" 16)—a poem Whitman apparently wrote during the 1856–57 creative period and rejected from *Leaves of Grass* in 1867. I am primarily concerned with the image of a problematic self which emerges out of the 1860 edition, but even more importantly out of the final *Leaves of Grass;* therefore, I am treating the two poems—"A Song of Joys" and "As I Ebb'd"—as virtual contemporaries, and I am using the final texts, for they are not essentially different from the 1860 text. Actually, they were not written during the same period: "A Song of Joys" was probably composed in the 1856–57 period of creativity: "As I Ebb'd" came later, probably in 1859, presumably during the period of depression Whitman experienced. The Whitman of psychological crisis apparently displaces the Whitman of confidence, but some sense of the problematic of self exists even during the earlier, confident period. "Leaflet" comments on that early inner conflict.

8. Given my view of the importance of relation in *Leaves of Grass,* I think Whitman's failure to find it is just that; whereas, Waskow argues (pp. 202–210) that Whitman's acceptance is an "existential act of faith" and, therefore, a successful awakening. I disagree with Waskow, obviously, not necessarily about what it is Whitman discovers, but about how one interprets it.

9. According to Fredson Bowers, "No poem on the pink paper can be dated after this time [Spring, 1857];" "I Sit and Look Out" was written on pink paper. Bowers, p. xlviii.

10. James E. Miller, Jr. p. 236.

11. Throughout this discussion I am speaking of the image of man Whitman presents; I know that Columbus is not necessarily an image of Walt Whitman.

CHAPTER FIVE

The Self, the World, and Things

Beginning my studies the first step pleas'd me so much,
The mere fact consciousness, these forms, the power of motion,
The least insect or animal, the senses, eyesight, love,
The first step I say awed me and pleas'd me so much,
I have hardly gone and hardly wish'd to go any farther,
But stop and loiter all the time to sing it in ecstatic songs.[1]

With these lines Walt Whitman identifies the first stage of the self's
meeting with the world; he sees and touches the actual, physical
world and thereby begins to develop an essential relationship which
provides one ground for partial fulfillment and self-transcendence.
At this primary level, Whitman's concern lies mainly with the thing-
in-itself: he apparently wishes to encounter and express, in Randall
Jarrell's terms, the "thereness" or "suchness" of the physical world.[2]
Whitman asserts as much in "Song of Myself" when he claims for that
world both primary and final significance:

I accept Reality and dare not question it,
Materialism first and last imbuing.

For Whitman this first pleasurable step oftentimes involves passionate, ecstatic contact:

You sea! I resign myself to you also—I guess what you mean,
I behold from the beach your crooked inviting fingers,
I believe you refuse to go back without feeling of me,
We must have a turn together, I undress, hurry me out of sight
    of the land,

Cushion me soft, rock me in billowy drowse,
Dash me with amorous wet, I can repay you.

He obviously sees and feels the physical world sexually. Although exploitation of the sexual idiom or metaphor intensifies Whitman's encounter and his conviction that a "kelson of the creation is love," he means quite literally that one meets and relates to the world in a deeply physical way. Whitman also claims in a number of poems that physical reality reveals meaning. However, meaning first arises from the contact or encounter itself. Therefore, I prefer to concentrate in this chapter on the essential relation of the self with empirical reality, valued for itself, because Whitman's "first step" concentrates on that relation.

"There Was a Child Went Forth" describes in clear, exact images this essential "first step"; to some extent it also reveals without elaboration the kind of perception involved in the meeting. The poem describes a young child becoming sensitive to and aware of the reality around him. He observes and becomes all of the external experience he meets. As he discovers the lilacs, grass, lambs, water plants, boys and girls, and the city streets that constitute external experience, he becomes them and they become him:

> There was a child went forth every day,
> And the first object he look'd upon, that object he became,
> And that object became part of him for the day or a certain part
>   of the day,
> Or for many years or stretching cycles of years.

He seems to enter into a mutual relation with the world, a dialogue in which the reality lies neither wholly in the boy or completely in the world, but in the meeting itself. The boy may partly define the world in terms of himself (he absorbs it into himself), yet he primarily defines himself in terms of the world, for it is through the encounter with a concrete other that he presumably changes and grows. The experience is an expansive one, yet it is limiting, too, because the child is relating to an objective world which in itself possesses limits. The child encompasses experience up *to* "the horizon's edge," but not beyond.

Since the relationship is reciprocal, it involves both reception and participation.[3] The child does not simply absorb passively; he goes forth *(a child went forth)* to encounter and to become part of the world he discovers. After the first four lines, the poem begins to

repeat "became part of him," and for that reason it seems to contradict the opening lines because it does not explicitly state "that object
he became." Whitman may be inconsistent, but more than likely he
selected the shorter phrase for effect, intending to imply the interaction the first four lines establish. Moreover, the poem implicitly maintains the reciprocal action by emphasizing the child's direction—
going forth.

The poem does indeed present a child-like kind of perception,
for Whitman does not evaluate or analyze the world the child encounters; he simply places it there for the child to experience.
The young boy not only responds to the pleasures or beauty he
discovers in nature; he comes to know, as well, "all the changes of
city and country wherever he went" and "the doubts of day-time
and the doubts of night-time." Although he looks on the unpleas-
ant, even terrifying, experiences with something of the same
wonder and freshness[4] with which he sees "the early lilacs," his
experience nevertheless is potentially broader and more complex
than the typical Romantic child's experiences. Both kinds of experience—the pleasurable and the painful—receive much fuller development in other Whitman poems.

I am suggesting that at this level of encounter and in this poem,
reality for Whitman is somehow dialogical. The world is not merely
an extension of the self (a projection of man's mind or a reality
capable of being removed into the self), nor is the self an adjunct or
extension of the world. The world the child or self meets is an independent other; however, it can be known through dialogue. Occasionally Whitman claims to know ultimate reality or absolute nature
beyond all limits or all relationship, but that is not the case here. The
nature the child meets is knowable (absolute nature, or x-nature in
Buber's terms, is irrelevant here) and knowing is reciprocal. In other
words the tune lies neither in the tree nor in "thee" but in the
encounter. This encounter involves the child totally; that is, the perception is spontaneous and intuitive, and it involves the whole self.
The dialogue also enables the child to begin to escape from himself
and discover the possibilities for being a self-in-the-world. The kind
of encounter dramatized in "There Was a Child Went Forth" and,
more broadly, in poems about the first mode requires an essential
trust in one's self and in experience as a whole. Such trust may seem
naive, child-like, and hopelessly Romantic in "There Was a Child
Went Forth", but if one considers Whitman's relations with empirical reality as a whole, he discovers that trust is not *simply* childish,

and in Whitman's poetry as a whole the question of confidence assumes considerable complexity.[5]

In his preoccupation with the factual, objective, world-for-itself,[6] Whitman not only presents that world in its "thereness" and "suchness"; he dramatizes, as well, the meeting of the self with that world. I have indicated something of the quality that experience assumes in "There Was a Child Went Forth," but the poem does not speak for all the poems. The quality of the experience varies with virtually every poem, but each is a variation on a few basic themes: 1) Whitman's sense of being a part of brute nature; 2) his ecstasy resulting from contact with things; 3) his delight and joy in the energy and fullness of life—expressed as innocent wonder or as a more mature pleasure in natural beauty; 4) his very occasional uncertainty and anxiety about the empirical or material world.

1) "We Two How Long We Were Fool'd" frankly states that "We are Nature." However, Whitman does not mean that he and his companion are, therefore, God-like, for he has in mind objective, empirical nature:

> We become plants, trunks, foliage, roots, bark,
> We are bedded in the ground, we are rocks,
> We are oaks, we grow in the openings side by side.

Although the lines imply a loss of self in this becoming of plants and trunks, the poem neither describes nor implies a loss of the self through its absorption into nature. Rather, Whitman recognizes the physical, brutish, rank, and "natural" in himself and the other almost as absolutes:

> We are also the coarse smut of beasts, vegetables, minerals,
> We are two predatory hawks, we soar above and look down,
> We are two resplendent suns, we it is who balance ourselves
>   orbic and stellar, we are as two comets,
> We prowl fang'd and four-footed in the woods, we spring on
>   prey. . . .

After having been fooled for so long (perhaps by Transcendental pretensions?), he discovers certain basic physical limits that paradoxically provide the ground for the freedom and joy he shares at the end with his lover. That is, Whitman accepts both the beauty and coarseness in his physical nature; simple acceptance of himself is pleasurable, and it releases him, perhaps, from the conventional guilt and shame associated with the "coarse smut" of the

human body. However, the discovery by the lovers of their physical beings—of their "natural" selves—does not free them from
the limits empirical reality imposes on them; instead, it immerses
them in it. The poem speaks of the *acceptance* of self, not the loss
of it, through immersion in nature. Even before he accepts his
sexuality or his capacity for relation with another, he must accept
his physicality. The first essential relationship, then, becomes the
ground for the others.

2) Whitman's longing for contact with the material world and his
ecstasy when he achieves it are probably the most unusual aspects of
this self-things relation. Whitman speaks of a kind of libidinous real-
ism. That is, his poems not only present the substance and detail of
the world, but they also express an intense sensual response to the
earth:

> I am he that walks with the tender and growing night,
> I call to the earth and sea half-held by the night.
>
> Press close bare-bosom'd night—press close magnetic nourish-
>   ing night!
> Night of south winds—night of the large few stars!
> Still nodding night—mad naked summer night.
>
> Smile O voluptuous cool-breath'd earth!
> Earth of the slumbering and liquid trees!
> Earth of departed sunset—earth of the mountains misty-topt!
> Earth of the vitreous pour of the full moon just tinged with blue!
> Earth of shine and dark mottling the tide of the river!
> Earth of the limpid gray of clouds brighter and clearer for my
>   sake!
> Far-swooping elbow'd earth—rich apple-blossom'd earth!
> Smile, for your lover comes.
>
> Prodigal, you have given me love—therefore I to you give love!
> O unspeakable passionate love.[7]

The self who experiences great sensual ecstasy in this relation resembles Whitman's "Spontaneous Me" who responds to every touch—
everything sensuous—in a *sensual,* erotic way. Indeed, he is so sensitive that his ecstasy threatens to overwhelm him. For this spontaneous self the whole world is defined by sexuality, as this surrealistic
image from "Song of Myself" indicates:

> Something I cannot see puts upward libidinous prongs,
> Seas of bright juice suffuse heaven.

A sky or heaven, yet, of "seminal wet"!

That image and the whole current of sexual energy that affects Whitman's contact with things indicate that his attraction to the earth and things involves something primitive—even magical. So doubtless he speaks in such passages with one of the *most* "forbidden voices . . . of sexes and lusts." To speak of copulation ("Copulation is no more rank to me than death is") or to acknowledge the auto-eroticism in the poems ("The scent of these arm-pits aroma finer than prayer") would not offend Whitman's readers so much as his ecstatic sexual response to things: "Winds whose soft-tickling genitals rub against me it shall be you!"

By describing such desire and passion he can express enormous energy with a power he could not otherwise achieve. But he is also expressing sexual passion, and he means it as just that! He achieves a coalescence of man and nature that Coleridge perhaps only dreamed of. The real danger in such a passionate merging with things lies in the possible loss of the self when one is completely overcome by "prurient provokers."

> The sentries desert every other part of me,
> They have left me helpless to a red marauder,
> They all come to the headland to witness and assist against me.
>
> I am given up by traitors,
> I talk wildly, I have lost my wits, I and nobody else am the
>   greatest traitor,
> I went myself first to the headland, my own hands carried me
>   there.
>
> You villain touch! what are you doing? my breath is tight in its
>   throat,
> Unclench your floodgates, you are too much for me.

Such a loss or diffusion of self does not occur significantly in "Song of Myself," however, because each orgasmic experience leads Whitman to new awareness of himself and his world and thus to a further discovery of self:

> I am cut by bitter and angry hail, I lose my breath,
> Steep'd amid honey'd morphine, my windpipe throttled in
>   fakes of death,
> At length let up again to feel the puzzle of puzzles,
> And that we call Being.

Nevertheless, the threat remains. There is temporary loss, some-times, and occasionally, in "Spontaneous Me," for example, the loss or diffusion of self seems definitive.

3) Whitman does not always respond to things in such a patently sexual way. Frequently, he expresses a general sensuous delight and joy in the energy, fullness, and beauty of life. In such moods he still values the empirical world for itself, and he finds meaning in it through relation or contact with it. Yet the quality of the experience differs from those intensely sexual reactions; it is not so intense or so exhausting as his orgasmic contacts with things. Whitman's poem "Miracles" quietly states the pleasure and joy he finds in each experi-ence; each moment of encounter with something or someone is suffi-cient cause for wonder and celebration:

> Why, who makes much of a miracle?
> As to me I know of nothing else but miracles,
> Whether I walk the streets of Manhattan,
> Or dart my sight over the roofs of houses toward the sky,
> Or wade with naked feet along the beach just in the edge of the
>   water.
>
> To me the sea is a continual miracle,
> The fishes that swim—the rocks—the motion of the waves—the
>   ships with men in them,
> What stranger miracles are there?

Whitman expresses here a pleasure or wonder that might be sus-tained—longer, at least, than the climaxes he experiences in his sex-ual encounters with the sea, the air, and the earth. The miracles he speaks of are moments in time—human experience—not really Tran-scendental or mystic moments, for Whitman fixes his attention, once more, on the "thereness" of the world. He renders a similar kind of experience in both "O Magnet-South" and "Mannahatta." Each poem celebrates the diverse, specific qualities of a place or region as the poet "goes forth" to meet and know the South and the City.

Whitman's encounter with things extends into the city as well as into nature. One seriously oversimplifies Whitman if he fails to recog-nize that the "thereness" of the world Whitman presents encom-passes the plenitude of city life as well as of the natural world. In "Crossing Brooklyn Ferry" the "glories" Whitman responds to are precisely those unique to the city: "the glories strung like beads on my smallest sights and hearings, on the walk in the street and the

passage over the river." Whitman responds with wonder and pleasure to the beauty and vitality of every aspect of the situation—to the
things of the river and to the living crowd. In "Give Me the Splendid
Silent Sun," Whitman actually rejects a relationship with the primal
sanities of nature and expresses both the necessity and excitement of
encountering life in the city. He seems to recognize that his desire
for a pure pastoral life is unrealistic and evasive. Although he is "tired
with ceaseless excitement, and rack'd by the war-strife," communion
with nature is not his way; instead, he must live "an intense life, full
to repletion and varied" in the city. In spite of his war weariness he
can look on the energy and fullness of Manhattan with excitement
and hope. If he expresses wonder, it is the wonder of a man who has
experienced the insanity of war, who recognizes he must reconstruct
his world in the city, and who is revived and stimulated by the
prospect. A man—not a child—goes forth in this poem, and as that
man, Whitman is as open to experience as the child.

In these poems about nature and the city Whitman predictably
suspends judgment, and he rejects abstract explanations of his contact with being. As he implies in "When I Heard the Learn'd Astrono-
mer," when he wants to "know" the reality over against him, he will
try to experience it, not understand it through the words of a scien-
tist:

> When I heard the learn'd astronomer,
> When the proofs, the figures, were ranged in columns before
>   me,
> When I was shown the charts and diagrams, to add, divide, and
>   measure them,
> When I sitting heard the astronomer where he lectured with
>   much applause in the lecture-room,
> How soon unaccountable I became tired and sick,
> Till rising and gliding out I wander'd off by myself,
> In the mystical moist night-air, and from time to time,
> Look'd up in perfect silence at the stars.

This rejection of intellectualizing something reduces Whitman's experience to a mere feeling-state or to a spasm of ecstasy, but more
often than not Whitman is aware of himself, his action, and his experience; he responds in such situations as a total person, not just as a
passionate, spasmodic Romantic poet. Experience for him often
seems new, fresh, spontaneous, uncontrolled, and unpredictable, but
at the same time his method and the dramatic situation in most
poems require that the speaker know the quality and direction of his

experience. He may not know dramatically (or even as the author) the particular form the process will assume or the particular end or goal of the direction; nevertheless, the speaker is aware at each moment of direction and of the relative incompleteness or fullness of his experience. This is evident in "There Was a Child"; the poet presents the child, perhaps as an image of what he once was, but he does not entirely identify himself with the child. The poem is a reminiscence, and as such Whitman dramatizes both the child's immediate responses and the poet's awareness of direction. In "Song of Myself," especially, the poet can anticipate and guess from the beginning what he may discover about himself and the world, but he does not know for sure. He must find out, and the drama arises from that search. The control and sense of direction, therefore, do not deprive the experience of adventure, newness, and openness.[8]

4) For the most part Whitman's confrontations with empirical reality result in wonder, ecstasy, contentment, and growth because he can trust his experience in the world. Occasionally, however, that world appears untrustworthy and threatens the poet as it does in "As I Ebb'd" and in "Yet, Yet, Ye Downcast Hours." At first, in "As I Ebb'd" Whitman feels secure with the immediate reality he faces— the shore and the sea—because he thinks he knows it. However, once he discovers his insignificance and his inability to understand the mystery represented by the ocean, he finds that his immediate experience is not so trustworthy after all, for it has become part of that "other" world which excludes and threatens the poet so completely. His failure to relate to any part of it results in the hopeless alienation of the poet which I described above. In "Yet, Yet, Ye Downcast Hours" Whitman finds his own physical nature, and by extension all matter, a threat because it limits him, confronts him with the finality of death and exposes him to complete loss of identity:

> Yet, yet, ye downcast hours, I know ye also,
> Weights of lead, how ye clog and cling at my ankles,
> Earth to a chamber of mourning turns—I hear the o'erweening,
>   mocking voice,
> *Matter is conqueror—matter, triumphant only, continues on-*
>   *ward.*

The poet cannot resolve it for himself, and he can do nothing for the anguished, despairing cries of others threatened by the irrevocable fact of matter.

More often, however, if Whitman does not simply accept or celebrate the smut, coarseness, rankness, rottenness, and limits of the physical world, he reconciles himself to the fact of materialism as he does in "This Compost." The innocent trust and the wonder of the child who goes forth into the world for the first time disintegrates in the first stanza of the poem, for the speaker has suddenly been threatened ("startled") "where I thought I was safest." Instead of beauty and goodness, he finds contamination. The "woods," "pastures," and the "sea" have been poisoned by "distemper'd corpses" and "with sour dead." Whitman has moved, in a sense, from the pure wonder and joy of "There Was a Child" to a momentary disillusion with and fear of his body and the natural world. He feels threatened not only by the rottenness in the external world but by the potential "foulment" in himself—by his own corporality. The poem presents, then, the negative of "There Was a Child" and of "We Two, How Long We Were Fool'd."

After the first section the poem moves carefully and systematically through two more stages that eventually resolve the dilemma and enable Whitman to transcend the earth without denying any aspect of its physical reality. In effect, Whitman's awareness broadens to perceive the life-death-rebirth cycle in nature. He recognizes specifically that life emerges from the "sour dead." Whitman continues to be aware of death and decay, but he also perceives beauty. In effect, he understands and accepts the entire cycle. It is that acceptance which inspires the wonder and excitement he expresses in the middle of section 2:

> What chemistry!
> That the winds are really not infectious,
> That this is no cheat, this transparent green-wash of the sea
>   which is so amorous after me,
> That it is safe to allow it to lick my naked body all over with its
>   tongues,
> That it will not endanger me with the fevers that have depos-
>   ited themselves in it,
> That all is clean forever and forever.

He does not respond with the innocent wonder of a child, but responds with wonder and terror at the striking fact of the total cycle:

> Now I am terrified at the Earth, it is that calm and patient,
> It grows such sweet things out of such corruptions,
> It turns harmless and stainless on its axis, with such endless
>   successions of diseas'd corpses,
> It distills such exquisite winds out of such infused fetor,

It renews with such unwitting looks its prodigal, annual, sump-
    tuous crops,
It gives such divine materials to men, and accepts such leavings
    from them at last.

Whitman of course prefers the positive direction—the resurrection
or restoration—but he no longer tries to separate the clean and the
vital from the "corruptions" of physical reality. He celebrates chem-
istry, natural growth, and the fullness of life. Through his encounter
with "this compost" he discovers something of himself, for he can
now accept an aspect of his physical being which repelled him at the
beginning of the poem. And I think he accepts himself and the world
for themselves, not as manifestations of some Transcendental
material reality.[9]

I was looking a long while for Intentions,
For a clew to this history of the past for myself, and for these
    chants—
And now I have found it . . .
It is in the present—it is this earth to-day.

Whitman apparently finds empirical reality valuable and meaningful for itself—not simply in "I Was Looking a Long While" but in
many poems that present the relation between the self and empirical
reality. The relationship constitutes a "first step" beyond the self into
the world and becomes thereby the initial ground for discovering
meaning-in-being. In a poem like "There Was a Child" Whitman
describes those very first meetings with otherness that awaken the
child both to himself and to the other. The encounter defines the self
by setting it at a distance from the world (the poem clearly presents
two entities—the child and the world he enters), and at the same
time the encounter establishes a potential relationship between the
child and the world which is necessary to the child's emergence as
a fully realized self. In other words, the poem dramatizes an initial
discovery by the Whitmanian persona of his situation in the world.
He responds to that discovery with wonder and delight. In "This
Compost" or "As I Ebb'd," for example, Whitman recgonizes that
acceptance of the world must include an awareness of its rottenness,
hostility, or mystery. By and large, however, the relationship between the self and empirical reality provides the basis for Whitman's
discovery that the self and the world are larger and better than the
child or the disillusioned man might think.
    The relationship is an initial or basic one, but it is not simply a "first

step." The self does not always respond with the sensibility and
innocence of the child. Rather, Whitman experiences the relation
repeatedly—at different levels and in various contexts—as part of a
constant process of relating to the world and as the basis for developing other essential relations. He finds value and meaning in the
relationship itself and in it as a ground for other relations. Thus, in
both instances he discovers meaning in the concrete. There is no
point in exaggerating the degree of fulfillment realized in this first
essential relation. It provides only a minimal way to self-awareness
and self-transcendence; in this sense it *is* just a first step. "Give Me
the Splendid Silent Sun" indicates how Whitman does and must press
on beyond things to the city and to the others. That is, the self can
remain solitary even if it experiences essential moments in relation
to empirical reality. So Whitman seeks to go beyond that to something solidary. Besides its limitations, the relationship also has its
negative results—the possible diffusion and subsequent loss of the
self, and the decline into a mere feeling-state. Sometimes, the relation is no more than an illusion, disguising a fundamental autoeroti-
cism in Whitman. Nevertheless, the dialogue between the self and
the world provides one basis for knowing the self and the other—one
way of beginning the long process of becoming whole.

NOTES—*Chapter V*

1. Whitman, "Beginning My Studies."
2. "Some Lines from Whitman," *Poetry and the Age* (New York, 1953).
3. V. K. Chari would probably not agree that the relationship is reciprocal as I mean it. He speaks of interpenetration between Whitman and the world (p. 56), but he emphasizes the primacy of subjectivity—the object flows, unites, and merges with the subject in "There Was a Child," as it does in all of Whitman's poetry. Again, our disagreement is basic; Chari says, in effect, that there is only one essential direction in Whitman (from object to self), that the self is a monad, and therefore, that meaningful experience is monological (see pp. 36 and 56).
4. Although Tony Tanner deals only with Whitman's early poetry, he exaggerates, I think, wonder, innocence, naivete, passiveness, and limitlessness in Whitman and, specifically, in this poem. See "Walt Whitman's Ecstatic First Step" in *The Reign of Wonder* (Cambridge, England, 1965), pp. 64–86.
5. Such trust seems far removed from our age, and thus, readers (Tony Tanner for one) often dismiss it as naive and foolish. But trust is not so far removed as some think. Think, for example, of these passages from Carl Rogers: "The basic nature of the human being, when functioning freely, is constructive and trustworthy" (p. 194). "This process of living in the good life involves a wider range, a greater richness, than the constricted living in which most of us find ourselves. . . . And the reason they can thus live fully in a wider range is that they have this underlying confidence in themselves as trustworthy instruments for encountering life." (p. 195). "This process of the good life, is not, I am convinced, a life for the faint-hearted. It involves the stretching and growing of becoming more and more of one's potentialities. It involves the courage to be. It means launching oneself fully into the stream of life. Yet the deeply exciting thing about human beings is that when the individual is inwardly free, he chooses as the good life this process of becoming" (p. 196). From *On Becoming a Person* (Boston, 1961). Surely the quality of the experiences and the historical contexts of Whitman and Rogers differ, yet both share an essential faith in the self and experience—even a conviction that experience is essentially good.
6. Cf. Stanley Coffman, "The World Dimensional in the Poetry of Leaves of Grass," *Emerson Society Quarterly* (22), pp. 8–10.
7. It is impossible for me to agree with V. K. Chari's point that Whitman —as the wise man—lives and acts in this world without passion or attachment (p. 147). Even if I accepted Chari's basic assumption about an achieved mystical state for Whitman, I would have difficulty discerning an imperturbable Whitman in these lines.

8. Tanner exaggerates the situation he perceives in Whitman's poetry: "You cannot adopt the naive wondering eye and at the same time appear to know what you expect to find" (p. 83). Whitman's dramatic point of view, where he stands "both in and out of the game," makes a dual perspective quite possible. He can be simultaneously naive and knowing, for in Whitman's poems events simultaneously are happening and have happened.

9. I have been discussing in this chapter Whitman's encounter with the empirical world exclusively as an encounter with *things*, and accordingly I have ignored his sense that things sometimes point to a reality or meaning beyond themselves. I have done so simply because, in the poems I have been discussing, Whitman is primarily and usually interested in things as things. His concern with them as signs is an aspect of the third essential relation—the self with the spirit.

CHAPTER SIX

The Self and Others

In "Give Me the Splendid Silent Sun" Whitman rejects the pastoral as a solution to the brutal facts of American experience. If the American pastoral ever existed, it no longer does. Nor do the presumably ideal relations with others that might have once existed in it. Whitman finds, instead, that he can leave the warstrife behind only by immersing himself in the city. In the second section Whitman enumerates the details of city life:

> Give me faces and streets—give me these phantoms incessant
> and endless along the trottoirs!
> Give me interminable eyes—give me women—give me com-
> rades and lovers by the thousand!
> Let me see new ones every day—let me hold new ones by the
> hand every day!
> Give me such shows—give me the streets of Manhattan!

He presents one great "turbulent . . . chorus"—the people, who are simply part of "the endless and noisy chorus" of the city. Whitman responds to the city as place or situation; he has replaced natural things with urban things. The poem ends where relationships with others might begin. As Whitman focusses momentarily on the faces and eyes emerging out of the "shows" and "the streets of Manhattan," he becomes aware not only that he will find others in the city; he also learns that he needs others. Things, place, and situation are not enough.

In both "Once I Pass'd Through a Populous City" and "City of Orgies" Whitman indicates that relationships with others possess much greater value for him than his encounter with the things of the city. He remembers the woman who "passionately clung" to him more than he remembers the "shows, architecture, customs, traditions." The relationship made the impression, not the place. Likewise, in "City of Orgies" Whitman passes beyond a response to things and people as objects. Life in Manhattan assumes meaning through communication with others. "City of Orgies" is also a short poem, and so Whitman does not develop or enumerate any real dialogue with others. Nevertheless, the final lines clearly indicate the relationships are personal and reciprocal:

> Not those, but as I pass O Manhattan, your frequent and swift
>   flash of eyes offering me love,
> Offering response to my own—these repay me,
> Lovers, continual lovers, only repay me.

He may refer here simply to a momentary communication with another achieved by a look or glance, or he may have in mind some extended relation with another; whichever, the relationships possess a depth and value for him that imply genuine dialogue, and such relationships offer greater possibilities for fulfillment than one's relations with things.

In this chapter I shall explore the various forms the self-other dialogue assumes in *Leaves of Grass,* and at the same time I will distinguish between those relationships which remain non-essential, those which are incomplete in some degree, and those few which become essential. It is relatively simple to point to the "categories" into which one might divide the poems—self and another, self and the many, love of men for women, of man for man—and these general forms are important. It is more difficult, however, to discover and describe the quality of each relationship—its completeness or incompleteness, its depth or superficiality. The variety of relationships—the tension between them (between, for example, homosexual and heterosexual love), the degrees of genuineness, and the masking of monologue with the appearance of dialogue—reveal the deep problematic of self which Whitman dramatizes in his poetry.

1. The Self and Another

In "Children of Adam," "Calamus," and in parts of "Drum Taps" Whitman attempts the essential task of communication with another, both through the body (by touch or gesture) and through the inner sphere in which one experiences the most complete human dialogue. Although Whitman only occasionally realizes in "Children of Adam" a genuine relationship with another, I do think he intends for the sexuality he celebrates to lead to genuine dialogue and mutuality. Nevertheless, the section as a whole actually speaks of a polymorphous sexuality that sometimes overwhelms the self instead of providing a direction toward completion. Whitman's subject and experience in such poems becomes sexuality rather than essential relationship. In "Calamus" and in certain "Drum Taps," on the other hand, Whitman concentrates much more successfully on a relationship between man and man and on the presence of another; at the same time the poems recognize tension, threat, and failure as real possibilities.

a. "Children of Adam"

My discussion of the self and empirical reality indicates how Whitman accepts and rejoices in the things of the world. Part of that celebration involves the recognition and acceptance of his own body in all its beauty, sensuality, and coarseness. "Children of Adam" concentrates on precisely that. Unconditional acceptance of the body becomes not only the basis of any relationship between man and woman (or between the poet and any other); it becomes the ground for all self-awareness. Whitman speaks of this acceptance in the last two lines of the closing poem:

Touch me, touch the palm of your hand to my body as I pass,
Be not afraid of my body.

The poet's voice here is quiet and gentle; the world he refers to is fresh and new; and the contact he urges is innocent and passionless. Such "relief, repose, content" might result from unconditional acceptance of one's body and sexuality, but this Adamic mood does not describe the whole experience. Whitman accepts and celebrates, as well, his grossest nature—the coarse, vulgar, brute, passionate self that longs for "libidinous joys only" and for reckless, raging love and orgasms:

> Give me the drench of my passions, give me life coarse and
> rank.

Besides accepting his own body in both its repose and its sexual turbulence, Whitman sees the world in sexual terms. He sees, first, attraction and attachment rather than repulsion or separation:

> Of that, of them and what goes with them my poems informing,
> Of the smell of apples and lemons, of the pairing of birds,
> Of the wet of woods, of the lapping of waves,
> Of the mad pushes of waves upon the land, I them chanting. . . .

Second, he responds sexually to the natural world as well as to individuals:

> The souse upon me of my lover the sea, as I lie willing and
> naked.
>
> I have perceiv'd that to be with those I like is enough,
> To stop in company with the rest at evening is enough,
> To be surrounded by beautiful, curious, breathing, laughing
> flesh is enough,
> To pass among them or touch any one, or rest my arm ever so
> lightly round his or her neck for a moment, what is this
> then?
> I do not ask any more delight, I swim in it as in a sea.

The poet finds pleasure and satisfaction—as "Spontaneous Me" indicates—in contact with every part of the external world. His response is polymorphous and sometimes indiscriminate; nevertheless, complete abandonment to his own sexuality—unconditional acceptance and confirmation of it—is a necessary step for Whitman before he can overcome fear of his own or of another's body. The step is a necessary "first step," because it provides the basis for Whitman's relation with the world and with others.

At this first level, then, Whitman values the body and sexuality for itself. He enjoys "being" and that is justification enough for the "mystic deliria" that sometimes overwhelms him. Furthermore, he regards sexuality as the essence of reality:

> Sex contains all, bodies, souls,
> Meanings, proofs, purities, delicacies, results, promulgations,

Songs, commands, health, pride, the maternal mystery, the
    seminal milk,
All hopes, benefactions, bestowals, all the passions, loves, beau-
    ties, delights of the earth, . . .
These are contain'd in sex as parts of itself and justifications of
    itself.

By abandoning himself to sex Whitman comes in contact with the
underlying creative energy in existence, and thus he penetrates a
little further into the meaning of the "being" he so joyously celebrates. Finally, he values sex because it provides a potential basis for
genuine communication between man and woman.

Throughout "Children of Adam" Whitman urges a free, lawless,
sexual love—the kind he celebrates in "One Hour to Madness and
Joy." The very absoluteness of Whitman's desire for free sexual
indulgence reveals both the possibilities and risks of such radical
action as few other poems do. Whitman apparently hopes that the
freedom he urges will result either in a kind of sustained orgasm
or, if not that, in such a magnificent one that it might last him his
whole life:

To escape utterly from others' anchors and holds!
To drive free! to love free! to dash reckless and dangerous!

To feed the remainder of life with one hour of fulness and
    freedom!
With one brief hour of madness and joy.

Although he obviously values sensation for itself, he nevertheless
implies that he will find in the climax he seeks an essential reality
which "ties," "conventions," and "gags" have suppressed.

Whitman would willingly risk dangers and destruction to realize
that apocalyptic "one brief hour of madness and joy." Although the
poem does not dramatize sexual climax (the excitement and agitation
in the poem come from anticipation), it points toward a fulfillment
that is primarily orgasmic, but can result in a measure of self acceptance and confidence:

To have the gag remov'd from one's mouth!
To have the feeling to-day or any day I am sufficient as I am.

Presumably, the sexually free man and woman need not suppress
their natural impulses, nor need they feel shame because of them.
They discover through self-acceptance and sexual encounter that

they are better than they thought, and they make that discovery, apparently, only through a genuine sexual relationship with another. Possibly—but one must look further to be sure.

At the same time that Whitman anticipates a personal relation which will catapult him "to the heavens of the love indicated to me," he inadvertently reveals how illusory that hope may be. The love he celebrates in "One Hour to Madness and Joy" is in fact auto-erotic. He does not envision any real person opposite him—anyone will do as long as Whitman makes it himself:

> O to be yielded to you whoever you are, and you to be yielded
>   to me in defiance of the world!

He speaks only of his own sensation; the other becomes merely an object. Moreover, the climax the poet imagines ironically threatens him with loss of self. He "courts destruction," not simply because he defies conventions but because he risks diffusion of himself in an overwhelming sensation or feeling state.

"One Hour to Madness and Joy" reveals two radically different possibilities. It does not hold them in tension, but it conveniently presents the real problematic for the self in "Children of Adam." I should like to explore that a little further by commenting, first, on Whitman's attempt to dramatize sexual love as a basis for self-transcendence and, second, on those poems in which the self is threatened by an indiscriminate, spontaneous sexual desire.

Whitman indicates several times that he is thinking of a genuine relationship between a man and a woman. In, "A Woman Waits for Me," for example, he speaks first of *a* woman and later directly addresses a "you". The first lines indicate that Whitman, apparently, sees the woman as an independent other person who can give him something he does not possess, and he announces what he can give her:

> A woman waits for me, she contains all, nothing is lacking,
> Yet all were lacking if sex were lacking, or if the moisture of the
>   right man were lacking.

Beyond that he intends to give her pleasure, love, and *athletic* children. Near the end of the poem Whitman speaks also of the interpenetration of "I and you." He also speaks of the inseparableness of "you and I"—of himself and the woman he loves—in "From Pentup Aching Rivers":

From my own voice resonant, singing the phallus,
Singing the song of procreation,
Singing the need of superb children and therein superb grown
    people,
Singing the muscular urge and the blending,
Singing the bedfellow's song, (O resistless yearning!
O for any and each the body correlative attracting!
O for you whoever you are your correlative body! O it, more
    than all else, you delighting!)

Ideally, then, copulation leads beyond sensation to communication
or love. Orgasm results in the discovery of one's self and of the other
in the relationship.

Sexual intercourse obviously begets babies, too, but Whitman is
more concerned with bodies, sex, communication, and self-discovery. The image of birth functions primarily in relation to self-discovery and self-transcendence. Man is reborn through his love of a
woman. He is renewed through orgasm, and thus his climax does lead
to discovery—not just of his own body but of himself as a man and
of the woman as another person. I have emphasized this possibility
as strongly as I have because I think Whitman intended it; he tried
to write genuine love poems, as well as sex poems. But instead of
expressing the genuine relationship he may have intended, the poems often express something else.

They express Whitman's fascination with sex and an essentially
auto-erotic sexuality. Three examples, in particular, should make my
point. In "From Pentup Aching Rivers" Whitman expresses his ache
for a woman with this line:

O for you *whoever you are* your *correlative* body! O *it* more
    than all else, you delighting! (Italics added.)

The language exposes Whitman's desire as primarily auto-erotic, for
he seeks anyone, any *body*, that will satisfy his longing. The body to
which he would make love possesses no identity ("whoever you are")
and little humanity. One might be able to feel sympathy, but hardly
desire, for a "correlative body." Whitman completes his dehumani-
zation of the woman when he effectively separates her body ("it")
from *her* (the "you"). If something does stand before him, it is a
faceless, nameless sexual object. Second, the phrase "female form" in
both "From Pent-up Aching Rivers" and "I Sing the Body Electric."
similarly reduces the woman to a mere object of the poet's intense
sexual desire. His separation of the person from the body confuses

Whitman's point about meaning-in-being—about the body as a gesture for the total person. Finally, there is Whitman's word "interpenetrate":

> I shall expect them to interpenetrate with others, as I and you
> interpenetrate now.

Whitman is apparently describing, as I suggested before, a genuine
personal relationship between "I and you," but since he has already
generalized his lover from woman to women, "interpenetrate" simply generalizes and impersonalizes the relationship further. While
the failure of language is not definitive of the section, it does indicate
that Whitman often fails to make the relationship between man and
woman concrete and essential and, therefore, that his stated meaning differs sharply from his dramatized meaning.

Rather than serving as the basis for self-transcendence and discovery, the sexual freedom and self-abandonment Whitman urges can
result in loss or diffusion of self when the self is overwhelmed by
uncontrollable passion. If not that, the self winds up as a monological
man wholly defined by the feeling-state in which he immerses himself. The irony of either condition is that the presumed freedom from
conventions yields a new enslavement—this time to the genitals
instead of to "ties and conventions." "Spontaneous Me" dramatizes
the dangers and limitations for Whitman of indiscriminate sexual
indulgence. Both the dramatized experience and the poem are
largely unstructured. Whitman expresses the varieties of his sexual
experience and response in a somewhat diffuse and repetitive sequence; the subjects, experiences, and responses rapidly follow one
another in this order: nature (seen sexually), the phallus, semen,
copulation, nature, lovers, a boy's sex dream, testacles, the phallus,
lovers, desire and ejaculation, masturbation and shame, nature, and
finally "the oath of procreation" that presumably unifies but actually
has nothing at all to do with the poem. Whitman seems to wander
randomly through the world vibrating like a tuning fork to everything he touches or imagines, carelessly sousing a good deal of it, and,
when he is not directly involved, vicariously enjoying the sexual
experiences of others.

The precise image of the self that one sees in "Spontaneous Me"
depends on one's assumptions about form. If the poem fails because
of its randomness and disorder—if it virtually explodes as Whitman
seems to—then one can argue that it unconsciously dramatizes a real

diffusion of the self into a series of feeling-states. But if the poem successfully presents the diffuse, polymorphous sexual sensibility of the poet, then it does dramatize an identifiable self—a supremely sensual man. Either way Whitman fails to engage in meaningful dialogue or relationship with another person. He responds to his world in terms of his own genitals, and transforms everything in that world into a sexual object—whether it is the ocean or another individual. Thus, he is unable to see the world of things from a detached, aesthetic point of view, and he possesses no sense at all of other persons. The poem presents the self, then, as little more than a series of autoerotic sexual spasms.

The "oath of procreation" Whitman swears near the end of the poem provides neither a formal center nor a thematic focus for it; because even though the oath does assert a transcendent value for sexuality, the assertion has nothing to do with the substance of the poem. One other element qualifies my interpretation further. Whitman's claim that once he indulges his desires he will achieve satisfaction and contentment ("wholesome relief, repose, content") is not so significant as he says. In the context of the poem the repose or contentment is largely physical; it probably results from sheer exhaustion after so many spasms of joy. Whitman may even be psychologically at rest, but his state of mind results, I think, from his physical emptiness. In other words, nothing in the poem suggests that he has achieved genuine fulfillment or awareness. Freedom in "Spontaneous Me" does not accomplish what radical action in "Song of the Open Road" does or even what the untrodden path Whitman follows in "Calamus" achieves. Ironically, this freedom confines Whitman completely to his own sensibility. Instead of becoming a potential ground for self-transcendence and self-realization, Whitman's discovery and acceptance of his body and sexuality lead to limitation and separation of the self. When one compares the failure here to escape genital enslavement with the genuine "I and you" relation Whitman at least talks about in "Children of Adam," one discovers the basic problematic for the self in the radical sexual action Whitman's sex poems urge. So if Whitman does not court destruction throughout "Children of Adam," he surely takes a tremendous risk (sometimes unconsciously) when he casts aside "creeds and schools" and "ties and conventions."

Whitman's statements about sexual relations indicate two important ways in which one might discover meaning in experience. Physi-

cal facts, sexuality specifically, assume meaning through self-awareness and the self's relationship to another or to the world. That
meaning is not limited to the physical, but it is not separable from
it, either. The link between copulation and communication exem-
plifies one specific way in which a physical act becomes a gesture or
a symbol for genuine human dialogue. Sexual intercourse possesses
value and meaning for itself, yet it expresses an inner reality that
becomes real only in the concrete gesture or act.

In the first poem in "Children of Adam" explicitly referring to
sexual love as "The love, the life of their bodies, meaning and being,"
Whitman simply says that meaning lies within the concrete reality
of human experience, and he sets out to dramatize and discover the
reality—meaning-in-being. In the sex poems, that meaning supposedly emerges in the reciprocal love which the physical act expresses and symbolizes. Through that reciprocal relation the poet
discovers himself as he finds the other. In line eight Whitman
confirms his sense that act and awareness fuse in the fully lived
moment when he says, "Existing I peer and penetrate still." Whitman combines in "peer" and "penetrate" the physical acts of looking
and entry with psychological seeing and understanding. He looks at,
touches, and penetrates physically and psychologically both the
world and his feminine lover, and in those essential relations he
discovers meaning. Both the act and the awareness occur simultaneously in the world—in "existing." The relationship of meaning and
being (or value and fact) is very similar to the one I described in
"Crossing Brooklyn Ferry." Whitman discovers meaning through
relationship—a relationship lived and known in time. Whitman's
description in "From Pent-up Aching Rivers" to parts of the body as
"act-poems," his reference to the phallus in "Spontaneous Me" as
"this poem drooping shy and unseen that I always carry;" and his
long list in "I Sing the Body Electric" of body parts make sense
primarily as examples of the poet's expression of meaning-in-being.
At one point Whitman even calls sexual intercourse an "act-divine";
besides expressing his opinion of it, he also means that it is divine
because it perpetuates life. Whitman simply means by "act-poems"
and "act-divine" that things, bodies, and acts are poems because they
not only possess value for themselves, but as gestures they also express and symbolize a meaning beyond themselves.

The problematic of Whitman's identity emerges in "Children of
Adam" through both the thematic and formal elements I have discussed. On the one hand, it exists in "Children of Adam" indepen-

dent of style. That is, some of the poems occasionally express tension, shame, and guilt resulting, apparently, from Whitman's radical sexual attitudes. Other poems present a basically auto-erotic love that is exclusively concerned with his own sexual sensations. Such an ego-centered sexuality interferes with and confuses Whitman's professed attempt to write poems about heterosexual love. The problematic becomes even more apparent when one considers the generative and illustrative function of form in the poems. In this respect, the limits of style both cause and reinforce the auto-eroticism, the isolation of the poet, and the failure of essential relation, and in doing so they expose a real problematic of the self, for the sexual conflict threatens to divide or confuse Whitman's essential identity. I am not suggesting that love in itself threatens the identity of Walt Whitman by somehow depriving him of himself. On the contrary, the poems are a kind of dialogue which provides one means of self-discovery and self-transcendence. The problematic lies in the personal conditions that distort or obstruct genuine dialogue—in short, in the thematic and formal conflicts I have described.

b. "Calamus"

"Calamus" concentrates on the other essential I and you relation Whitman dramatizes in *Leaves of Grass*—the relationship, literally, between man and man. This relationship leads him into untrodden paths, but he welcomes them—for all the psychic disruption and personal risk they cause—because he knows that only there will he discover and experience, without fear or shame, his real self which has been stifled and hidden. When Whitman speaks of walking "in paths untrodden," he refers both to a situation and to his poetry. That is, he presents a situation—a person, a place, and a relationship— which functions as a dramatic reality, but he also recognizes that through the poems themselves he engages in a dialogue with his reader which sometimes achieves an openness and a fulfillment not present in the dramatic situation or in the life of the man. In both ways, Whitman rejects "all the standards hitherto publish'd" to seek personal and poetic meaning in the "standards not yet publish'd." Although his poetic innovations are surely important, the personal direction and experience Whitman dramatizes—his rejection of sexual and social conventions—are far more radical than his rejection of poetic conventions.

Besides indicating Whitman's need to step outside of society, "In

Paths Untrodden" introduces the basic "Calamus" situation in other
ways, as well. The poem implies that the "published standards" are
clearly repressive and alienating. Not only do the prevailing sexual
and social values fail to express the poet; they would destroy him
besides, either by converting him into a conventional man or by
forcing him to feel guilty and ashamed and to question and despise
his own personal nature. So to find the real "me," the reality that
expresses and fulfills his "soul," Whitman must follow the path seldom taken by others. He must seek meaning and satisfaction "away
from the clank of the world" in secrecy: "No longer abash'd, (for in
this secluded spot I can respond as I would not dare elsewhere.)"
Seclusion does not mean isolation, however; instead, Whitman
repudiates the accepted standards so that he can imagine and experience a deep, mutual relation with another which will express and
fulfill him as the conventional values and relations do not:

> From all the standards hitherto publish'd, from the pleasures,
>   profits, conformities,
> Which too long I was offering to feed my soul,
> Clear to me now standards not yet publish'd, clear to me that
>   my soul,
> That the soul of the man I speak for rejoices in comrades.

The poet does not speak simply of an unconventional sexual relation
here (if he does mean that); he speaks, as well, of an intimate, personal relationship that one can describe only as an I-Thou dialogue.
The physical reality becomes an expression and symbol for the inner
mutuality Whitman dramatizes. That inner reality remains largely
unexposed (part of the "standards not yet publish'd"), yet it is so
essential that it "contains" all the rest; that is, the relationship between man and man can resolve some of life's deepest confusions and
tensions, and it can establish a basic meaning and direction for a
person. Without such a relationship Whitman would remain alone,
either in or out of society, and completely alienated. In this sense,
then, the poem provides the ground for personal discovery, fulfillment, and meaning.

Even though Whitman freely expresses his inner secret self and
although he celebrates the "need of comrades," he cannot yet live
that reality openly and fully in the world. Therefore, he continues to
experience tension and anxiety; he evidently fears exposure; he still
feels some guilt; he remains divided between his real and public
selves; and even if he no longer feels ashamed, he recalls a time when

he was deeply "abashed" over his desire for "manly attachment." In presenting Whitman's impulse toward freedom, as well as his continuing anxiety, the poem isolates the two primary tensions that inform the entire *Calamus* section.

(1) The poems dramatize a continuing struggle in Whitman to overcome fear, guilt, and shame and to accept himself and a free relationship of man with man. This conflict is intensified by internal as well as external pressures. Although Whitman apparently repudiates public standards, he is sensitive to them. They cause him some anxiety; otherwise why does he "not dare" respond except in secrecy? Besides such public pressure he also fears his own inner impulses. "There is something fierce and terrible" in him which frightens and distresses him, which he "dare not tell . . . in words." Yet this impulse he fears directs him toward a potentially meaningful and fulfilling relationship. So he is divided within, as well as without.

(2) The poems also present a basic tension between the fear and pain of loneliness and the confidence and security an "I and you" relationship brings. Whitman potentially isolates himself by revealing his inner nature and by repudiating public standards. If no relationship with another develops, then he would be left completely alone, incapable of participating in the superficial security of an inauthentic society and prevented from experiencing a meaningful I-Thou relation with another. "The sick, sick dread" Whitman mentions in "Recorders Ages Hence" could be the result of his isolation. But should he succeed in finding that "other" who responds fully to the love Whitman offers, then the risks would prove to be worthwhile. The dilemmas, the fears, and the risks evident in these basic tensions reveal how deeply problematic the self and experience are for Whitman in *Calamus*.

The persistence of his fear of exposure, his continuing guilt, and the lingering moments of shame are apparent in several of the *Calamus* poems. In what was the penultimate poem in the section Whitman says directly that his poems do expose him:

> Here the frailest leaves of me and yet my strongest lasting,
> Here I shade and hide my thoughts, I myself do not expose
> them,
> And yet they expose me more than all my other poems.

One hears more than a direct statement of fact in these three lines. Whitman concentrates in them a disturbing paradox about himself.

The emotion or impulse (his sexual ambiguity) that most exposes, endangers, and distresses him (the "frailest" part of him) seems to be the most real—it is the "strongest lasting." Because of social conventions and his fear of his own homosexuality Whitman would naturally prefer to protect himself by masking the reality his poems expose. But if he were to repress or hide his "thoughts," he would deny part of himself, and Whitman cannot do that. Instead, he evidently must express himself and he must try to establish a genuine relationship with another person. He has no choice, therefore, but to open and expose himself. He regrets it; he fears the exposure; yet he must assume the risk. "Trickle Drops" expresses the overwhelming sense of shame exposure can cause.

Whitman's attempt to accept himself, his subsequent rejection of conventional values, and his search for meaning in relation with others expose him also to loneliness, for he isolates himself with no guarantee that he will find meaning in "the life that does not exhibit itself" and with no promise that he will succeed in finding others who will respond to him. "Calamus" does not present Whitman as a strong, self-sufficient individual who can easily tolerate the isolation his rebellion causes. The situation is quite the opposite. Whitman so needs and depends on the love of another that he feels a "sick, sick dread lest the one he [loves] might secretly be indifferent to him." Loneliness does not simply distress or upset the poet; it could, as Whitman recognizes in "I Saw in Louisiana A Live-Oak Growing," virtually silence him or cast him into despair. Whitman compares his own dependence on the love of his friends to the independence and self-sufficiency of the live-oak. He could not go on, as the tree does, "uttering joyous leaves . . . without a friend or a lover near." His loneliness would be too great. Whitman does not say whether he would turn to leaves of despair or whether he would be paralyzed and thus become silent. Either possibility indicates, however, the devastating effect isolation and loneliness would have on his poetry. The "Live-Oak" poem indicates that Whitman not only needs love, but that the specific relationship between man and man provides the essential meaning for his life and his poetry.

Although loneliness and its consequent despair do indeed threaten Whitman, the dialogue he seeks can diminish tension and fear and actually enable him to transcend his separation and limitations. The I-Thou relationship the *Calamus* poems dramatize not only relieves the pain of loneliness, it establishes, as well, an essential meaning for the life of Walt Whitman. I am saying that the Calamus love, as

Whitman presents and experiences it, is not basically destructive; on the contrary, it is potentially fulfilling, and more convincingly portrayed than the heterosexual love Whitman strives to present in "Children of Adam." There is no doubt that the love between man and man Whitman speaks of is deeply problematic, for it exposes him to failure, despair, dread, and alienation—to a real psychological destruction. Nevertheless, it can result in a supremely transcendent experience in which Whitman possesses himself fully. The moment or the relation is neither mystic nor spiritual in the conventional sense, yet it does resolve contradictions, answer doubts, and overcome division; it frees Whitman from guilt, shame, and fear; and it banishes loneliness and delivers him from time:

> To me these and the like of these are curiously answer'd by my
>   lovers, my dear friends,
> When he whom I love travels with me or sits a long while
>   holding me by the hand,
> When the subtle air, the impalpable, the sense that words and
>   reason hold not, surround us and pervade us,
> Then I am charged with untold and untellable wisdom, I am
>   silent, I require nothing further,
> I cannot answer the question of appearances or that of identity
>   beyond the grave,
> But I walk or sit indifferent, I am satisfied,
> He ahold of my hand has completely satisfied me.

Even a poem such as "Scented Herbage of My Breast" supports my view of the positive direction of the Calamus love. Although some critics argue that the poem definitively exposes the destructiveness of that love (Whitman after all links love with death and not with life, as he did in "Children of Adam"), the poem actually presents a liberating and fulfilling discovery by the poet. Even so the liberation does not emerge fully until the end of the poem. Before that one has a clear sense that Whitman's situation is highly problematic and that the kind of dilemma "Scented Herbage" defines does not inevitably lead to a positive conclusion. Whitman presents the conflict by concentrating (1) on the struggle in himself between secrecy and openness and (2) on an association of the poem and the poet's unhappiness with a destructive love—with death, actually.

(1) The first part of the poem reveals how difficult it is for Whitman to speak his mind. He wants to confess, but he is confused by the meaning of what he might say. Besides, revelation of the shame and pain associated with what seems to be a perverse, guilty love disturbs

him a great deal: "You are often more bitter than I can bear, you burn
and sting me." Nevertheless, he must speak his heart, although it is
a real struggle for him to do so. Whitman intensifies the confessional
quality of the poem by suggesting that poem, meaning, and experience are physically and psychologically him:

> O slender leaves! O blossoms of my blood! I permit you to tell
>   in your own way of the heart that is under you.

When he utters the poem, he expresses himself, and that is painful
—because of the exposure and the repeated (experiencing) of bitter-
ness.

(2) The first part of the poem also connects what he would say
(what it is that "burns and stings" him so) with death. In the third line
he speaks of his poems—his leaves—as "tomb-leaves":

> Scented herbage of my breast,
> Leaves from you I glean, I write, to be perused best afterwards,
> Tomb-leaves, body-leaves growing up above me above death.

The leaves express the poet's psychological and emotional death—a
dying that has left him in the state of despair, tension, and confusion
with which the poem begins. These poems of despair or confusion
remain ("growing up above me above death") after the poet's
spiritual "death." The same line also suggests the conventional idea
that the poems will achieve the permanency of art and continue to
express the poet after he is literally dead. Both meanings are valid
and important to the development of the poem. Whitman also connects his leaves with death in the tenth line: "Yet you are beautiful
to me you faint tinged roots, you make me think of death." The
bitter, unhappy leaves that burn and sting him with shame make him
think of death. Since the poems do expose a disruptive and even
personally destructive psychological condition (the shame, guilt, and
the spiritual and emotional death Whitman may have in mind), one
might think that Whitman's thoughts here are suicidal. The beauty
of those "tomb-leaves" may be the beauty of death as a release from
the emotional turmoil he has experienced.

The beginning of the poem clearly indicates that Whitman's identity and world are being threatened, and he may even be thinking
of suicide. But the poem soon dismisses that possibility. The leaves
are bitter, yet they are beautiful, as well. That is, Whitman associates
them with the shame, guilt, and fear he has felt, but at the same time

he recognizes that they express love and relationship—a love that is potentially "beautiful" and personally creative. At this point, Whitman seems to separate death, beauty, and love from the emotional turbulence that has heretofore been an integral part of his love. He idealizes the three but inclines toward death rather than life:

> Death is beautiful from you, (what indeed is finally beautiful
>   except death and love?)
> O I think it is not for life I am chanting here my chant of lovers,
>   I think it must be for death,
> For how calm, how solemn it grows to ascend to the atmosphere
>   of lovers,
> Death or life I am then indifferent, my soul declines to prefer,
> (I am not sure but the high soul of lovers welcomes death most,)
>   . . .

Life produces psychological turmoil and guilt: it forces him to conceal what he is. Death, on the other hand, may bring a permanent state of beautiful love fully realized. In other words, by connecting beauty, love, and death as he does, Whitman envisions an ideal situation where he can celebrate and experience that part of himself he has so long concealed. In such a situation he would be unafraid to reveal his hidden self—to confront, accept, and live the real person that he is.

Before, the poems *exposed* him: they revealed his impulse toward homosexual love; they confessed his consequent shame and fear; and they showed how he was threatened with serious psychological breakdown. Now, the leaves *express* him: they reveal the same secret or real self but from a wholly different psychological point of view. Whitman is beginning to discover the liberating and fulfilling possibilities of accepting himself and loving another. Therefore, the leaves begin to mean "precisely the same as" death means because the poet now sees that they express love and beauty, not perversion and ugliness. They express, as well, a self that no longer frightens and shames him; but one he is now ready to accept, announce, and live:

> Grow up taller sweet leaves that I may see! grow up out of my
>   breast!
> Spring away from the conceal'd heart there!
> Do not fold yourself so in your pink-tinged roots timid leaves!
> Do not remain down there so ashamed, herbage of my breast!
> Come I am determin'd to unbare this broad breast of mine, I
>   have long enough stifled and choked;

Emblematic and capricious blades I leave you, now you serve
    me not,
I will say what I have to say by itself. . . .

Whitman has reversed the conventional equations, and any interpretation that fails to account for that simply cannot explain the
poem as the speaker experiences it. Instead of presenting life as
creative and death as destructive, he thinks of life—*as he has suffered
it*—as psychologically destructive, and he views death—as he regards
it aesthetically—as essentially creative. Love and death are the same,
then—creative, liberating, and fulfilling. They become a means to
self-transcendence, yet at the same time they provide a way to
recover and liberate Whitman's essential self.

It is not always easy to decide in Whitman's poetry when he uses
death as a physical or metaphysical fact and when he uses it as an
image or symbol. In "Scented Herbage," he may think of it as a fact
in the third line, but after that, he views death as an aesthetic state
(as an image or symbol) rather than a physical or metaphysical one.
For Whitman death symbolizes a permanent condition—first, of love
and beauty and, second, of genuine mutuality between man and
man. In this way it becomes an ultimate reality ("the real reality") or
a transcendent state, but it does not refer to immortality, nor does
it refer to some mystic state in which the poet gets out of himself. On
the contrary, he recovers himself in that condition. In effect, he seeks
a kind of death-in-life—an unchanging, exhilarating experience of
beautiful love—liberated from the appearances (the masks), disrup-
tions, and madness of ordinary life. Yet he wants that experience (as
a good Romantic would) in-the-world; he wants the aesthetic state he
images in death to be definitive of existence. No matter how un-
characteristically Romantic or aesthetic the solution may be for
Whitman, one must remember that the image fixes and idealizes the
personal and the relational; that the poem presents love as fulfillment
and not deprivation; and that Whitman seeks meaning not in death
as "beyond" but in death (an aesthetic condition) as existence—he
seeks, in short, meaning-in-being through openness and relation.

Whitman writes again of the untrodden paths he follows in "These
I Singing in Spring"; but in it he expresses no anxiety, shame, or guilt.
He recognizes, of course, that every lover experiences sorrow, but
for the moment he has escaped it. Therefore, he can speak with
unqualified joy about his dear friends and those "that love as I myself
am capable of loving." He speaks really of two modes of relation. He

establishes dialogue with others (1) through poetry (the spoken word) and (2) through memory and imagination (he recalls the past and he makes present in the moment both his former and current friendships).

(1) In the first sense, Whitman sings his poems as an expression of love for others, and he collects and offers them to the other hoping for a response that will establish a dialogue between him and his reader:

> These I singing in spring collect for lovers,
> (For who but I should understand lovers and all their sorrow
>   and joy?
> And who but I should be the poet of comrades?)

One can easily associate several of the images Whitman includes ("collects," actually) with particular poems in "Calamus" and *Leaves of Grass* so it is apparent that he regards the natural objects as images for his poems. Every image or object serves also as a symbol (or "token") of Whitman's love for others:

> And this, O this shall henceforth be the token of comrades, this
>   calamus-root shall,
> Interchange it youths with each other! let none render it back!)
> And twigs of maple and a bunch of wild orange and chestnut,
> And stems of currants and plum-blows, and the aromatic cedar.

Thus, each image or each poem, in some way addresses a person and calls for his response. The Calamus root is the central symbol, however; it concentrates all the diverse, natural images into one, just as the "Calamus" poems, perhaps, function as the essential expression of relation between man and man in *Leaves of Grass:*

> But what I drew from the water by the pond-side, that I reserve,
> I will give of it, but only to them that love as I myself am capable
>   of loving.

Whitman attempts, then, to speak to others through the poem, and in this sense, he presents himself as one with others through the spoken word—through the poem as dialogue.

(2) In the second sense, Whitman presents an actual situation in which the poet's relationships with his friends and lovers play a central role. Whitman describes himself wandering alone "along the pond-side," "by the post-and-rail fences," and "far in the forest." As

he goes, he collects tokens from nature as gestures of love toward the "dear friends" who appear in the poem. He does not, however, encounter others directly—no troop of people physically accompanies him or gathers round him; rather he recreates through memory and imagination all of the meaningful relations he has had with others, and he concentrates them in the present moment. He engages really in a kind of silent dialogue with those he calls forth out of his consciousness. Both the past and present friendships are valid for Whitman, and, therefore, they sustain him even when he is alone. Indeed, they assure him that he is *not* alone in any definitive or absolute sense. From this point of view, the Calamus root still functions as the central symbol in the poem, and surely it carries masculine or phallic implications. Whitman does mean love between men and, in some sense, I suppose such love is homosexual. It is also clearly sensual or physical, for touch seems to be an important expression of it. There is, however, no evidence that "Calamus" speaks of or advocates specific homosexual acts, and it is absurd to say or imply that it does. But more importantly the Calamus root symbolizes an essential relation—a genuine, deep mutuality that only a few can experience.

One last poem from "Calamus" will summarize what I have to say about dialogue and relation in the section. In "Of the Terrible Doubt of Appearances" Whitman indicates a concrete way in which dialogue between man and man fulfills him. The poem focusses, first, on the doubts and anxieties of experience—on the problematic nature of Whitman's situation. Whitman simply says that he does have moments of uncertainty when he is confused and frustrated by mystery:

> Of the terrible doubt of appearances,
> Of the uncertainty after all, that we may be deluded,
> That may-be reliance and hope are but speculations after all,
> That may-be identity beyond the grave is a beautiful fable only,
> May-be the things I perceive, the animals, plants, men, hills,
>   shining and flowing waters,
> The skies of day and night, colors, densities, forms, may-be these
>   are (as doubtless they are) only apparitions, and the real
>   something has yet to be known,
> (How often they dart out of themselves as if to confound me and
>   mock me!
> How often I think neither I know, nor any man knows, aught
>   of them.)

In this case, his anxiety does not seem to be based on his ambiguous sexuality or on his "manly" relations. The poem then goes on to show how these uncertainties "are curiously answer'd" by his lovers. In other words the love between him and another gives a meaning to his life that liberates him from confusion. Although the I-Thou relation he describes does not answer his questions directly, he does discover that meaning in experience arises in relationship rather than in knowledge. His "dear friends" enable him to be what-he-is in the midst of doubt; they enable him to find a meaning-in-experience that diminishes anxiety and displaces cosmic questions.

C. "Drum Taps"

The middle poems in "Drum Taps" convey an overriding sense of loneliness, loss, waste, destruction, and death. Whitman clearly understands that war interrupts the flow of life; that it prevents personal relationships from developing, and that it often destroys those relations that exist. Yet Whitman recognizes, as well, that in the midst of carnage men can establish genuine personal relations. Once the abstractions disappear, the cause is forgotten, and the war becomes real, these comradeships provide the only value for a man in the midst of a terribly destructive war. The personal relationships between man and man also become a key in the reconstruction of Whitman's private world at the end of the war. Whitman can rebuild his world in the public sphere by immersing himself in the city ("Give Me the Splendid Silent Sun") and by rediscovering the principle which finally justifies the war ("Over the Carnage"), but identification with the turbulent mass of the city and recovery of the principle of union supply only a partial solution. Whitman must also find a deeply personal way to put his torn world back together.

In "Vigil Strange I Kept on the Field One Night" the destruction and deprivation of the war is clear. The young man has been slaughtered, and the speaker has been deprived of a loved and loving comrade. Nonetheless, the poet recognizes that the two men did share a reciprocal love that, just possibly, kept them going—on the "march in the ranks hard-prest, and [along] the road unknown"—and thus enabled them to find something of value in the war. The war made the relationship possible, and it gave the friendship, perhaps, a depth and immediacy it might not have had in other circumstances. Therefore, the surviving comrade will remember the personal I-Thou relationship that did exist, as well as recall the death that deprived him of his friend. The old soldier maintains a vigil that is at once a lament *and* a celebration. It is a vigil he can never forget because it reminds him of both love and death: "Vigil of silence, love and death, vigil for you my son and my soldier."

"The Wound-dresser" only suggests the kind of relationships Whitman established during the war with the men in the hospitals. Yet the poem says enough to show that Whitman tries to give more than pity, solicitude, and aid to the men. If he could, he would experience the other's pain, fear, and death:

> I am firm with each, the pangs are sharp yet unavoidable,
> One turns to me his appealing eyes—poor boy! I never knew you,
> Yet I think I could not refuse this moment to die for you, if that would save you.

Whitman's willingness to become that man and to suffer and die for him demands a deep understanding of the other and an extraordinary commitment of the self to him. The dialogue is silent, momentary, and only suggested, yet it is there.

The poem dramatizes Whitman's sympathy, consideration, and his ability to identify with the other, but it says virtually nothing about his limitations. The Civil War prose, however, does; Whitman indicates that he cannot possibly establish a genuine dialogue with each and every man he meets in the hospitals:

> Reader! How can I describe to you the mute appealing look that rolls and moves from many a manly eye, from many a sick cot, following you as you walk slowly down one of these wards? To see these and to be incapable of responding to them, except in a few cases (so very few compared to the whole of the suffering men), is enough to make one's heart crack.

> . . . but as there is a limit to one's sinews and endurance and sympathies etc., I have got in the way, after going lightly, as it were, all through the wards of a hospital and trying to give a word of cheer, if nothing else, to everyone, then confining my special attentions to the few where the investment seems to tell best, and who want it most.[2]

Yet he extends himself as much as he can. He values each man as a person and tries to meet each as a man with his own story, needs, and personality.

The value of his presence to the men is, again, only implicit in the poem. It describes primarily Whitman's function as a wound dresser and says little more. But Whitman also brought the men gifts and necessities, he talked with them, and above all he gave himself to them:

> It was in such an experience as of the war that my heart needed
> to be fully thrown—thrown without reserve. I do not regret it
> —could not regret it. What was a man to do? The war had much
> to give—there were thousands, tens of thousands, hundreds of
> thousands needing me—needing all who might come. What
> could I do?
>
> . . . I never once questioned the decision that led me into the
> war . . .
>
> . . . When once I am convinced, I never let go; after I first took
> hold of this thing, I never let go. I had to pay much for what I
> got; but what I got made what I paid for it—much as it was—
> seem cheap . . . What did I get? Well, I got the boys, for one
> thing . . . I gave myself for them—myself.[3]

He gave them the comfort and love that only the personal presence
of a man deeply interested in them and, in his own way, sharing their
suffering, can give. Whitman briefly describes his value to the men
in the final lines of the poem:

> Thus in silence in dreams' projections,
> Returning, resuming, I thread my way through the hospitals,
> The hurt and wounded I pacify with soothing hand,
> I sit by the restless all the dark night, some are so young,
> Some suffer so much, I recall the experience sweet and sad,
> (Many a soldier's loving arms about this neck have cross'd and
>   rested,
> Many a soldier's kiss dwells on these bearded lips.)

He made their suffering slightly more tolerable, and perhaps he even
made the dying feel that they did not face death absolutely alone.
They faced it with a bold, true, loving comrade at their sides.

Although "As I Lay with My Head in Your Lap Camerado" seems
like a "Calamus" poem, it is very important to "Drum Taps." In one
sense, it is a poem about poetry. In it Whitman resumes the poetic
journey the war had interrupted; he enters the open road, once
again, not knowing whether he will succeed or fail as a poet. The
outcome, however, makes no difference to him—he is willing to take
the risk—but the act itself and the relationship he establishes with his
reader do make a difference. The dialogue between the poet and his
reader provides one essential way for Whitman to rebuild his world
after the personal and public disruption caused by the war.

But the poem may also mean something more. It is so like the
"Calamus" poems that it invites one to extend its meaning to include
the Calamus love. In this sense, "As I Lay" focusses on the personal

dialogue Whitman needs to transcend the psychic damage of war and to restore a personal meaning to his life. The radical relationship —the Calamus love and freedom—Whitman urges possesses its own danger and death: "I know my words are weapons full of danger, full of death." Yet after the dreadful experience of war, Whitman simply must take the risk:

> Dear camerado! I confess I have urged you onward with me,
>   and still urge you, without the least idea what is our destina-
>   tion,
> Or whether we shall be victorious, or utterly quell'd and de-
>   feated.

Whitman must, once again, follow the untrodden paths he describes in "Calamus," recognizing full well the dangers of personal guilt, loss, or rejection and of public rebuke and persecution. At this point, however, hell, heaven, and social approval mean nothing; only personal relationship possesses meaning for him. And if he succeeds in finding a Calamus love, he will be satisfied—he will have escaped the "war-strife":

> But I walk or sit indifferent, I am satisfied,
> He ahold of my hand has completely satisfied me.
>   ("Of the Terrible Doubt of Appearances")

The poem's place in "Drum Taps"—as a poem of resolution—and its explicit assertion of risk show that transcendence for Whitman is still a process and that the situation of the self continues to be problematic. Whitman survives the war, but he does not achieve a state of transcendence as a result. Instead, he commits himself once again to the life long endeavor of living—to the long process of becoming whole.

2. The Self and Others

In "Democratic Vistas" Whitman discusses two major principles— the individual and the aggregate. Individualism arises from man's desire to be himself, and the mass develops from man's need and desire to live with others. The first isolates men from one another, and the second brings them together: "individualism which isolates . . . adhesiveness or love that fuses, ties, and aggregates, making the races comrades, and fraternizing all." Whitman recognizes that "the two are contradictory," but he explains that "our task is to reconcile them."

His great concern with individuals and their relationships to one another shows Whitman's clear sense that America is not simply things, places, and politics. America is, instead, an idea and a political institution that expresses the unique inner man—"the precious idiocrasy and special nativity and intention that he is"—and that enables him to realize the special "quality of Being" he possesses better than any conception or institution ever has. Whitman argues for the personalist basis of Democracy and America. This personal reality lies "underneath the fluctuations of the expressions of society," and unless it becomes the primary value, the political forms will be meaningless. At one point Whitman goes so far as to say that the "aggregate" does not simply consolidate a great many simple separate persons into a compatible mass; it develops as a genuine community based on concrete I-Thou relationships between man and man. Whitman's statement that America must reconcile the individual and the mass implies the necessity of relationship between individuals. But he goes further than that. He believes that Democracy *means* community. The political structure is not just a convenience to nurture "individual separatism"; it provides, as well, for "the highest forms of interaction between men." Whitman looks forward to a community in which "perfect personalities . . . meet," and that community will be based on concrete relations between persons. "Intense and loving comradeship—the personal and passionate attachment of man to man" must exist if a genuine community is to exist. "I say democracy infers such loving comradeship, as its most inevitable twin or counterpart, without which it will be incomplete, *in vain*, and incapable of perpetuating itself" (italics added). Whitman seems to understand that without personal relationships and without the extension of these into a genuine community, democracy would become a meaningless abstraction, a collection of incomplete egocentric individuals, or a materialistic and vulgar pseudo-community—the Gilded Age America Whitman exposes in the first part of "Democratic Vistas."

I am not saying that Whitman intellectually anticipated Martin Buber's sense of the "essential We"—the poet did, of course, "know" it existentially. I am simply pointing out the political writer's major concern with relationships within the society and with the relationships of the self to the many. These are the same concerns that often preoccupied the poet in his political or American poems—those, for example, once grouped as "Chants Democratic" and some of the other songs he added later. In them he praises democracy, he celebrates ensemble, and he glorifies the individual. But he seldom writes a poem in which he actually dramatizes the relations between the self and the many or the existence of a genuine community. That is astounding and ironic. Except for a few unusual (and major) instances, the Poet of Democracy—the great promoter of the States— did not dramatize, and therefore did not make essential in his drama of identity, the relationship of the self to the many. He valued the self and many sphere very highly—as his major concerns in "Democratic Vistas" show—but he simply did not make "ensemble" concrete.

In *Calamus* Whitman speaks of his relationships with other single persons. Occasionally he projects those *I* and *Thou* relationships into a social or communal context, as he does in "For You O Democracy," in which he says that the "life-long love of comrades" will provide a firm basis for Democracy. Whitman surely has in mind the concrete relations between man and man he speaks of in other *Calamus* poems, and he seems to be thinking also of larger circles of companionship ("I will plant companionship as thick as trees") that would make up the community and which would necessitate a genuine relation between the self and the many. In context the poem probably implies the concrete, personal relationships dramatized in other poems, and the images in lines 4 and 5 at least try to make companionship concrete. But on the whole the poem simply asserts a value —one very similar to the principle of community Whitman states in "Democratic Vistas." It is a value that informs other poems, but oddly enough, Whitman seldom succeeds in making it concrete or real.

"Crossing Brooklyn Ferry" is one of the major exceptions. I commented on it in Chapter 3, and so I shall simply recall a few of its relevant major features. In the poem Whitman establishes a relationship with others in two ways. (1) He dramatizes an I and you—an *I-Thou*—and finally a "we" relationship in the poem itself. Whitman and the other New Yorkers who will ride the ferry share a common experience; they share, as well, a common humanity which is not confined to place and time—to the city or to the ferry; and they share, finally, an inner spiritual reality which joins the living and the dead in a communal relation that transcends both time and space. Whitman presents the relationship as the central action or event in the poem. (2) The poem also establishes an "I and you" and an essential "we" relationship through its language—through the address of the poet to his readers and through their response to his call. Both the fictional others in the poem and the present and future readers of it, experience the genuine "we." The poem itself constitutes the shared experience for the reader and is analogous to the fictional characters' ferry ride. The common humanity (the reciprocal sharing of knowledge about one another) and the shared inner spiritual reality are the same for both the fictional others and Whitman's present and future readers.

Both dramatically and verbally, then, Whitman addresses other persons across time, and in speaking to them, he says "we" with genuineness. He presents and creates a relationship between the self and the many that is concrete and that depends on essential relations between persons. Martin Buber explains the principle this way: "The genuine We is to be recognized in its objective existence, through the fact that in whatever of its parts it is regarded, an essential relation between person and person, between I and Thou, is always evident as actually or potentially existing. For the word always arises only between an I and a Thou, and the element from which the We receives its life is speech, the communal speaking that begins in the midst of speaking to one another."[4] Whitman addresses each other person individually; yet at the same time, his address binds the others and himself into We, and thus Whitman establishes for himself a genuine relationship between the self and the many. In that relationship he realizes and verifies himself both in and across time in a way that few other poems dramatize or achieve.[5]

If, as I say, Whitman does not dramatize a genuine relation between the self and the many in the poems about Democracy, America, and Ensemble, then what does he do? First, he does indeed speak of comradeship and the community, but without making them real. They are either facts and values he assumes or political and spiritual abstractions he promotes. As such, the States or Democracy exists in only the future—as the embodiment of "a new politics." Second, Whitman celebrates America as a place where people live and work, and to some extent he does succeed in making America present as a place.

1) "For You O Democracy" states what Whitman would *like* to have happen in America, and it implies, I think, what he would like to express and dramatize in his poetry. Other poems also mention and praise comradeship and ensemble. As Whitman says in "Song of the Broad-Axe," America is the place "where the city of the faithful-

est friends stands." According to the poet, that city of friends is one of the most important "shapes of Democracy," but unfortunately it is only dimly outlined in the poem. Whitman is more interested in *all* the different "shapes" of America than he is in relationship. He seems really to *assume* the existence of genuine self and many relationships in the "ensemble" he values, and so he limits his direct concern to references, brief sketches of people (occasionally in relationship), and apostrophes such as his cry in "A Broadway Pageant":

> Superb-faced Manhattan!
> Comrade Americanos! to us, then at last the Orient comes.

Oftentimes "ensemble" or comradeship appears in a poem as the main subject and value, but it remains either an abstraction or eternal principle that exists somewhere beyond the world; in neither form does it have anything to do with a concrete relation between the self and the many. "Thou Mother With Thy Equal Brood" serves as an obvious case in point. The number of capitalized nouns alone in it reveals as much about the poem and about Whitman's penchant for abstract universals as anything. Whitman shows no sense here of a personal relationship of the self with others—with society or with the community. In the first section he announces:

> I'd sow a seed for thee of endless Nationality,
> I'd fashion thy ensemble including body and soul,
> I'd show away ahead thy real Union, and how it may be accomplish'd.

But he never does "fashion . . . ensemble" in any concrete way. If the poem does anything besides exasperate its readers, it deals with the relation of the self to an abstract ideal—"Thou! mounting higher, diving deeper than we knew, thou transcendental Union!" In another section Whitman sets concrete existence even further aside by making "ensemble" one with eternal principle:

> (Lo, where arise three peerless stars,
> To be thy natal stars my country, Ensemble, Evolution, Freedom,
> Set in the sky of Law.)

Ensemble becomes part of "thou New, indeed new, Spiritual World!" It no longer has anything to do with the relational and communal Whitman beautifully dramatizes in "Crossing Brooklyn Ferry."

Nor does ensemble possess any present reality, for Whitman envisions it as part of a prophetic future. The poet ends "Thou Mother" by saying,

> Thou mental, moral orb—thou New, indeed new, Spiritual
>   World!
> The Present holds thee not—for such vast growth as thine,
> For such unparallel'd flight as thine, such brood as thine,
> The FUTURE only holds thee and can hold thee.

And he looks forward in "Song of the Redwood-Tree" to "the new society at last":

> Fresh come, to a new world indeed, yet long prepared,
> I see the genius of the modern, child of the real and ideal,
> Clearing the ground for broad humanity, the true America, heir
>   of the past so grand,
> To build a grander future.

It is quite true that Whitman could not predict the exact shape of the future—the new politics in a new world—and he could not imagine what concrete relationships would be like in the future. The poems I have been referring to do not even indicate that present relationships between the self and others are necessary for the new world to emerge. These poems, instead, project a principle, and that ideal, presumably, will justify and develop the concrete forms and relationships that will emerge. Whitman does not base the forms on the present and the concrete. His claim in "Song for Occupations":

> Will you seek afar off? you surely come back at last,
> In things best known to you finding the best, or as good as the
>   best,
> In folks nearest to you finding the sweetest, strongest, lovingest,
> Happiness, knowledge, not in another place but this place, not
>   for another hour but this hour,
> Man in the first you see or touch, always in friend, brother,
>   nighest neighbor—woman in mother, sister, wife,
> The popular tastes and employments taking precedence in po-
>   ems or anywhere,
> You workwomen and workmen of these States having your own
>   divine and strong life,
> And all else giving place to men and women like you.

does not describe what actually occurs in the Democratic chants. Whitman has, in effect, inverted the structure of the experience in "Crossing Brooklyn Ferry," for in it place, self, and relationship are the source and verification of the spiritual reality Whitman discovers. This is not the case in the poems about Democracy and Ensemble.

I am simply saying that for ensemble—for the relation of the self to the many—to become essential, the ideal must be situational and topical. It must emerge, that is, from concrete relationships; it must appear, in short, as the genuine We. However, in poems like "Thou Mother" and "Song of the Broad-Axe" it does not. Ensemble and comradeship stand free as abstract universals with no effective concreteness or presentness.

2) Whitman does convey a sense of America as a place where people live and act. "Our Old Feuillage" is one of several poems that evoke and celebrate places and people. But except for an occasional sketch Whitman does not really portray the people in direct, concrete relations with one another or with the many, and except for an occasionally good line that effectively describes place, the poem becomes a kind of guided tour or geography lesson. Whitman also repeatedly locates himself in America—he makes it his scene—and he explains how important place and others are to his personality and to the forms and values he and others adopt. But neither "Song of Occupations" nor the other poems dramatize Whitman's relationship to America with anything close to the success of "Song of Myself."

There is not really a great deal to say about the self and the many at this point because, for the most part, Whitman does not make that relationship genuine. In the Democratic chants and in other similar poems, Whitman's relationship to America and the relation of the self to the many remain curiously and ironically theoretical. For that reason the poems come very close to making each person that makes up "the divine average" or "Ensemble" part of an abstraction or part of a collective mass which has lost the sense of relationship that keeps a community from being a collective. Whitman proclaims his confidence in ensemble and association—and in a few great poems he makes it real—but his uncertainty about the relationship of self and many (uncertain because he seldom makes it concrete and genuine), his easy reliance on abstract universals and the unintended emergence of a collective rather than a communal America make the relationship between the self and the many more problematic than Whitman ever knew.

NOTES—*Chapter VI*

1. Cf. Clark Griffith, "Sex and Death: the Significance of Whitman's 'Cala-
    mus' Themes," *Philological Quarterly,* XXXIX (1960), 18–38; and Rob-
    ert C. Tuttle, *The Identity of Walt Whitman: Motive, Theme, and Form
    in Leaves of Grass,* (unpublished dissertation, University of Washing-
    ton, 1965), pp. 123 ff.
2. Walt Whitman, *Walt Whitman's Civil War,* ed. Walter Lowenfels
    (New York, 1961), pp. 91 and 145.
3. *Ibid.,* pp. 15–16.
4. Martin Buber, *The Knowledge of Man* (New York, 1965), p. 106.
5. Cf. Maurice Friedman's explanation, *Martin Buber: The Life of Dia-
    logue* (New York, 1960), pp. 208–209.

CHAPTER SEVEN

The Self, Death, and Spirit

In "Whispers of Heavenly Death" Whitman concludes one of his poems ("Thought") with three questions:

> Sinking there while the passionless wet flows on—and I now
>   pondering, Are those women indeed gone?
> Are souls drown'd and destroy'd so?
> Is only matter triumphant?

The three really ask one question—what is death? Whitman gives *no* answer in "Thought" because in that moment and in that state of mind he has no answer. He cannot even respond with the confidence or assurances on which he often relies in his other encounters with uncertainty or with mystery. The poem describes the sudden disruption of Whitman's cheerful, festive, thoughtless mood by thoughts of death and shipwreck:

> As I sit with others at a great feast, suddenly while the music
>   is playing,
> To my mind, (whence it comes I know not,) spectral in mist of
>   a wreck at sea.

The interruption of Whitman's "life" at the feast parallels the abrupt end of the women's lives described in the poem: "A huge sob —a few bubbles—the white foam spirting up—and then the women gone." Both Whitman's situation and the sinking of the ships suggest the way thoughts of death disrupt and destroy life even during its most joyous moments. Not only that, the strange disappearance of

the *President*—"the solemn and murky mystery"—suggests the attitude toward death that Whitman expresses; it, too, is a solemn and
murky mystery. No one knows the fate of the steamer, but more
importantly Whitman does not know—nor can he guess—the fate of
the people who went down with the ship. In this poem Whitman
stands before the unknown—the fact of death, and he asks the ultimate questions: "Are souls drown'd and destroy'd so?" "Is only matter triumphant?" At the end of the poem he has no answer. A question—uncertainty—the mystery of death remain.

The equally uncertain situation of the self (of the soul) in relation
to spirit (to some unknown, yet ultimate reality) emerges in another
"Whispers" poem—"A Noiseless Patient Spider." Like the spider
tirelessly seeking to connect with something beyond him, so Whitman's soul—"surrounded, detached, in measureless oceans of space"
—tries to establish a relationship with the spheres beyond it. The
poem clearly suggests that the soul *might* connect with something
"somewhere," and surely the ceaseless striving for relationship suggests that the poet *is* confident about the future. But the poem offers
no assurance that spiders or souls, after enduring a period of isolation
and loneliness, will inevitably succeed in bridging the vast spaces
separating each from some other. As a matter of fact, it emphasizes
the tenuousness of the attempt and the connection by focussing on
the flimsy filament the spider unreels and on the "gossamer thread"
the soul hopes will catch somewhere.

In the same poem Whitman also indicates the consequences of the
soul's failure to find relationship. Along with the spider, it would
continue to exist alone, in the "*vacant* vast surrounding" and in "
measureless oceans of space" (italics added). The means of connection and the present and continuing isolation of the soul (it will
remain so until some future time that itself is unknown) underscore
the uncertain situation of the self as it tries to discover some connection with spirit. Even if one accents only the positive—the soul *will*
"catch somewhere"—one cannot ignore the uncertainty of that:
somewhere, but *where?*

Although the questioning, uncertain nature of these two poems
does not definitively describe Whitman's attitude, they do indicate
that death and man's relationship to spirit were as unknown and
problematic for Whitman as any aspect of existence. They are problematic because they remain essentially unknown (even in many of
the most trustful of Whitman's poems) and because Whitman is
finally uncertain about them. He sees death, for example, in a variety

of ways—as a passage into oblivion, as a completion and fulfillment of one's human existence, as a release from suffering, as a passage into a new, conscious life; to some extent each attitude excludes the others.

Because death is a mystery and spirit is seldom fully available to Whitman, his poetry about death and spirit is predominately a poetry about human existence. For that reason D. H. Lawrence's description of Whitman as a great poet of the end of life satisfies me much more than any of those descriptions which transform Whitman into a poet of spiritual law, immortality, or some mystic consciousness. Whitman may try to discover the truth about the Absolute or the infinite, but he recognizes, all the while, his humanity and his ultimate inability to penetrate death and spirit.

He hears whispers about them (the possibility for dialogue exists), but they are not always the same; and he finds faint clues and indirections, but they, too, differ from one another. At best, then, Whitman can express only the whispers he hears and the clues he finds. He can express his attitudes toward death and spirit; he can somehow describe his encounters with them as a man in-the-world; but he cannot say what they *are*.

"Whispers of Heavenly Death" and "Songs of Parting" reveal the essential problematic I find in Whitman's death poetry, for they include many of the attitudes toward death that Whitman dramatizes in *Leaves of Grass.* The sections include both pre-war and post-war poems, and I suppose one could relate Whitman's response to death in a given poem to a particular period in his life. But the point is that Whitman placed all of the poems in the final edition of *Leaves of Grass,* and he placed them in sections that deal quite clearly with parting, death, and spirit. Together they reveal the poet's lifelong uncertainty about death and his recognition of the essential problematic of his relation to spirit.

(1) In many poems Whitman expresses a genuine belief that death is a passage or a journey—a new beginning—into another, Transcendental life. Whitman does not try to describe what follows death (because he obviously does not know), and often he is unsure of the exact "purport" of it. Nevertheless, he possesses in such poems an overwhelming trust in the unknown—in God. And that is what he describes: his conviction, his confidence, that "Heavenly Death provides for all." "Assurances" offers one of the clearest and most direct

statements of Whitman's confidence. The poet needs no assurances because his trust is complete: "I do not doubt that the passionately-wept deaths of young men are provided for, and that the deaths of young women and the deaths of little children are provided for." The poem expresses Whitman's belief in a Transcendental unity which informs all of human existence and which "provides for all." Heavenly Death frees man from "temporary affairs" and provides the way to eternal life. Whitman is not saying, however, that he will become part of a vast, unlimited, undifferentiated eternity; he speaks rather of relationship and unity and, thus, even if he does not name it, of participation in a spiritual life after death. So in this way, death and spirit actually are fused in the poem.

Even though Whitman assures his reader that spirit provides for everything, he indicates that one fully understands it only in death. The clear separation between life and spirit—between the temporal and the eternal—is similar to the separation that informs "To Think of Time." This conception of death concentrates on its ultimate Transcendental meaning rather than on the human meaning—the immediate personal significance it has for and about man-in-the-world.

(2) In other poems, however, Whitman encounters death not as if it were a gateway to another life and in that sense a release from limits or from pain, but he accepts it as a fact and he thinks of it as a means of completion, fulfillment, and justification. That awareness gives greater depth and meaning to life; it frees Whitman from regarding death as a threat and from the subsequent anguish and despair; and at times it gives him a sense of renewal and joy. It makes no difference, therefore, if death provides a passage or if it brings oblivion, for Whitman focusses on the human side—on the meaning of death for one's human life. When he speaks from this perspective, he is truly the poet of the end of life.

In "Of Him I Love Day and Night," the poet states very simply that death is an essential part of life. In fact it actually dominates life, for Whitman discovers that the places of life are "vastly fuller of the dead than of the living." Whitman dreams that he has lost a friend, and in the dream he searches for him "among burial-places." But he fails to find him, nor does he discover any assurances that his friend is alive and well somewhere else. Instead, he finds that all places are "burial-places" and are inhabited by the dead:

And I found that every place was a burial-place;
The houses full of life were equally full of death, (this house is
    now,)
The streets, the shipping, the places of amusement, the
    Chicago, Boston, Philadelphia, the Mannahatta, were as
    full of the dead as of the living,
And fuller, O vastly fuller of the dead than of the living.

Whitman means only that he becomes aware of the constant presence of death in life through his recognition of the millions who
have died and have disappeared from the places of the living. He
does not mean that all the dead are somehow spiritually present
because if they were, they would in some way be alive to him as
others are in "Crossing Brooklyn Ferry." Nor does the imagery in
the poem seriously imply resurrection and rebirth for his friend;
the echoes of resurrection are at best faint, and Whitman says
nothing about rebirth. He accepts death as a reality that means
nothing but itself. He does not fear it, nor does he worship it:

And now I am willing to disregard burial-places and dispense
    with them,
And if the memorials of the dead were put up indifferently
    everywhere, even in the room where I eat or sleep, I should
    be satisfied,
And if the corpse of any one I love, or if my own corpse, be duly
    render'd to powder and pour'd in the sea, I shall be sat-
    isfied,
Or if it be distributed to the winds I shall be satisfied.

Whitman may not feel threatened by death or obsessed with it because he values the experience—the love of a friend—life gave him.
He may, therefore, view death as a completion because he now sees
the relationship as a completed, meaningful action. Therefore, he
can say "I shall be satisfied." The acceptance of death as a part of
human life and not as a passage to eternal life constitutes the central
meaning of the poem.

Whitman expresses a similar awareness of the constant presence of
death-in-life in "As the Time Draws Nigh," the opening poem of
"Songs of Parting." In this poem, however, he speaks of his own
coming death, rather than of the death of another, and he regards
that death as both a mystery and a threat—as a dark unknown which
he dreads:

As the time draws nigh glooming a cloud,
A dread beyond of I know not what darkens me.

Whitman refuses, however, to be paralyzed by his fear. Instead, he asserts his continued will to live and to fulfill himself as Walt Whitman and as a poet:

I shall go forth,
I shall traverse the States awhile, but I cannot tell whither or
    how long,
Perhaps soon some day or night while I am singing my voice
    will suddenly cease.

He recognizes he could die any moment—suddenly, without warning—and naturally he dislikes the possibility of a premature death. Nevertheless, he is satisfied because he has existed positively, and he has worked toward self-realization through his concrete actions as a poet:

O book, O chants! Must all then amount to but this?
Must we barely arrive at this beginning of us?—and yet it is
    enough, O soul;
O soul, we have positively appear'd—that is enough.

Death will end his life, but it will also define it and give it meaning. Whitman's awareness of his relationship to death has already given meaning and depth to his life, and it has freed him from the dreadful cloud that threatens him. In this poem, Whitman once again concentrates on the human side—on the personal meaning death has for the poet in the lived human moment.

(3) "Yet, Yet, Ye Downcast Hours" presents the Whitman who regards death as a threat instead of a promise and who fears it instead of trusting it. In the poem the poet is the object of "despairing cries [that] float ceaselessly toward" him from those who cannot trust and who fear death. None of the voices knows "Whither I go"; each is uncertain and alarmed; each seems to think that *"matter is conqueror"*; and therefore, they fear that death means oblivion. In this poem Whitman shares their anguish and their mistrust: "I understand your anguish, but I cannot help you." He cannot answer them, comfort them, or even share *his* confidence with them because he has none. He, too, believes *"matter is conqueror—matter, triumphant only, continues onward."*

Yet, yet, ye downcast hours, I know ye also,
Weights of lead, how ye clog and cling at my ankles,
Earth to a chamber of mourning turns—I hear the o'erweening,
    mocking voice,
Matter is conqueror—matter, triumphant only, continues on-
    ward.

Whitman does not ask a question about matter, as he did in
"Thought"; he says directly that it is the final reality. The poem ends
with a question, but it is the question of the young man who desires
to escape the oblivion of death— *"Shall I not escape?"* The implied
answer is no. The unknown now appears as a threat; and that in itself
reverses Whitman's whole attitude. Instead of trusting, he doubts;
instead of joy or peace, he experiences anguish and fear. And more
than that; he loses contact before death with those who have been
closest to him:

Despairing cries float ceaselessly toward me,
The call of my nearest lover, putting forth, alarm'd, uncer-
    tain. . . .
I understand your anguish, but I cannot help you.

The threat of the unknown seems to separate persons. The poet's
inability to communicate with the other or to comfort him in the face
of this ultimate experience prevents the mutuality from taking place
that exists in some of the death scenes in "Drum Taps." The failure
of confidence here not only effectively discredits the possibility of
eternal life: it removes, as well, a degree of depth and an awareness
of spirit from human existence.

(4) In "So Long" Whitman accepts his coming death with calmness
and even with hope, for he understands that death will bring the
completion and fulfillment of his poetic life and of his identity:

So I pass, a little time vocal, visible, contrary,
Afterward a melodious echo, passionately bent for, (death mak-
    ing me really undying,)
The best of me then when no longer visible, for toward that I
    have been incessantly preparing.

The best of him—what Walt Whitman has been and what he *means*
as a poet and person—will emerge out of that death, or at least it will
be potential in the poems he leaves. So paradoxically, when Whitman
dies (when "decease calls" him "forth"), he springs "from the pages
into our "arms." The death the poet anticipates at any moment will

give the man and poet more fully to us—not because he will be available in some spiritualistic way but because he is somehow there as a presence in the words of his poems:

> Camerado, this is no book,
> Who touches this touches a man,
> (Is it night? are we here together alone?)
> It is I you hold and who holds you,
> I spring from the pages into your arms—decease calls me forth.

Whitman announces one future in the poem, and he knows he will not directly participate in it. He anticipates another future, however; he senses that he will return ("I may again return") as a presence embodied in the spoken words of his poetry. Whitman will leave history only to return as a kind of mythic figure—as a presence that, time and again, engages a reader in genuine dialogue. The last lines, then—

> An unknown sphere more real than I dream'd, more direct,
>   darts awakening rays about me, *So long!*
> Remember my words, I may again return,
> I love you, I depart from materials,
> I am as one disembodied, triumphant, dead.

—clearly refer to Whitman's discovery that the other sphere of existence lies in his poetry; it is real, yet unknown; spiritual, yet not mystic. These same lines may imply the poet's passage to a spiritual other world—and if so, they almost seem to be an afterthought. More likely, they imply his return through poetry and his participation in the spiritual depths of existence through a dialogue between poet and reader.

(5) Whitman suggests another view of death in "Pensive on Her Dead Gazing." Although it it not so central to "Whispers of Heavenly Death" and "Songs of Parting" as the other conceptions, it is nevertheless important. In the poem Whitman imagines that the voice of the nation ("The Mother of All") charges America to absorb into its soil, streams, and air—into its life—the young men. America must embrace these dead so that they will live on in the national memory as heroic figures who will be forever present to the nation. In this way the dead achieve an immortality that possesses a current meaning. Whitman does not say so in this poem, but he makes clear elsewhere that the poet can help preserve the dead in memory and thus give them immortality. Whitman does this in "Drum Taps," of course, and

he says as much about the poet's function in "Spirit Whose Work Is Done." Whether the poet preserves the memory of one—the fallen comrade of "Vigil Strange"—or of many—the dead of the Civil War —he defines the meaning lives have assumed through death. The fate of the men whose memory is evoked in "Pensive" is neither oblivion nor a personal immortality (the poem simply does not consider the second); rather, they achieve a continuing existence in the mythic life of the nation. The achievement of immortality for the Civil War dead through poetry generalizes Whitman's sense of a personal immortality through poetry. The emphasis, however, is somewhat different. In "Pensive" and in "Drum Taps" Whitman concerns himself mainly with preservation through memory; whereas, the poet in the poem is clearly a living personal presence.

This introductory discussion outlines the conceptions and experiences of death and spirit that Whitman dramatizes in his poetry. The ones I describe may not exhaust the possibilities, but they do demonstrate Whitman's uncertainty about death and spirit and therefore about himself, and they indicate as well his repeated efforts to come to terms with death and spirit—realizing that unless he did his experience would remain radically incomplete. Although he sought final knowledge and a definitive relationship to spirit, he achieved neither, and that is the point. Throughout his poetry Whitman confronts death and searches for spirit as a man and a poet living a concrete situation in-the-world. For such a man unwavering confidence, definitive answers, and a sustained relationship with spirit are not possible.

I have assumed up to now a close connection between the two relationships—between the self and death and the self and spirit. The connection may be obvious, but all the same, I want to state it before I begin discussing self, death, and spirit in four of Whitman's major poems. First, Whitman's encounter with the fact of death and his subsequent transcendence of despair or of the threat of his own death yield a fuller and deeper awareness of the self and of existence. As the poet realizes himself more completely, both in relation to time and to eternity (death), he comes into closer proximity—perhaps even into momentary contact—with spirit—with the mythic and eternal in life. The experience is similar to the spiritual one in "Crossing Brooklyn Ferry"; however, the modes of encounter differ. Second, since death is the ultimate definitive human experience, it reveals the depth and meaning of a life. It reveals how fully (how spiritually) one has lived. Death gives shape to a life by concluding it, and thus it shows to what extent an individual experienced and revealed the Absolute-in-the-moment. Third, as the final human experience death also brings the poet to the edge of the Absolute, mystery, or spirit, and thus it brings him into an unknowable relationship with it. Finally, death provides a passage to a spiritual "other" world; it is the means through which the poet gains immortality. In this case, death is the fulfillment of the moment-in-the-Absolute. It marks the instant of the final disappearance of the phenomenal into the ideal.

1. "Out of the Cradle Endlessly Rocking"

"Out of the Cradle" is essentially a poem about love and death and about awareness and poetry. Through the mature poet-narrator Whitman dramatizes in the voices of the boy, the bird, and the sea several attitudes toward nature and death which the poet finally encompasses in his own personal vision. The action and experience of the poem—and the subsequent discovery and understanding by the poet—centers on his childhood confrontation with the fact of death. The narrator presents the central action through the dramatic device of a reminiscence. The narrator presents it as a kind of play within a play—as a narrative within a larger narrative-lyric poem and thereby gives the boy, bird, and the sea immediacy as characters he *presents*—not simply as characters or points of view he *describes*.[1] The simultaneous distance and relation situation enables the poet to dramatize the boy's experience—and thus to participate in it—and at the same time it allows him to encompass and transform the various visions into his own personal sense of love, death, and poetry.

In the first part of the poem—lines 1–22—the poet identifies his song and sets the scene for his reminiscence. He sketches the place, outlines the experience, identifies himself, and anticipates his own translation and transcendence of the tremendously disruptive and threatening experience at the center of the poem. The single sentence which opens the poem foreshadows the boy's experience by revealing that the promise of love and union will give way to the actuality of loss and separation. The security of the ninth month midnight (the security and peace of the womb) will abruptly change into the uncertainty of a midnight of loss, sorrow, and mystery.

The reminiscence begins with the appearance of the two birds and with the assured, joyful celebration of their love by the male bird:

Shine! shine! shine!
Pour down your warmth, great sun!
While we bask, we two together.

With the sudden disappearance of the bird's mate the whole tenor
of his song changes. No longer ecstatically confident, he waits, puzzled, confused, and sorrowful. He begins to lament his loss, and he
also begins to call to his mate and to nature—hoping for a response
from somewhere:

Loud! loud! loud!
Loud I call to you, my love!
Land! land! O land!
Whichever way I turn, O I think you could give me my mate
*   back again if you only would.*

But the only sounds he hears are the whistle of the wind and the
surge of the sea—nothing but the noise of a savage, fierce, natural
force. There is no response from his lover or from nature—no voice
to assure him or to tell him what has happened. His repeated failures
to discover the fate of the she-bird make him desperate for an answer, but still none comes. The song of sorrow begins with a loud call,
shifts to a murmur as the bird listens one last time, and ends in silence
as the sick, sorrowful bird realizes that his song—his call—is useless.

At the end of his song the bird is overwhelmed by his loss and his
loneliness. He is cut off completely from nature, from his loved one,
and from spirit; and he is divided and despairing within himself. With
his past life destroyed and with a seemingly meaningless future
before him, he finds himself absolutely alone, faced with a threatening, destructive, natural world. From this limited point of view death
appears only as an ultimate threat to personal life—it destroys life
and personality—and as a psychological threat to continued personal
existence—it disrupts life and personality. Death has destroyed the
bird's mate, and it leaves him desperate and despairing.

At the end of the song nothing changes:

The aria sinking,
All else continuing, the stars shining,
The winds blowing, the notes of the bird continuous echoing,
With angry moans the fierce old mother incessantly moaning,
On the sands of Paumanok's shore gray and rustling.

The place and the conditions remain the same. Nothing changes
except the boy. He escapes the hypnotic hold of the song, and he

begins to develop and define (to translate) the personal meaning the bird's experience and song have for him. Through them the youth has encountered the brutal fact and the overwhelming mystery of death; he has come face to face with the reality of personal loss and despair; and he has experienced the intense grief expressed in the song. Yet the boy is not only tearful, he is ecstatic. He is filled with the love so eloquently expressed in the midst of its loss:

> *Hither my love!*
> *Here I am! here!*
> *With this just-sustain'd note I announce myself to you,*
> *This gentle call is for you my love, for you.*

That overpowering experience has released emotions and thoughts heretofore unknown to him. He feels sorrow *and* passion: he understands the bird's anguish, and he is aware of loss; yet he knows how deep and intense love can be. Therefore, he can see beyond the bird's despair and desperation without in any way denying or ignoring it. His deeply felt loss enables him to feel love more intensely, and his stark confrontation with the fact of death makes him more aware of the possibilities of life. At this point, the young Whitman is ready to be a poet—to understand and express the "sweet hell" aroused within him:

> Demon or bird! (said the boy's soul,)
> Is it indeed toward your mate you sing? or is it really to me?
> For I, that was a child, my tongue's use sleeping, now I have
>   heard you,
> Now in a moment I know what I am for, I awake. . . .

And he is ready to be a man, too—to encounter life and all its pain, joy, contradiction, and mystery. Not only is he ready; he *must* confront it and speak about it:

> Never more shall I escape, never more the reverberations,
> Never more the cries of unsatisfied love be absent from me,
> Never again leave me to be the peaceful child I was before.
> . . .

Whitman's openness, his heightened sensitivity, and his confidence in his destiny do not immediately supply him with an understanding of "the unknown want" or with a means of expressing the sweet hell—the complex of emotions, questions, and awareness—

that has been aroused within him. He is momentarily uncertain and confused:

> O give me the clew! (it lurks in the night here somewhere,)
> O if I am to have so much, let me have more!

The original version of the poem expressed much more uncertainty and doubt:

> O give me some clew!
> O if I am to have so much, let me have more!
> O a word! O what is my destination?
> O I fear it is henceforth chaos!
> O how joys, dreads, convolutions, human shapes, and all shapes,
>   spring as from graves around me!
> O phantoms! you cover all the land, and all the sea!

There, as well as in the final version, Whitman's commitment to discovery and his confidence that he can express the meaning of his reminiscence conquer his uncertainty:

> A word then, (for I will conquer it,)
> The word final, superior to all,
> Subtle, sent up—what is it?—I listen;
> Are you whispering it, and have been all the time, you sea-
>   waves?
> Is that it from your liquid rims and wet sands?

The lines suggest that the word has always been there before him in existence, and that the word or meaning of the experience emerges only through the poet's encounter with the world: the meaning arises between the poet and the other he confronts. The world or spirit calls, demands openness and commitment from the poet; the poet addresses the world by facing it with his whole being; and from that encounter the answer ("Whereto answering, the sea . . .") or the word ("Lisp'd to me the low and delicious word death") arises. The poet actually supplies the sound—*he* says death —but he does so in response to the demand nature, life, and spirit make on him, not as part of a process of naming and creating a world of his own.

In the bird's definitive silence and despair, Whitman finds the word, the present meaning of his past experience. There *is* a response for the poet; whereas for the bird there was none. The answer is not so direct as the one the bird sought, nor does it correspond to his simplified version of existence (day *or* night). The answer (the word "death" in which every aspect of the experience coalesces) reveals, instead, the complexity and contradiction in existence. Whitman tries to see life as a whole, whereas the bird could not. The bird found himself alone in a fragmented, disintegrating world; he could speak his grief, but for him no possibility for transcendence existed. Whitman, on the other hand, discovers that he can unconditionally accept the threats, betrayals, *and* promises of existence and that he can express his awareness. Whitman's quest ends, then, with the discovery of a language that expresses an experience through which the poet discovers himself:

> Whereto answering, the sea,
> Delaying not, hurrying not,
> Whisper'd me through the night, and very plainly before day-
> break,
> Lisp'd to me the low and delicious word death.

Whitman finds himself in the word.

The syntax—"whisper'd me" not whispered *to* me—is repeated in the final line, so it must be intentional. It confirms my point that Whitman finds himself in the word—in the answer the sea gives him. The sea does whisper *to* him—it answers him; that is, Whitman discovers meaning in his meeting with the sea, and thus, it "answers" him. At the same time, the sea whispers *him.* By uttering the word death—

> Lisp'd to me the low and delicious word death,
> And again death, death, death, death—

the sea utters the key to the awakening experience. The experience has enabled the boy to say: "Now in a moment I know what I am for, I awake." In this sense the sea utters the poet—it *whispers* him. The experience reveals the meaning of death to the poet (the sea whispered death to him), and the experience becomes the means by which the boy discovers himself (the sea whispers him).

The poet's knowledge of death involves far more than a sentimental longing for a soothing, blissful death. The young poet is momentarily tempted by the serenity and security the quiet sleep of death might bring (the return to the mother); the hissing melody that softly envelops him suggests this. After recognizing the hostility of the sea and of nature and after seeing how death destroys and disrupts hu-

man life, one might well be inclined to dismiss the painful disturbing
parts of it all and embrace the peacefulness which death could bring.
That possibility persists virtually until the end of the poem:

> The word of the sweetest song and all songs,
> That strong and delicious word . . .

But it does not prevail, for Whitman's poem will

> . . . fuse the song of my dusky demon and brother,
> That he sang to me in the moonlight on Paumanok's gray beach,
> With the thousand responsive songs at random,
> My own songs awaked from that hour.

The poem will encompass each song (the bird's, the boy's, and the
sea's) as real, if partial, responses to death in the mature poet's comprehensive vision. Whitman accepts death unconditionally; he recognizes it as a destructive, disruptive force that ends life and identity
as he knows it. Whitman also realizes that death is the ultimate limit
which one must face in order to live, for unless one lives with death,
as Whitman discovers he must, he cannot fully possess his humanity.
Whitman is tempted to evade that awareness by a sentimentally
satisfying explanation of death (by a regressive return to the mother)
but he rejects it. Whitman discovers, finally, a knowledge of death
that frees him to live and to sing. It provides him with a new life as
a man and a poet living in the world, attempting the overwhelming
task of genuine communication.

That new life brings him into an essential relationship with the
Absolute or with spirit. First, Whitman's complete openness to existence, his unconditional acceptance of death, and his transcendence
of the painful limit-situations dramatized in "Out of the Cradle"
enable him to experience something of the infinite and the Absolute.
There is nothing mystic about the dialogue of self and spirit here.
Whitman participates in the infinite by facing death and by contem-
plating mystery, yet he remains wholly human and finite all the
while. Second, the poet's attempt to penetrate the meaning of death
and to understand, thereby, something of its mystery constitute his
full response to life, and that total giving of himself brings him into
contact with the spirit that is happening in the world and within
himself.

As the mature poet-narrator, the "chanter of pains and joys, uniter
of here and hereafter," Whitman participates in the finite and in the

infinite and, thus, in history and myth. He fuses past, present, and future, yet he lives in the present moment; he transcends existence, yet he lives within its limits. Through his encounter with death and spirit Whitman experiences himself as a whole man—as *Soul-I*. His willingness to risk the total confrontation achieves an awareness that prepares him for a further encounter with the fact of death and for the subsequent transcendence he dramatizes in "When Lilacs Last in the Dooryard Bloom'd."

2. *"When Lilacs Last in the Dooryard Bloom'd"*

The poet confronts the same broad threat in this poem as he did in "Out of the Cradle." He is faced with the fact of death, and he is threatened by personal dislocation and psychic disruption because of the great loss he has suffered and the intense grief he is experiencing. He encounters death as directly and starkly as before and, at first, sees it only as the definitive human limit and as the annihilation of life and self. He is forced at first to accept the fact of death unconditionally; he then goes on to seek a meaning in it that will enable him to transcend the fact without evading it; and he finally discovers a meaning for death that obtains to man's situation in the world—to the experience of Walt Whitman in the lived human moment.

At the beginning, the poet is faced with the agonizing fact of Lincoln's death. Whitman knows he must try to reconcile death with life and with his own personal situation, but at first he cannot. Therefore, his grief imprisons him, and his experience breaks down into discrete segments. He stands helpless before the "black murk" that envelops the world—the black murk of his grief and the blankness of a threatening incomprehensible death:

O powerful western fallen star!
O shades of night—O moody, tearful night!
O great star disappear'd—O the black murk that hides the star!
O cruel hands that hold me powerless—O helpless soul of me!
O harsh surrounding cloud that will not free my soul.

Yet at the same time, Whitman can recognize and appreciate the beauty and richness of early spring. But at this point the visions are unrelated; life and death occur in the world, but Whitman cannot yet connect them. The two faces of the natural world resemble the two Whitman described in "Out of the Cradle." However, the irony is much greater in "Lilacs," for the death of Lincoln—and Whitman's returning thoughts—occur in the midst of spring, and that makes for a basic contradiction Whitman cannot presently cope with.

Whitman introduces the bird and its song in section 4. The poet knows the bird sings about death, and he is aware the bird has found language to express the meaning of death. It sings an "outlet song of life." By that Whitman means that the song releases and consoles; it transforms fact into meaning; once heard and understood the song opens into life. But for now the song and the meaning are hidden from the poet because he is still bound by the painful fact of death:

> Solitary the thrush,
> The hermit withdrawn to himself, avoiding the settlements,
> Sings by himself a song.

Sections five and six reinforce one's awareness that death clouds and disrupts the joy that typically accompanies spring. Whitman's brief description of the coffin and the corpse passing "over the breast of the spring, the land, amid cities" makes real the actual loss which caused the poet's grief and reveals his inability to reconcile human experience with the seasonal cycle. The promise of spring for the moment means nothing. The wheat may grow anew from its shroud, but nothing indicates that the dead Lincoln will. The corpse and the coffin "shall rest in the grave." So instead of promise and hope, Whitman encounters death and loss.

The two sections also expose the inadequacy of the standard gestures of mourning. The processions, the long lines filing past the coffin, the church services, the dirges, and the gifts of flowers, all express the grief and demonstrate the love Whitman and the nation feel, but they do little more. The gestures simply show that the cloud of grief still encloses him and prevents any transcending awareness. The gestures are also inadequate because Whitman is trying to use symbols of the natural cycle to solve the problem of human death. He does not succeed, for the two realms are still quite discrete. Even though section seven faintly prefigures that Whitman's ability to sing a carol of death (his language, "sane and sacred death", echoes the words of the bird,) the poet can only mourn.

> (Nor for you, for one alone,
> Blossoms and branches green to coffins all I bring,
> For fresh as the morning, thus would I chant a song for you O
>   sane and sacred death.
>
> All over bouquets of roses,
> O death, I cover you over with roses and early lilies,

> But mostly and now the lilac that blooms the first,
> Copious I break, I break the sprigs from the bushes,
> With loaded arms I come, pouring for you,
> For you and the coffins all of you O death.)

Still deeply troubled, Whitman indulges his grief but cannot escape it.

In section eight Whitman once again speaks of his depression. Not only does the star remind him again and again of his lost loved one; it also represents the *fact* of death. The star possesses no mystic meaning, nor does it suggest that Lincoln lives on in some spiritual other world. It disappears—it is *"lost* in the netherward black of the night" (italics added)—and as a result, Whitman sinks into despair:

> As my soul in its trouble dissatisfied sank, as where you sad orb,
> Concluded, dropt in the night, and was gone.

The grief intensifies and the tension increases in the ninth section. Whitman says simply that he *must* go on speaking of the star, for he cannot escape the mastering hold of his mental state and of the fact of death. He hears the song and the call to transcendence, but he cannot yet fully experience its meaning. Whitman is no longer just trapped by grief and death; the turmoil is greater than that. Now he understands his condition, and he tries to will a new awareness, but he cannot.

The questions Whitman asks in Sections 10 and 11 show that he himself recognized the inadequacy of his earlier forms of mourning. They may have provided some comfort through the ritual expression of grief, but they did not help him escape his sorrow or transcend the fact of death. Those earlier forms actually immersed him further in his sorrow and intensified the conflict. In sections 10 and 11, however, he discovers a new way:

> Sea-winds blown from east and west,
> Blown from the Eastern sea and blown from the Western sea,
>   till there on the prairies meeting,
> These and with these and the breath of my chant,
> I'll perfume the grave of him I love.

He will "perfume the grave of him I love" with signs from the whole expanse of America, instead of with spring flowers. Whitman once again "adorn[s] the burial-house" with signs of life, but previously the signs were not particular and relevant enough to supply a personal

meaning—an understanding by *Walt Whitman* of Lincoln's death
and of death as it figures in Whitman's own life. He selects signs of
life now—"Pictures of growing spring and farms and homes" and
"the city at hand with dwellings so dense"—from Lincoln's and his
own America. This discovery changes Whitman's whole outlook, for
now he celebrates, rather than mourns:

> Lo, the most excellent sun so calm and haughty,
> The violet and purple morn with just-felt breezes,
> The gentle soft-born measureless light,
> The miracle spreading bathing all, the fulfill'd noon,
> The coming eve delicious, the welcome night and the stars,
> Over my cities shining all, enveloping man and land.

He celebrates the land; and he celebrates day and night (life and
death) together. Darkness no longer threatens or confuses him as it
did, nor does it negate the day.

Even though his language anticipates the bird's song, Whitman is
not yet ready to "tally" that carol. He does not move abruptly from
grief to a longing for *"lovely and soothing death."* Through his
search for a meaningful way of expressing and of escaping his grief,
Whitman discovers a perspective which enables him to celebrate life
and death and to think of death as a completion or fulfillment of life
rather than a destroyer of it. He identifies the American scenes with
Lincoln, and he implies that the President helped make them great
by preserving the Union. The America Lincoln led becomes part of
him and he becomes part of it. Death has, in effect, fully defined the
public identity of Lincoln, and thus it has become the culmination
and fulfillment of his life. With this recognition Whitman begins to
reconcile himself to death by focussing on the human experience to
which death has given a final shape and meaning. Whitman's discovery, however, is by no means complete at this point, nor has he
escaped the inner tension that was so acute before.

At the beginning of Section 14, Whitman reaffirms his situation in
the midst of human life, and there both the thought of death—the
cloud that overwhelmed him, at first—and the knowledge of death
—the awareness Whitman discovers at the end of the long, black trail
—come upon him:

> Falling upon them all and among them all, enveloping me with
>   the rest,
> Appear'd the cloud, appear'd the long black trail,

> And I knew death, its thought, and the sacred knowledge of
>   death.

At first, Whitman is clearly suspended between the two—between the oppressive fact and the knowledge that will finally release him from it.

The journey he undertakes with the two "companions" takes him to a place similar to the one in which he experienced despair (see Sections 2 and 8, e.g.), yet the situations are not exactly the same. Whitman is no longer faced only with the blackness of an incomprehensible and impenetrable fact. Instead, he *enters* the "deep secluded recesses" that paralyzed and repelled him before. This confrontation dramatizes the poet's emerging awareness that he can transcend death only by unconditionally accepting it as a fact and a mystery and by finding meaning in and *through* it—and not by transforming it into something other than itself.

Not only does Whitman unconditionally accept the fact and the mystery of death, and thus encounter the infinite or the Absolute; he simultaneously engages in a dialogue with the bird. The carol of death arises from that dialogue. That is, the song emerges both from within the poet and from without. On the one hand, Whitman supplies the language and the interpretation as he "tallies" the meaning of death in "Lilacs," and he also expresses a feeling for death that has attracted him before—in "Out of the Cradle" and in earlier lines in "Lilacs." So in one sense the vision *is* his. It may not be definitive of the poet's final awareness of death in "Lilacs," but it does arise partly from within him. At the same time, the bird—a voice and sensibility quite different from Whitman—utters the song; at least his song expresses a vision of death that arises quite independently of Whitman, even though the poet interprets it in the particular words of the poem. So the song results from a genuine dialogue or interaction between Whitman and the world (represented both by the bird and the two companions):

> And I in the middle as with companions, and as holding the
>   hands of companions,
> I fled forth to the hiding receiving night that talks not . . .
>
> And the voice of my spirit tallied the song of the bird.

The carol itself passionately celebrates death. Death will bring peace, comfort, and restful joy to the dead:

> *Prais'd be the fathomless universe,*
> *For life and joy, and for objects and knowledge curious,*
> *And for love, sweet love—but praise! praise! praise!*
> *For the sure-enwinding arms of cool-enfolding death.*

It offers a loving, blissful fulfillment radically different from that Whitman describes in Sections 10–12. The song also proposes a transformation of the old rituals into new ones that will celebrate death and the peace of the dead rather than express grief and incomprehension:

> *From me to thee glad serenades,*
> *Dances for thee I propose saluting thee, adornments and feast-*
>   *ings for thee,*
> *and the sights of the open landscape and the high-spread sky*
>   *are fitting,*
> *And life and the fields, and the huge and thoughtful night.*

The man who died rests in peace. Knowing that, the living can find comfort in the fact of death, and they can look forward to the ecstasy of their own deaths. The resolution that the bird's song proposes is really an aesthetic one that envisions death as a beautiful, blissful state in which one experiences a kind of continuing aesthetic pleasure. Somewhat hedonistic and sexual indeed, the ecstasy is nonetheless primarily aesthetic and unrelated to the *"dense-pack'd cities"* of Lincoln's and Whitman's America.

The key, however, in "Lilacs" is the meaning of death for the man who lives. Whitman has been seeking, and he discovers in the end, a personal meaning that enables him to live moment by moment in the world. A view of death which repudiates life because it is either so painful or so vastly inferior to the ecstasy of death, which looks forward to a state following life, does not provide the resolution Whitman seeks. Therefore, tempting as the vision is—and it is expressed so much more persuasively and passionately than in "Out of the Cradle"—the bird's song alone cannot reconcile Whitman to death. He must possess the meaning of the song, but he must go beyond it as well. The bird's vision of death is simply one part of Whitman's total perspective.

The "long panoramas of visions" Whitman describes in Section 15 indicate that his awareness (the "sight" that "unclosed") encompasses more than the star (Whitman includes *all* the Civil War dead) and more even than the bird's song. Whitman makes the "knowledge of death" concrete rather than wholly subjective, aesthetic, or mystic; he relates it to an objective situation similar to the one from which the original dismay and grief arose:

> I saw battle-corpses, myriads of them,
> And the white skeletons of young men, I saw them,
> I saw the debris and debris of all the slain soldiers of the war,
> But I saw they were not as was thought,
> They themselves were fully at rest, they suffer'd not,
> The living remain'd and suffer'd, the mother suffer'd,
> And the wife and the child and the musing comrade suffer'd,
> And the armies that remain'd suffer'd.

Whitman envisions repose for the dead—an escape from suffering—and perhaps he implies they will enjoy the loving bliss the bird describes. But he has taken a major step beyond the song: he has translated his awareness into his own personal language (different from the formal, elegiac diction of the song); he has made it concrete in his personal situation; and he has, once again, unconditionally accepted suffering and death as facts of life. His understanding, however, is still limited to the knowledge discovered in the bird's song, and it excludes, for the moment, the crucial meaning he enunciates in Section 12. Whitman must pass beyond even this.

> Passing the visions, passing the night,
> Passing, unloosing the hold of my comrades' hands,
> Passing the song of the hermit bird and the tallying song of my
>   soul . . .

Whitman passes beyond each separate element of his experience to an encompassing awareness which holds the complex, seemingly contradictory experiences of the whole poem and the whole man in tension—in a total vision. One response, one state of mind, one meaning for death does not replace another: "Yet each to keep and all, retrievements out of the night." Nor are the elements any longer perceived discretely, for Whitman's experience is no longer fragmented. He "knows" full well that life *is* contradictory and diverse —it consists of sadness and joy, love and loss, life *and* death. Whitman must accept life unconditionally, but he also knows that it has meaning and that he can find that meaning-in-being through his relationship with existence. Thus Whitman transcends his grief, his sense of death as both a threat and an incomprehensible mystery, and even his belief in death as a blissful state, but he denies nothing. He transcends (passes beyond) these and each separate element only to return to the world with unconditional acceptance and a sense of wholeness:

> Yet each to keep and all, retrievements out of the night,
> The song, the wondrous chant of the gray-brown bird,
> And the tallying chant, the echo arous'd in my soul,
> With the lustrous and drooping star with the countenance full
>   of woe,
> With the holders holding my hand nearing the call of the bird,
> Comrades mine and I in the midst, and their memory ever to
>   keep, for the dead I loved so well,
> For the sweetest, wisest soul of all my days and lands—and this
>   for his dear sake,
> Lilac and star and bird twined with the chant of my soul,
> There in the fragrant pines and the cedars dusk and dim.

He ends his poem and reaches his fullest realization by affirming the human situation. At the same time, his comprehensive vision and his unreserved openness to the unknown allow him to encounter and affirm the infinite or the Absolute, but he does so in wholly human terms.

Whitman seeks and discovers in "Lilacs" the meaning of death *in* and *for* life. He says nothing really about an after life, and so it seems to me irrelevant whether the soldiers and Lincoln live on in any way other than through memory. Whitman provides no firm basis for speculating otherwise because he describes the condition of the dead only insofar as he says "They themselves were fully at rest." He engages in a dialogue with the world and with the unknown and the infinite—and so with spirit—but he does not address it as God or even suggest that a presence exists in the unknown—as he *did* imply in "Out of the Cradle." Whitman does not, in other words, presume to comprehend the unknown in any but a human way. What Whitman discovered in "Out of the Cradle" is rediscovered and fulfilled in "Lilacs." He accepts death as a limit and a threat. Yet he recognizes it, also, as the fulfillment of a life: it shapes and gives meaning to a life, and it completes it so that the dead can be present to the living in memory—or in poetry. Recognition of the contradictory nature of death—its factualness and mysteriousness, its threat and promise—provides a new life for Whitman. He can now live with death—and live, therefore, more fully—and he can now sing about death—and fulfill, thereby, the impulse to expression aroused in "Out of the Cradle."

3. *"The Sleepers"*

In "The Sleepers" Whitman dramatizes a dream vision or psychological journey in which he penetrates a realm of existence—both within himself and in the world—that transcends time and space and finite human limits. The first line indicates that the poem is a vision: "I wander all night in my vision," and three later lines indicate that Whitman is entering another realm:

> Now I pierce the darkness, new beings appear,
> The earth recedes from me into the night,
> I saw that it was beautiful, and I see that what is not the earth
>   is beautiful.

The day gives way to the night, and the earth yields to another sphere. The night world differs so radically from the daytime reality that Whitman finds himself "Wandering and confused, lost to myself, ill-assorted, contradictory." He loses himself and he loses the earth, but the losses release him from conventional limits and enable him to discover a new self and a new world. Now he can "become the other dreamers," and thereby participate in the lives and deaths of the persons his dream encompasses: "I am the actor, the actress, the voter, the politician." What he achieves in "Song of Myself" through intuitive identification and genuine dialogue, he achieves here through a dream; but he does dream an ideal world in which the inter-human prevails, and his dream also provides him with a new vision of death and with an awareness of the infinite—of the spirit that exists before, during, and after the poet's daytime life.

The dream actually involves two distinct visions of darkness, sleep, and death, and at the beginning it involves contrasting moods as well —peace and discontent, depression and excitement. (1) In section 2–5 Whitman speaks about several forms of violent death and thus dwells on the fact of death:

> Steady and long he struggles,
> He is baffled, bang'd, bruis'd, he holds out while his strength
>   holds out,
> The slapping eddies are spotted with his blood, they bear him
>   away, they roll him, swing him, turn him,
> His beautiful body is borne in the circling eddies, it is continu-
>   ally bruis'd on rocks,
> Swiftly and out of sight is borne the brave corpse.

He cannot, for the moment, escape it: "I turn but do not extricate myself, confused, a past-reading, another, but with darkness yet." Apparently, Whitman must encounter death in this way—he must accept it as a brutal fact of life—before he can break through to another perception. In his dream, Whitman immerses himself in death and suffering, and thus it becomes a way of exploring the darkness, pain, and chaos of the mind and of the world as well as of the beauty Whitman later discovers. The dream, therefore, is not an escape or a denial; it becomes, instead, a means of encounter and, then later, of transcendence.

(2) The experience Whitman narrates in section 6 about the visit of the squaw to his mother's childhood homestead marks the change from one vision to another. In the original text of the poem (1855), the section also revealed the continuing confusion of the poet and the ambiguity of his situation. Whitman included six additional lines in the earlier version:

> Now Lucifer was not dead—or if he was, I am his sorrowful
>   terrible heir,
> I have been wronged—I am oppressed—I hate him that op-
>   presses me,
> I will either destroy him, or he shall release me.
>
> Damn him! how he does defile me!
> How he informs against my brother and sister, and takes pay for
>   their blood!
> How he laughs when I look down the bend, after the steamboat
>   that carries away my woman!

The exclusion of the lines may diminish the sense of conflict and contradiction in Whitman's vision—his awareness of the problematic nature of the "other side"—and the poem may lose something as a result. Nonetheless, the final version defines the direction of the poem more sharply by focussing unequivocally on the extremely important relationship between the two women. The position and function of the story in the poem suggest how moving and essential an experience Whitman finds this. For a brief time two persons from very different worlds experienced a genuine, mutual relationship that momentarily released them from themselves and their respective worlds. To experience even that degree of openness and mutuality, the two women had to transcend the ordinary limits of relationship, and they also had to break down conventional racial and

social categories. That is precisely what Whitman's dream enables
him to do, and from this point on he enters an "unseen" realm—"a
contact of something unseen"—where men and women are transformed, where beauty exists, and where genuine dialogue between
persons becomes possible.

In this unseen realm men and women are returned to their homes
—to familiar, secure worlds of love:

> Elements merge in the night, ships make tacks in the dreams,
> The sailor sails, the exile returns home,
> The fugitive returns unharm'd, the immigrant is back beyond
>   months and years,
> The poor Irishman lives in the simple house of his childhood
>   with the well-known neighbors and faces,
> They warmly welcome him, he is barefoot again, he forgets he
>   is well off, . . .

and along with innumerable others, they are restored to the health
and goodness that, for Whitman, constitutes man's essential condition:

> The homeward bound and the outward bound,
> The beautiful lost swimmer, the ennuyé, the onanist, the female
>   that loves unrequited, the money-maker,
> The actor and actress, those through with their parts and those
>   waiting to commence,
> The affectionate boy, the husband and wife, the voter, the nom-
>   inee that is chosen and the nominee that has fail'd . . .
>
> I swear they are averaged now—one is no better than the other,
> The night and sleep have liken'd them and restored them.

In that realm where "the wildest and bloodiest is over, and all is
peace," Whitman comes upon the beauty of his own soul and of the
universe:

> The soul is always beautiful, it appears more or it appears less,
>   it comes or it lags behind.

Finally, he discovers a world where relationships between persons
become the rule:

> The sleepers are very beautiful as they lie unclothed,
> They flow hand in hand over the whole earth from east to west
>   as they lie unclothed,

> The Asiatic and African are hand in hand, the European and
>   American are hand in hand,
> Learn'd and unlearn'd are hand in hand, and male and female
>   are hand in hand,
> The bare arm of the girl crosses the bare breast of her lover,
>   they press close without lust, his lips press her neck,
> The father holds his grown or ungrown son in his arms with
>   measureless love, and the son holds the father in his arms
>   with measureless love, . . .

Love becomes genuine, no longer egocentric or lustful. Nationality
and convention—the roles and situations that often divide people—
disappear, so that each person can stand in direct, open relationship
to the person opposite him. In short, Whitman discovers spirit as it
manifests itself in human experience.

The world of darkness provides the ground for a transforming,
transcending experience that renews Whitman and those with
whom he identifies and those he observes. He recognizes that the
night enfolds the happy and the healthy as well as the wretched and
the wounded. It equalizes them all:

> I swear they are averaged now—one is no better than the other,
> The night and sleep have liken'd them and restored them.

Whitman doubtless means that sleep or death makes Presidents and
commoners the same. But the dream also makes him aware of a
common reality every man shares that involves far more than a
simple "averaging" of men and women. The vision introduces Whitman into a mythic realm beyond conventional time and space limits.
This new realm reveals to the poet the essential health and capacity
for love everyone possesses:

> I swear they are all beautiful,
> Every one that sleeps is beautiful, every thing in the dim light
>   is beautiful,
> The wildest and bloodiest is over, and all is peace;

it provides ideal conditions for the expression of youth and love and
for the fulfillment of maturity:

> O love and summer, you are in the dreams and in me,
> Autumn and winter are in the dreams, the farmer goes with his
>   thrift,
> The droves and crops increase, the barns are well-fill'd;

and it makes possible genuine I-Thou and communal relations. Death is no longer a threat; indeed, it possesses very little significance. Whitman does not deny its reality; he simply finds the central meaning of life in the relationships and renewal made possible by the expanded awareness of the dream vision and by the transforming force of spirit he ultimately discovers.

Whitman must enter the dream world—a radically different realm and mode of perception—in order to break away from the limits that would prevent transcendence and close off the world of spirit. In his dream he penetrates the surfaces of human experience and discovers the depths where he can directly confront the Absolute and engage in dialogue with it. He turns to it, responds to it, and gives his trust to the informing mystery—the spirit which is both the source and end of life:

> I too pass from the night,
> I stay a while away O night, but I return to you again and love
> you.
>
> Why should I be afraid to trust myself to you?
> I am not afraid, I have been well brought forward by you,
> I love the rich running day, but I do not desert her in whom I
> lay so long,
> I know not how I came of you and I know not where I go with
> you, but I know I came well and shall go well.
>
> I will stop only a time with the night, and rise betimes,
> I will duly pass the day O my mother, and duly return to you.

Through his dream, then, Whitman participates in the infinite and discovers his place in relation to it. He does so, however, without ever losing his humanity, for at no time does he think he *is* the infinite or the "mother"; at no time does he claim to be at one with spirit. He claims relationship but not identity, and he thinks that at some future time he will become one with spirit, but that time is beyond the present situation and the poem.

The final lines also show that Whitman recognizes he must return to the world—to history and humanity—in its unrenewed state. He must, it seems, break off his dialogue with spirit. Nevertheless, his encounter has produced an essential trust in the unknown and thus in existence and in himself. He carries that trust with him, knowing that he has been and is part of the infinite—even if it will no longer be so immediately present to him.

Through his dream the poet confronts the chaos and confusion of the mind and the facts of suffering and death. He discovers spirit, as well, and thereby comes to know the possibilities for *human* life. He possesses all of existence through his vision—sometimes experiencing it, sometimes only observing it—and by doing so, Whitman more surely possesses himself as a man in the world.

4. *"Passage to India"*

Whitman seems reluctant to return to the daytime world in "The Sleepers"; nevertheless, his final direction is into the world. He moves away from it to recover a lost humanity, and he then returns. The poet's direction in "Passage to India" is just the opposite, and so his encounter with spirit in "Passage to India" differs considerably from the dialogue he dramatizes in "The Sleepers" or for that matter from those he presents in "Crossing Brooklyn Ferry," "Out of the Cradle," and "Lilacs." In a way Whitman has moved *from* a passage along an open road and *from* passing beyond death (or beyond human limitation) *back* into the world *to* a mystic passage to God. The main value and goal in "Passage to India" is a mystic union with God.

Whitman strives for this ultimate union through three stages of transcendence. First, the technological and electronic forms of communication Whitman celebrates in the poem transcend time and space in the present and bring Whitman closer to other people and lands. In effect, they enable him to begin to discover his past—the historical and cultural past represented in the old world east of Suez. Second, the physical achievements of the modern world become symbolic of man's transcendence of time and space through mythic time. By possessing the human past, Whitman penetrates to the mythic source of human life. Finally, that transcending experience yields another—the ultimate transcendence of time and space through union with God.

In the first section Whitman introduces his three major symbols— the Suez canal, the trans-continental railroad, and the trans-oceanic cables; in the second section he refers to them as manifestations of "God's purpose from the first," and in the third, he elaborates on two of them (he says little about the cables) and thereby firmly establishes the technological linking of previously separate places. Whitman makes a gesture toward the specific and the concrete in this section, but he is far more interested in the significance of the achievements

—in their part in God's plan—than he is in conveying any real sense
of their physical reality. He does not convey, for example, the sense
of location he does in "Crossing Brooklyn Ferry," nor does the poem
depend on the continuity of place and act as "Crossing Brooklyn
Ferry" does. The Brooklyn Ferry is a real one, but the railroad in
"Passage to India" is a Transcendental Railroad in disguise. Whitman
and the poem, therefore, move very quickly to the second stage of
his quest for India.

Starting with section 4, Whitman begins to imaginatively span all
history:

> Along all history, down the slopes,
> As a rivulet running, sinking now, and now again to the surface
>   rising,
> A ceaseless thought, a varied train—lo, soul, to thee, thy sight,
>   they rise.

And he evokes, as well, man's mythic past:

> Down from the gardens of Asia descending radiating,
> Adam and Eve appear, then their myriad progeny after them,
> Wandering, yearning, curious, with restless explorations,
> With questionings, baffled, formless, feverish, with never-happy
>   hearts,
> With that sad incessant refrain, *Wherefore unsatisfied soul?* and
>   *Whither O mocking life?*

The significance of his quest deepens. He does not just seek other
lands; he searches for more—for the "hidden prophetic intention"
behind the "vast Rondure, swimming in space."

Whitman's introduction of the poet here—"the true son of God"
—is appropriate, for the poet comes after the technological achievements and translates the meaning of those facts: he expresses their
symbolic or mythic meaning; he discovers God's purpose in them;
and he eventually will write the mystic poem which will join "Nature
and Man":

> Then not your deeds only O voyagers, O scientists and inven-
>   tors, shall be justified,
> All these hearts as of fretted children shall be sooth'd,
> All affection shall be fully responded to, the secret shall be told,
> All these separations and gaps shall be taken up and hook'd and
>   link'd together,
> The whole earth, this cold, impassive, voiceless earth, shall be
>   completely justified,

> Trinitas divine shall be gloriously accomplish'd and compacted
>   by the true son of God, the poet . . .
>
> Nature and Man shall be disjoin'd and diffused no more,
> The true son of God shall absolutely fuse them.

The poet will discover the meaning of life and will thus complete
every Romantic's quest to reconcile the opposite and discordant
qualities in it. Although Whitman seeks a shared, communal past in
history and through literature, the passage about the poet actually
indicates that meaning and the union he seeks lie elsewhere and not
in this world at all.

Whitman's transcendence of history and his discovery of the
mythic significance of technological communication return him to
the "soothing cradle of Man"—to the historical, cultural, and mythic
source of his life. Walt Whitman and America exist as the climax of
the long evolution *from* the "soothing cradle"—"the river Euphrates
flowing"—*through* the emergence of Asia and the discovery of
America *to* the nineteenth century present where Whitman stands
"Curious in time." But even this source of life is not the spiritual
origin Whitman longs to find and to merge with. For that he must
pass to more than India. And he prepares for that spiritual journey
in section 7 when he explicitly identifies the goal of his mythic quest
and terminates that stage of his search:

> Passage indeed O soul to primal thought,
> Not lands and seas alone, thy own clear freshness,
> The young maturity of brood and bloom,
> To realms of budding bibles.
>
> O soul, repressless, I with thee and thou with me,
> Thy circumnavigation of the world begin,
> Of man, the voyage of his mind's return,
> To reason's early paradise,
> Back, back to wisdom's birth, to innocent intuitions,
> Again with fair creation.

The communal past he seeks is literary and historical; it is tempo-
rally and spiritually removed from the present; and it is very abstract
—quite unlike the shared human experience Whitman dramatizes in
"Crossing Brooklyn Ferry." Earlier in "Passage to India," Whitman
was very impatient with the concrete and factual and he also
becomes impatient with the limits placed on him by the communal-
mythic experiences he has spoken of in Sections 4–7:

O we can wait no longer,
We too take ship O soul,
Joyous we too launch out on trackless seas.

He moves very quickly from myth—something he can at least know
dimly from history and literature—to mystery—an unknown which
he can know only through mysticism.

Whitman prepares for this ascension in two ways. He rejects his
humanity and turns exclusively to his soul:

With laugh and many a kiss,
(Let others deprecate, let others weep for sin, remorse, humilia-
    tion,)
O soul thou pleasest me, I thee.

And he imagines himself ascending into the infinite where he will
melt "in fondness in his [God's] arms." In this ninth section Whitman
explicitly repudiates human limits, empirical reality, and others:

Passage, immediate passage! the blood burns in my veins!
Away O soul! hoist instantly the anchor!
Cut the hawsers—haul out—shake out every sail!
Have we not stood here like trees in the ground long enough?
Have we not grovel'd here long enough, eating and drinking
    like mere brutes?
Have we not darken'd and dazed ourselves with books long
    enough?

If one compares Whitman's willingness in "Passage to India" to
suffer for others and his actual suffering *as* the other in "Song of
Myself," one can readily comprehend the radical difference between
the two poems and the situation of the poet in each. Whitman does
not identify personally with another in "Passage to India"; he expresses merely a vague abstract willingness to suffer because of the
joy it will bring. Nor does he dramatize any personal, concrete experience other than his own imagined union with God (and even that
is very abstract). Whitman speaks of suffering for others in "Passage
to India," but he dramatizes no others and he experiences no pain.
He gives up everything ("What cheerful willingness for others' sakes
to give up all?") *not* for others, but for the purity, perfection, and
strength of God; and in doing so he gives up both the personal and
suffering. In the bliss he seeks, there is no pain—only endless joy and
excitement—just as there is no risk in sailing forth so recklessly.

In the final section Whitman forecasts, once again, the fulfillment of his journey—"Passage to more than India!"—and he claims a willingness to take any risk:

> Sail forth—steer for the deep waters only,
> Reckless O soul, exploring, I with thee, and thou with me,
> For we are bound where mariner has not yet dared to go,
> And we will risk the ship, ourselves and all.

Whitman hardly steers for Melville's deep waters; he does not even steer for the deep waters he has explored himself in other poems. There is no risk because the unknown retains no mystery. Although Whitman achieves no union in the poem, he expresses complete confidence in God and the trackless seas, and so the risk is meaningless. Beginning with "Song of the Open Road," however, and continuing through many of the other poems I have discussed Whitman's encounter with the unknown involves real risk. The seriousness of it of course differs from poem to poem, but in some—"As I Ebb'd," "Out of the Cradle," "Lilacs," for example, when Whitman faces death or the unknown he *does* "risk the ship, ourselves and all."

The spirit of God Whitman encounters in "Passage to India" differs radically from the spirit Whitman relates to in "Crossing Brooklyn Ferry," "Out of the Cradle," and "Lilacs," for Whitman does not discover this spirit in existence. He does not find him in "letters . . . dropt in the street"; he cannot "hear and behold God in every object" ("Song of Myself," 48); he does not encounter spirit or "eternity in men and women" (*Preface,* 1855); nor does he discover spirit through a dialogue with another or in the experience of the essential We. The God he addresses in "Passage to India" exists beyond time and space, and he can be reached only as the moment is absorbed into the Absolute. This God is the same one Columbus addresses in "Prayer of Columbus." Only in "Passage to India" Whitman has complete confidence in his vision and in his destiny; whereas Columbus's vision and confidence fail, and he falls into despair, knowing *nothing* of his destiny.

In spite of the closing euphoria of "Passage to India," death and spirit nevertheless maintained their problematic natures for Whitman. "Passage to India" may dramatize supreme confidence, but reading it, one inevitably recalls the despair of "Prayer of Columbus" and the serious doubts of "Yet, Yet Ye Downcast Hours." "Passage to India" may also outline a three stage movement that leads to an

overwhelming confidence in a mystic union with God, but one cannot help remembering the three stages in "Crossing Brooklyn Ferry"
which result in Whitman's steady confidence in himself as a man-in-
the-world. And finally, Whitman's intense longing in "Passage to
India" to escape human life and its limits makes one think of Whitman's acceptance of those limits and his immersion in life in "Out of
the Cradle" and "Lilacs." So as I said, a conviction of immortality and
an unwavering confidence in death and spirit do not dominate Whitman's poems. The problematic nature of death and spirit—and thus
of the self—dominate them, instead.

NOTES—*Chapter VII*

1. Time, narrative method, voice, and vision, then—as Howard Waskow
   has explained so well—maintain the separation of the narrator from the
   other "characters" in the poem; while the experience itself—presumably a childhood experience of the narrator—links the poet to the situation, event, and the other characters.

CHAPTER EIGHT

"Song of Myself"

"Song of Myself" forms a major part of Whitman's poetic achievement; it is very likely his most important poem. Therefore, any discussion of Whitman and *Leaves of Grass* must come to terms with the long poem, for it is not only central to his poetry; it is the ground of all of *Leaves of Grass,* and as a kind of microcosm it includes most of the experiences that take shape within the whole work. Thus, "Song of Myself" dramatizes the central action of *Leaves of Grass,* and it presents Whitman's drama of identity more fully and more coherently than any other poem or section in the book. In a sense Whitman anticipated and dramatized it all at the beginning of his poetic career. From that point on he defined, elaborated, rediscovered, qualified, and fulfilled the self he discovered in 1855. Oddly enough, Whitman's beginning becomes my conclusion, but his beginning includes in some fashion the multitudes Walt Whitman contained and discovered in his lifelong search for wholeness. Therefore, "Song of Myself" serves very well as the ending of this volume.

1.

The poem moves essentially from concentration on the monological self to a discovery of the dialogical self—the man who shares his being and experience with the external world and with others. The movement develops in six stages. At the beginning, the "idle, unitary" self—the separated self—dominates the poem. He announces himself and asserts that he contains a multitude of characteristics. Many of them are similar to those possessed by the self that emerges at the end of the poem. But in this first stage Whitman's poetic identity has yet to be realized, threatened, and confirmed. Therefore, he can only speculate about what he might contain; he does not yet know. In the second stage, after his sudden expansion of consciousness, he begins to recognize the world beyond him and to establish relations with it. Nonetheless, the self and others remain essentially separate because the dialogue is still incomplete. Whitman begins absorbing all to himself; he recognizes his own and the world's diversity; but he sees that world as little more than a reflection of himself. In the third stage Whitman experiences the full mutuality toward which the entire first half of the poem moves. He realizes the uniqueness and reality of the world and he opens himself completely to it. As a result, in the fourth stage, he risks his whole person, and that risk becomes apparent when the poet's identity is threatened and almost destroyed. But Whitman survives, and in the fifth stage he emerges intact with his discoveries both earned and confirmed. He has unconditionally accepted existence, and he has experienced transcendence. Finally, the drama of identity ends as the self is absorbed into the world—leaving his reader with his experiences of encounter and his vision of wholeness.

The first lines of the poem anticipate the essential dialogue developed in it:

> I celebrate myself, and sing myself,
> And what I assume you shall assume,
> For every atom belonging to me as good belongs to you.

Although he senses from the beginning that in some way he shares identity and existence with others, he does not yet know how, nor does he know how incomplete his awareness is. Although he seems ready to extricate himself from his own limitations and the trivia that surround him, he has not committed himself to engagement and dialogue, and thus he stands idle and unitary—alone in effect—with no real basis for his initial confidence and with no real awareness that the "I" and "you" *do* share every atom of their beings. He appears at the beginning of the poem, in one sense, as a satisfied, complacent, self-sufficent Romantic hero, yet in another sense, he half knowingly sets the stage for the self-realization and self-transcendence that will follow and in the end confirm his confidence.

The assured, complacent, and passive Whitman who simply waits for experience to come to him dominates the first four sections. He may be *ready* to engage the world, but in no way does he go to meet it as he will later in the poem. He begins his celebration, as he loafs on the grass waiting, apparently, for the apocalyptic sexual union that will take place momentarily between the "I" and his soul. Even that transformation will leave him incomplete, however; it will simply launch him on a long process of self-discovery and confirmation. But at this initial point Whitman seems satisfied—as if there were nothing more for him to know or experience. He claims to "speak at every hazard" of "Nature without check with original energy," but his contentment prevents any real sense of risk from emerging in these early sections. All his other claims about experience—except for the immediate sensuous ones of section 2—seem highly abstract, in spite of his assertiveness, as he seems detached and quite separate from existence.

This basic separation of the self from the not-self stands out very clearly in Section 4 when Whitman says that the life around him is not part of his essential self:

These come to me days and nights and go from me again,
But they are not the Me myself.

That "Me myself" stands apart from existence:

Apart from the pulling and hauling stands what I am,
Stands amused, complacent, compassionating, idle, unitary.
. . .

The "pulling and hauling" Whitman rejects here not only refers to the "trippers and askers,"—those inauthentic, desperate men Whitman exposes and challenges in "Song of the Open Road"; the experience includes as well sickness, loss, depression, and "the horrors of fratricidal war"—those "fitful events" he can neither deny or escape if he wishes to discover his genuine identity. Although he insists that he stands both in and out of the game (in a vague way the necessary condition for dialogue), the context confirms that he is "in and out" only insofar as he is a split or dual self. Apparently his "real" self (that "what I am") stays apart, "watching and wondering," never entering into dialogue with the world, while the sensuous self not only "sniffs" the green leaves and enjoys the sound of belched words but deals also with the trippers and askers the "real" Whitman rejects.

At the same time the passive, complacent self insists on his detachment and imperturbability, he also makes a series of claims that
describe the necessary conditions for self-discovery and that clearly
anticipate many of the attitudes the emergent self in the poem will
hold. His initial claims do not differ generally from the assertions he
makes late in the poem; yet in a dramatic sense, they differ a great
deal because the dramatic context and the self change considerably
in the course of the poem. As he recognizes more and more clearly
that the authentic self emerges only in dialogue, his person and his
ideas assume greater concreteness and meaning than they have at
the beginning of the poem. Nevertheless, the claims are crucial, even
if they are untested and unconfirmed.

First, Whitman urges the same radical action here that he calls for
repeatedly in his poetry. He casts aside creeds and schools, so that he
might free both his physical and psychical selves—his total self—for
contact, openness, and meeting; he seems to ready himself, in effect,
for the long series of contacts with nature and with others that constitute the action of "Song of Myself." Second, he must accept, as part
of his rebellion, the clarity and sweetness of existence: "Clear and
sweet is my soul, and clear and sweet is all that is not my soul." At
least, he seems *ready* to accept all unconditionally. Third, he also
recognizes that the meaning he will discover lies in-the-world. As a
matter of fact, Section 3 indicates that ultimate reality exists *only* in
the present. Whitman does not "talk of the beginning or the end,"
for

> There was never any more inception than there is now,
> Nor any more youth or age than there is now,
> And will never be any more perfection than there is now,
> Nor any more heaven or hell than there is now.

Each moment possesses its potential perfection, yet each moment
differs from every other. Whitman envisions no state of transcendence here; instead, as in many of his poems, he presumes that life
is a dynamic process moved forward by the procreant "urge and urge
and urge." Fourth, in such a dynamic situation, one experiences
transcendence and realizes his authentic self only in-the-world. He
may find his "Hell" in the creeds and schools that limit him or in the
psychically devastating experiences of war, guilt, or alienation. He
may experience whatever of "Heaven" he finds in dialogue and
through transcendence. Finally, Whitman recognizes a fundamental

condition for complete dialogue; he indicates that man exists both at a distance from and in relation to others: "Always a knit of identity, always distinction, always a breed of life." Identity (relation) and distinction (distance) yield life—a life fully experienced through dialogue rather than monologue.

If the Whitman persona recognizes so much in these early sections, there might seem to be little left for him to discover, but of course he does not yet "know" all he presumes to say. Not only is he untested and inexperienced, he has not yet overcome the two fundamental dichotomies in his world—that between his soul and body and the one between the "Me myself" and the world. So he possesses no real basis for his complacent claims about unity and completeness. He understands this to some extent when he refers to the mystery that persists in spite of his assurance—"I and this mystery here we stand." Surely he means the poem is a mystery, but he means as well that his body, his mind, and his life are mysteries, too. "Song of Myself," then, must solve these mysteries for both the self of the poem and his reader.

After the introduction of the self, the poem begins moving toward unity of the soul and the body and of the self and the world. The first climactic surge of awareness that begins the long process of encounter occurs in section 5 as the soul and body merge in a strange sexual union. Whether one calls the experience in this section mystic, transcendental, or simply consciousness-expanding, the experience—an apocalyptic, sexual one—suddenly expands the narrator's awareness, as soul and body, presumably become one. The experience symbolizes the union of soul with body; it is, therefore, both physical and psychical, not masculine and feminine, and thus quite strange. It resembles in its concrete obscurity the sexual experience of woman, man, and darkness in "The Sleepers." The essential point, however, is that the expansion of awareness occurs in the lived, sensual, orgasmic moment—a moment which intensifies and perhaps even exaggerates the basic sense of contact and relation the entire poem dramatizes.

Whitman's vision immediately encompasses all of existence from the most extensive, the oneness with God he speaks of, to the intensive—almost microscopic—"mossy scabs of the worm fence." The juxtaposition, in effect, of the "hand of God" and the "poke-weed" insists on the inseparability of the ultimate and the immediate. That recognition and the specific discovery that "a kelson of the creation is love" establishes a basis for reconciliation, contact, and dialogue.

The awareness also initiates the transformation of Whitman from a
passive to an active self. In succeeding sections, he begins to question
and participate rather than simply to witness and wait. In the broad-
est sense, the apocalyptic experience enables the poet to transcend
time and space, in section 5, and achieve the awareness of the *Soul*.
The first five sections, then, prepare the Romantic hero for his entry
into the world where he will discover his essential humanity in the
concrete drama of self and world.

2.

At the beginning of Section six Whitman fixes on one of his major
symbols, the grass, and uses that symbol to provide continuity and
meaning for the whole second stage (Sections 6-17). He begins with
the child's simple question, *"What is the grass?"* and concludes with
a deceptively simple answer: "This is the grass that grows wherever
the land is and the water is." Before he comes to that, however,
Whitman involves himself in a diverse and complex series of experiences. In effect, the simple question opens out into all existence as
any question must in the Whitmanian world where every detail—
"the moth and the fish-eggs," as well as the grass—assumes a place
in the totality of life. At first the poet simply guesses at answers—"I
guess it must be the flag of my disposition"—but he soon recognizes
that he can find meaning (an answer) in the grass only by confronting
actual experience.

So in these sections Whitman begins to meet the world outside—
the world he earlier refused to accept as a part of the "Me myself."
Throughout these sections he presents himself watching, wondering,
questioning, and even participating, but he never quite *becomes*
another person or a part of nature as he will in a later stage. Although
section 5 begins the transformation from the passive to the active
self, in this second stage Whitman mainly *sees* and *listens*—he receives and does not give; therefore, his dialogue with the world is
not yet complete. In effect, he absorbs everything to himself; and
therefore the dialogue of self and world remains incomplete. By
absorbing everything into himself he converts the external world
into his inner world and views that "other" as little more than an
extension or a reflection of himself. He implicitly denies its otherness; and so he lives with it as simply a "part of myself" in an essentially monological relationship. Occasionally, however,
Whitman indicates his awareness that the dialogue is incomplete,

and he now and then imagines himself actually becoming an-other. Nevertheless, the relationship is primarily reflexive; com-plete reciprocity is yet to come.

Before Whitman's consciousness-expanding experience in Section 5, he claimed that he had "no mockings or arguments"—probably no doubts or questions, either—for he felt satisfied. In Section 6, how-ever, he begins to speculate, wonder, and to suggest answers to the key question—what is the grass?—in a way that differs from his initial manner. (He sees that the grass may be a sign of the self, life, God, or death; he guesses that it may be a symbol of unity ("a uniform hieroglyphic"), yet he recognizes that he can only *guess* at answers.) He wishes he "could translate the hints about the dead young men and women," but apparently he is not sure that he has. Even when he offers his answer about the grass and death,

> All goes onward and outward, nothing collapses,
> And to die is different from what anyone supposed, and luckier,

it becomes tentative in context. Whitman's cry in Section 33, for example, "Space and Time! now I see it is true, what I guess'd at," confirms the tentative quality of these early sections and the incom-pleteness of Whitman's experience and identity. So if nothing else, the erotic experience of Section 5 has removed some of his compla-cency, and it has opened him to new possibilities. In Section 7 Whit-man continues to give tentative answers to the highly complex question about the grass; he speaks about the self and the earth, others, death and spirit. At the end of the section, he finally embarks on the long journey of discovery and confirmation.

Parallel images of movement and observation run through the next several sections and establish the situation of the self as a partici-pant-observer. Whitman projects himself into many different scenes, but he generally enters them as a witness, as *another* person:

> The youngster and the red-faced girl turn aside up the bushy
>   hill,
> I peeringly *view* them from the top. (8)
> I *witness* the corpse with its dabbled hair. (8)
> I *saw* the marriage of the trapper in the open air. (10)
> Where are you off to, lady? for I *see* you. (11)
> I loiter *enjoying* his repartee and his shuffle and break-down.
>   (12)
> I *behold* the picturesque giant and love him. (13)
> I *see* in them and myself the same old law. (14) (Italics added.)

Occasionally his participation virtually makes him one with the others because he either acts ("I am there, I help, I came stretch'd atop the load") or because he imagines himself in genuine dialogue with another. Nevertheless, reciprocal relationships occur infrequently in these sections; and the identification Whitman does achieve is less complete than it is in the third stage.

If one compares the runaway slave episode in Section 10, for example, with the hounded slave scene in Section 34, the essential distinction becomes clear. In the first the runaway slave stops at the house of the person Whitman imagines himself to be. The poet helps him and meets him in complete trust and sympathy:

> He staid with me a week before he was recuperated and pass'd
>   north,
> I had him sit next me at table, my fire-lock lean'd in the corner.

Yet he does not quite become that runaway slave as he later becomes the *hounded* slave who winces "at the bite of dogs." He greets him with openness, gives him complete sympathy, recognizes the slave as a person, but he does not project himself into the other man's reality; thus, he does not really experience that man. But the scene in Section 10 carries dialogue further than any other in this second stage. In the later episode Whitman imaginatively penetrates the specific reality of the other person; he does not ask "the wounded person how he feels, I myself become the wounded person." General sympathy or solicitude is not enough:

> I am the hounded slave, I wince at the bite of the dogs,
> Hell and despair are upon me, crack and again crack the marks-
>   men,
> I clutch the rails of the fence, my gore dribs, thinn'd with the
>   ooze of my skin,
> I fall on the weeds and stones,
> The riders spur their unwilling horses, haul close,
> Taunt my dizzy ears and beat me violently over the head with
>   whip-stocks.

In these lines Whitman makes the other present as the poet momentarily experiences the other's fear and pain. The difference may be simply a matter of degree, but the dialogue achieved in Section 33 differs considerably from the incomplete dialogue and apparent monologues of sections 6-17.

The explicit key to my reading of the second stage in "Song of

Myself" appears in the poet's own explanation of the self and other
relation in section 13:

> In me the caresser of life wherever moving, backward as well
>   as forward sluing,
> To niches aside and junior bending, not a person or object
>   missing,
> Absorbing all to myself and for this song.

In these lines he speaks both as a poet and as a man. In the first
instance, he simply wishes to contain everything ("not a person or
object missing") in his poem. In the second, however, he points
directly to the way he encounters the world in these sections: he
watches it and absorbs it into himself. In effect, he removes external
reality into the self. So even though he has surely moved beyond his
original simplistic sense of assurance and self-sufficiency, he has not
escaped his limits as a Romantic hero.

Although an essentially monological relationship with the world
prevails in these sections, a few explicit lines and certain experiences
anticipate the dialogue between self and world that will emerge fully
in later sections. It's as if the essence of the third stage develops
underneath and out of the second, much as later stages of recognition
struggle to break out in Sections 1-5. Whitman does not let it all out
at once, however; he cannot, for the search for self discovery is a long
process. Nevertheless, one glimpses his readiness for openness and
mutuality in the slave episode. Likewise, in section 14, one can sense
that Whitman is almost ready to encounter the world and to recognize it as a separate other:

> What is commonest, cheapest, nearest, easiest, is Me,
> Me going in for my chances, spending for vast returns,
> Adorning myself to bestow myself on the first that will take me,
> Not asking the sky to come down to my good will,
> Scattering it freely forever.

Whitman accepts here as part of the "Me" (the essential self) the
experiences he rejected in the first four sections. He also prepares to
"bestow" himself on another—a suggestion perhaps that he will go
to *meet* that other rather than absorb it. He indicates, as well, that
he does not ask the sky to come to him; instead, he "scatters" his good
will—perhaps himself—toward it. The lines suggest a relationship
that, at the end of section 15, Whitman anticipates even more
clearly.

There he refers explicitly to a reciprocal action between the self and the world, and he speaks again both as poet and man:

> And these tend inward to me, and I tend outward to them,
> And such as it is to be of these more or less I am,
> And of these one and all I weave the song of myself.

Besides explicitly referring to meeting, the first line suggests the equality of inner and outer as well as the objective reality of each. The second line emphasizes even more strongly the reality of the outer by indicating that the self achieves meaning only as part of the vast diversity Section 15 includes. Whitman does not say *it* is part of *him* as he did earlier; rather he is part of it. These are the first lines that clearly focus on the necessary conditions for essential existence. Whitman has not yet experienced full self-awareness, nor has the poem consistently dramatized mutuality. Nevertheless, at the close of the second stage one finds the subjective explanation inadequate. That is, Whitman does not simply project his own diversity into the world, and thus, conveninetly enough find himself there; nor does he simply remove the world into himself and call it "me." Moreover, he has already recognized in the first stage that he was not simply an adjunct of the earth—not part of the earth's diversity. Whitman seems to guess, instead, that the reality might lie in between. With that possibility the poem comes to a temporary rest; the poet has partly answered the child's question:

> This is the grass that grows wherever the land is and the water
>   is,
> This the common air that bathes the globe.

3.

Another movement begins almost immediately, however, as Whitman troops forth beating drums and blowing cornets, calling all to join him on his quest. He devotes his main effort in this third stage (Sections 18-32) to continued description and definition of the emerging self. Whitman returns to many of the ideas and situations he had "guess'd at" in the early sections, but he sees them differently from before because their meaning has changed as the self has progressed further towards essential existence. The ideas have a firmer basis in concrete experience than they did before. The main action of Sections 18-32, then, involves a continual definition and explanation that expands and extends one's sense of Whitman's poetic identity. The poet achieves this extension by allowing various themes and voices to appear and reappear as well as through sheer accumulation. The sections attempt to *shape* an identity, however, so that one cannot say that Whitman's real Me emerges *simply* by accumulation —as the sum of all his experiences.

Until Whitman experiences the orgasmic "touch" in 26, he attempts, primarily, to dramatize the same kind of self-world interaction that he had developed through the second major stage in the poem. When he is "quivered" to a new identity by the sound of the soprano's song, he begins to look forward to the exuberant recognition of Section 33 that confirms all his previous guesses, and thus he moves closer to a situation of genuine dialogue. Through most of the third stage, relationship seems to be largely reflexive; that is, the poet says he *is* this and that and so are the "you" and all men and women because they are extensions or versions of Walt Whitman—the cosmos. Although the poet thereby represents all men, he still absorbs them, as well as things, to himself. Nevertheless, the context of his seeing and hearing differs from what it was before; Whitman has reached a new stage of relationship or potential dialogue. This is apparent, for example, in the pronounced awareness of "I and you." The poet begins recognizing in Sections 18 and 19 that his poem is a dialogue—a shared experience—with the reader, and this awareness parallels the experience of the poet as man in the drama of the poem. He has not yet realized an I-Thou relationship with the world; nevertheless, he knows of it and he continues to work toward it.

In this stage (Sections 18-32) Whitman achieves coherence (1) by concentration on his poetic identity as a man and a poet, (2) by the continuing accumulation and development of basic attitudes and characteristics, and (3) through a consistent progression toward the "touch" and the new identity that emerges and confirms all he had guessed.

Whitman's series of questions in section 20—"what is a man anyhow? What am I? what are you?"—ask in effect one question because the I and you share a common human identity. By discovering what any one of the three is, Whitman discovers the other two because "In all people I see myself." Although the line could imply that he finds himself in others, in context he seems to mean that other persons act simply as reflectors of him; he sees himself in them as in a mirror. Thus he absorbs something from them, but does not yet give to or become them. Nevertheless, they do share a common identity that somehow exists between them. The relationship Whitman presents here is clearly problematic—perhaps, as the poem happens to work out, appropriately so. For the relationship between self and world is developing; the Whitman *persona* has not yet arrived at a clear or complete sense of his identity. Problematic as the relationship might be, it has assumed a good deal more concreteness and meaning for Whitman than it possessed in the opening lines of the poem.

Whitman's assertion of complacency and self-sufficiency also means something different from his expression of satisfaction in Section 3. If one removes the lines from context, he can argue that the Romantic self, as unchanged and as egocentric as ever, is still sounding off, but context is the key. Whitman asserts:

> I exist as I am, that is enough,
> If no other in the world be aware I sit content,
> And if each and all be aware I sit content.

The transforming orgasm in Section 5 and the succeeding rush of experience change the poet. So even if these particular lines look back to Whitman's initial self-satisfaction, they also refer to the emerging self who is closer to unconditional acceptance of existence and to essential living than the original Whitmanian hero of the opening sections. The lines, therefore, look forward to Whitman's recognition that contradiction exists as an absolute, but that one can contain it through an awareness of the wholeness of experience. Whitman's claim that he is content and sufficient as he is implies, as well, his sense that the lived moment (now) manifests as much perfection as one can know until the next fully lived moment. The self does not attempt to will what he cannot will (more awareness, more perfection, more good than there is now); instead, he flows with the totality of his experience toward greater and greater self-realization. He sees, in effect, with an awareness that corresponds to the transcending vision of the *Soul*. Therefore, he is content. At the same time, something of the Romantic self remains in this complacency, for his present confidence and contentment prevent him from anticipating the serious threat to his identity that occurs at his most expansive moment.

In the next several sections Whitman turns to the physical facts of the natural and human world—as he continues to explain himself as man and poet. In Section 23, he declares his acceptance of empirical reality:

> I accept Reality and dare not question it,
> Materialism first and last imbuing.

These lines and the succeeding ones, in which he cheers "positive science," establish a center for the extraordinary flood of sexual and natural images in Section 21–24. Whitman accepts time and space—empirical reality—as absolutes, yet he has and does in "Song of My-self" transcend them:

> Gentlemen, to you the first honors always!
> Your facts are useful, and yet they are not my dwelling,
> I but enter by them to an area of my dwelling.

Whitman simply enters through the facts ("by them") to meaning and identity. He does not deny "materialism," nor does he see the empirical world as some lesser reality. Instead, he enters into relation with it (he virtually becomes nature, while simultaneously remaining a person) and thereby discovers meaning in it. Whitman dramatizes the dialogue through sexual imagery that intensifies his contact with nature and thus metaphorically expresses a very close relationship. However, the longing to touch and be touched by the earth, his desire to be dashed by the "amorous wet" of the waves, and the ecstasy he hopes to experience in his sexual contact with nature mean what he says. Desire and ecstasy become one means of tran-scending the limits of one's self.

Whitman's oneness with nature assumes a slightly different form in Section 24 when he begins speaking of the "forbidden voices" that he clarifies and transfigures. When he looks at his own body as a sexual object and agent, he sees it in terms of things in nature, almost as if it were separate from him. When he speaks of the touch of nature, he attributes human sexual features to it, virtually making it a part of him:

> If I worship one thing more than another it shall be the spread
>   of my own body, or any part of it,
> Translucent mould of me it shall be you!
> Shaded ledges and rests it shall be you!
> Firm masculine colter it shall be you!
> Whatever goes to the tilth of me it shall be you!
> You my rich blood! your milky stream pale strippings of my life!
> Breast that presses against other breasts it shall be you!
> My brain it shall be your occult convolutions!
> Root of wash'd sweet-flag! timorous pond-snipe! nest of guarded
>   duplicate eggs! it shall be you!

Mix'd tussled hay of head, beard, brawn, it shall be you!
Trickling sap of maple, fibre of manly wheat, it shall be you!
Sun so generous it shall be you!
Vapors lighting and shading my face it shall be you!
You sweaty brooks and dews it shall be you!
Winds whose soft-tickling genitals rub against me it shall be you!
Broad muscular fields, branches of live oak, loving lounger in
    my winding paths, it shall be you!
Hands I have taken, face I have kiss'd, mortal I have ever
    touch'd, it shall be you.

Whitman's images, obvious as they are in one sense, are almost impossible to explain unless one recognizes that self and nature virtually disappear as separate entities as they meet in *between* subject
and object. From that meeting meaning arises.

Whitman quite clearly indicates, in Section 22, that meaning
emerges through meeting: "You sea! I resign myself to you also—I
guess what you mean." The earth, the sea, and his own body have
meaning, but it emerges, initially, in the transcending experience of
self encountering empirical reality. The fascinating juxtaposition of
knowledge and "live parts" in Section 25 comfirms this essential
condition of meaning-in-being that the poet discovers: "My knowledge my live parts, it keeping tally with the meaning of all things."
The antecedent of "it" is speech, but speech encompasses both
knowledge and live parts. That is, speech joins them by expressing
their relation, and thus it participates (as a symbol) in that reality. The
line ends with the "meaning of all things"—a cryptic indication that
the self-nature dialogue can yield the meaning of existence. Here,
too, Whitman presents himself as man and poet: the man engages the
world in a series of orgasmic touches that yield the meaning that the
poet discovers through his vision and encompasses in his symbolic
language.

Even though Whitman asserts, at the beginning of Section 26, that
"Now I will do nothing but listen," he goes right on talking, ac-
cumulating, and responding to experience. His device of listening
acts simply as a counterpart to the speaking in Section 25 and more
generally as a further extension of his exploration of the world
through his senses. The main flow of this part of "Song of Myself"
continues uninterrupted. For what he hears, as Section 26 develops,
functions as touch has all along and brings him to another point of
physical or sexual ecstasy that yields insight. All his senses, then,
somehow function as contacts—ways of meeting and merging with
the world—that yield, first, a kind of instant physical response, usu-

ally described with sexual imagery, and, second, some degree of transformed awareness. In sections 26–29, the pattern develops twice. The first orgasm occurs as Whitman listens to "the train'd soprano":

> I hear the train'd soprano (what work with hers is this?)
> The orchestra whirls me wider than Uranus flies,
> It wrenches such ardors from me I did not know I possess'd
>   them,
> It sails me, I dab with bare feet, they are lick'd by the indolent
>   waves,
> I am cut by bitter and angry hail, I lose my breath,
> Steep'd amid honey'd morphine, my windpipe throttled in
>   fakes of death,
> At length let up again to feel the puzzle of puzzles,
> And that we call Being.

As he comes out of the ecstasy brought on by the soprano, he recognizes ("feels") "the puzzle of puzzles"—"And that we call Being." He arrives "at length" at some form of cognition which emerges out of ecstasy.

In Section 27 Whitman turns back specifically to touch:

> I merely stir, press, feel with my fingers, and am happy,
> To touch my person to some one else's is about as much as I can
>   stand. . . .

He immediately relates the touch, and the excitement touch stimulates, to the discovery of identity: "Is this then a touch? quivering me to new identity?" He moves here toward another experience—similar to the previous one and to the apocalyptic experience of Section 5. As so much of the world presses in on him, touches and quivers him, he begins talking wildly; he loses control, and the floodgates open again:

> You villain touch! what are you doing? my breath is tight in its
>   throat,
> Unclench your floodgates, you are too much for me.

He pursues the sexual imagery into Section 29, but there he generalizes it into natural or fertility images. His ecstasy emits a "rain" from which "sprouts take and accumulate." The sprouts, of course, refer to the recognition or meaning emerging out of and because of the orgasm that occurs as self and world meet. Section

30 confirms this, for Whitman states there some of the "truths" revealed to him:

> Logic and sermons never convince,
> The damp of the night drives deeper into my soul.

He sees, in effect, the meaning of that which he has just experienced. The poem comes to another point of rest (Sections 30–32) as Whitman allows the new identity and awareness to take shape before another wave of experience begins that will define, threaten, and finally confirm the emergent identity of the poet. During this momentary pause and recovery, Whitman returns to previously expressed ideas, but now he stands much closer to full realization and confirmation than he did before. He reasserts, for example, his sense that traditional hierarchies which elevate one aspect of reality over another falsify existence; in Section 31 he also implies that one discovers the "eternal" or the "spiritual" only in the present, lived moment:

> I believe a leaf of grass is no less than the journey-work of the
>   stars,
> And the pismire is equally perfect, and a grain of sand, and the
>   egg of the wren,
> And the tree-toad is a chef-d'oeuvre for the highest,
> And the running blackberry would adorn the parlors of heaven,
> And the narrowest hinge in my hand puts to scorn all machin-
>   ery,
> And the cow crunching with depress'd head surpasses any
>   statue,
> And a mouse is miracle enough to stagger sextillions of infidels.

He refers, again, to his own very curious oneness with nature—

> I find I incorporate gneiss, coal, long-threaded moss, fruits,
>   grains, esculent roots,
> And am stucco'd with quadrupeds and birds all over.

And he re-emphasizes the relation to time and space he has consistently maintained through most of the poem. He transcends the conventional sense of temporal and spatial limits, and at the same time he recognizes a mythic or human continuity through them. He reasserts, in short, the awareness of the *Soul.*

In the movement of the whole poem the two climaxes in Section 26–29 amount really to one major surge that functions much like the apocalyptic experience of Section 5. That section flowed into the explosive outburst of recognition and experience which culminated in Section 15. Similarly the transforming experiences of Sections 26–29 flow into the triumphant burst of recognition in Section 33. This overall pattern closely resembles the particular movements within sections that carry Whitman into ecstasy and then from it to recognition. Although he arrives time and again at meaning through very concrete and at times quite sticky *being,* the poem does not simply repeat the same process, for each time the poet emerges he has advanced further toward self-discovery.

4.

That sense of totality and the new identity which has been forming for many sections hits Whitman with the same suddenness and excitement found in the initial transcending recognition he experienced in Section 5. He realizes that all he had anticipated, hoped, and experienced has been confirmed:

> Space and Time! now I see it is true, what I guess'd at,
> What I guess'd when I loaf'd on the grass,
> What I guess'd while I lay alone in my bed,
> And again as I walk'd the beach under the paling stars of the
>   morning.

The lines refer directly to the fifth and sixth sections, and in a general sense emphasize the structure and progress of the poem that I have been outlining. More specifically, the lines confirm the tentativeness and incompleteness of Whitman's early assertions. When he *guessed* what the grass meant—as he started to translate the vision of Section 5—he did just that—he guessed. In one sense, the word implies "I imagine" or "I suppose"; that is, Whitman suggests many possible and simultaneoulsy valid meanings for the grass. But he also *guesses* because he does not know for sure. In section 33, he finally does; he sees that what he "guess'd at" *is* true. Whitman seems to be aware of this himself as he cries "I am afoot with my vision"—as if he has not been before.

Whitman has moved *from* the largely Romantic self—the simple separated, monological man who stands apart from others and the world as a supposedly self-sufficient and complete identity—*toward* the dialogical self. In section 33 Whitman clearly identifies *with* others as unique, separate persons; he no longer absorbs the world to himself, nor regards others as simply extensions of himself. He participates in existence with others and thus no longer simply watches or observes the world. When he claims to be the man—to "become the wounded person," to "take part," and to "see and hear the whole"—he enters into the existence of others; he experiences the specific person and pain of another. His relation to others ceases to be monological as he tries to meet the other with the poet's own authentic being. By establishing a mutual relationship with the world and, then, with others, Whitman shows that the conventional division (duality) of the self and the world simply ceases to exist as the self and world meet in the in-between where each remains separated, yet where both share a certain oneness.

In Section 33 and the one following, Whitman's vision is both tremendously expansive and surprisingly intensive. Whitman dramatizes the expansive nature of his vision by emphasizing his continuing freedom from conventional time and space limits. The images at the beginning of Section 33 dramatize this emancipation by distorting and disrupting ordinary conceptions of the self in space:

> My ties and ballasts leave me, my elbows rest in sea-gaps,
> I skirt sierras, my palms cover continents.

Likewise, as he speeds through space and as he flies "those flights of a fluid and swallowing soul," he shows that space does not limit his vision. By becoming the clock ("I am the clock myself"), Whitman measures himself and his existence by a mythic or human time rather than by chronometric time. In effect, he humanizes time and he skirts space. He clearly is not confined to a particular realm, for he experiences a world (the totality of existence) through his awareness. He transcends time and space, yet he experiences that transcendence and he discovers his essential humanity within them—in the world.

Whitman presents this double awareness—he is truly both in and out of the game now, at a distance from *and* in relation to it—throughout the section by juxtaposing concrete (intensive moments) with metaphors suggesting escape from time and space. At one point he asserts "I help myself to material and immaterial." The structure of the sections and the line imply that he helps himself to both at the same time: he stands within time and space, yet transcends them—he lives in the material and there discovers the immaterial. In short, he discovers the meaning-in-being. But he does so only by existing in the world and by discovering meaning through it.

Whitman seems to have made it. He swallows all experience; he loves the taste; and he makes it his("it becomes mine"). Likewise, he reaches out to the world and becomes others. The meeting between self and world seems complete. He has arrived at a stage of awareness that confirms his guesses about the grass, life, death, and God. At that point he has escaped the limits of the Romantic self, and he has become virtually a dialogical rather than a monological man. But ironically, at this stage of apparent success and triumph Whitman steps onto a slide of imaginative identification that rapidly carries him to a point where "dull unintermitted pain" and suffering virtually overwhelm him and practically crush the transcending self that has just emerged confident and triumphant.

The slide begins almost imperceptibly in the last third of Section 33. Whitman is enjoying the great wealth and variety of experiences his vision encompasses and in which he participates. Up to now, the section has celebrated life, but in the last few episodes, before the line "All this I swallow, it tastes good, I like it well, it becomes mine," the poet turns to a battlefield, a ruined city, the drowned man's body, and the threat of death at sea. He seems, for the moment, simply to recognize that death and suffering do exist in the midst of life. So without being excessively naive or insensitive to pain, he can still savor the experiences he knows and dramatizes. With the next line, however, "I am the man, I suffer'd, I was there," the gesture becomes a slip, and his movement through suffering, pain, violence, war, and despair does not cease until they possess and almost silence him. Through the rest of section 33, agonies, indeed, become "one of . . . [his] changes of garments" as "I myself become the wounded person." For a time, actually, he assumes agonies as his only change, and that is the "usual mistake" he almost makes. His participation in the suffering, violence, and death of the world continues until he finally recognizes what is happening and shouts, "Enough! enough! enough!"

Throughout "Song of Myself," and particularly in Section 33, Whitman attempts to encompass all of existence. In effect, he *accepts* it all and that becomes the basis for discovery of the self-in-the-world. He has achieved, as well, complete openness to others as he imagines himself to be the other man. From the very beginning, my theory about Whitman's poetry emphasizes—and Whitman repeatedly recognizes—the potential hazards, as well as rewards, that total acceptance and complete openness hold. The danger, of course, arises from the possible reversal; instead of resulting in transcendence, openness may lead to exposure and subsequent despair. That is precisely what happens to Whitman. From an apparent *triumph* of identity he finds himself in the midst of a *crisis* of identity in which his very person is threatened, if not with obliteration, surely with extreme reduction.

There is no triumph in the last three lines of Section 36:

> The hiss of the surgeon's knife, the gnawing teeth of his saw,
> Wheeze, cluck, swash of falling blood, short wild scream, and
>   long, dull, tapering groan,
> These so, these irretrievable.

After those anguished lines, Whitman finally recognizes how he has slipped and how he is threatened, but he cannot yet control the dying, the suffering, and the victims crowding in on him. The situation differs considerably from the touches and the outsiders that overwhelm him in Section 28. There he reaches an orgasmic peak; here he falls into impotent depression. Before, the touches "quivered" him to a new identity and then to new awareness. Here the "outlaw'd" and the "suffering" threaten that new identity. He sees himself in prison, and he imagines that he walks handcuffed beside the mutineer. The usually garrulous Whitman becomes the silent one whose lips twitch, but do not really speak. He lies, for the moment, as a man and perhaps even as a poet "at the last gasp." He can do nothing but "project . . . [his] hat, sit shame-faced, and beg." The innumerable agonies he has put on reduce him virtually to nothing —to the utter despair of "I Sit and Look Out."

However, Whitman does not succumb to the disillusioning, terrifying, and depressing brute facts of life as he does in "I Sit and Look Out." In the poem "reality" has driven him to inaction and silence; "these sights on the earth" virtually paralyze him as he yields and makes the usual mistake. But in "Song of Myself" he refuses— "Enough! enough! enough!" He is stunned, but not quite helpless, and so he fights back. He knows that he cannot forget or deny the mockers and insults; instead, he must find a place for them at the center of his existence, for they have crowded in there and refused to be excluded. Whitman recognizes, at the same time, that he would indeed make a serious mistake (the usual mistake) if he dwelled only on "the blows of the bludgeons and hammers." So he resumes the "overstaid fraction"—he has given too much, almost all, to a part of the whole—and troops "forth replenish'd with supreme power." He recovers the new identity and direction he discovered in Section 33. It is a kind of supreme power because he has escaped the paralyzing abyss of despair and thereby has both earned and confirmed anew the confidence which his experiences have given him. In context, the power is supreme because Whitman has survived every possible challenge to his person—except, perhaps, the imminent threat of his own death—and he will meet no other in the action of the poem.

Whitman troops forth with a renewed energy and confidence that allows him to "force surfaces and depths" more fully and completely than he has before. He has dwelled too long on the surfaces, on objects and sensations, and on suffering and death. Now, however, he discards his partial vision as he resumes his attempt to see life as a totality—to discover the meaning-in-being. With his renewed confidence in both the world and himself, he once again can translate existence; he can resume his dialogue with the reader and with the "other" of the poem; and he can continue his efforts to revive and transform those who make the usual mistake either by succumbing to despair or by living an easy, but really desperate, life on the surface of existence. His song becomes a genuine song of all, and at the same time it continues to be a song of the self.

The self, however, has changed. He survives, yet he never blinks, in these final sections, the absolute necessity to recognize and accept the brute facts of existence:

Ever the hard unsunk ground . . . ever the trestles of death. (42)

Nor does he float off to some transcendental observation post where he need only notice or look at suffering and death. On the contrary, he still becomes the other man and continues to put on the agonies of the world:

Down-hearted doubters dull and excluded,
Frivolous, sullen, moping, angry, affected, dishearten'd, atheistical,
I know every one of you, I know the sea of torment, doubt, despair and unbelief.

But now he also speaks of the joys of experience. He has, in fact, become one of the world's citizens:

> This is the city and I am one of the citizens,
> Whatever interests the rest interests me, politics, wars, markets,
>   newspapers, schools,
> The mayor and councils, banks, tariffs, steamships, factories,
>   stocks, stores, real estate and personal estate.

How different this recognition from Whitman's earlier rejection of
the trippers and askers and the other "unreal" aspects of the city!
Although in Section 42 Whitman calls others to hear his message—

> A call in the midst of the crowd,
> My own voice, orotund sweeping and final,

—the real demand for openness and committment does not originate
with him; nor does it come from any traditional God or religion. It
comes, if anything, from the world, and Whitman both hears it and
responds to it through the dialogue in which he engages with that
world. He hears it initially because he trusts existence and is, therefore, willing to risk himself in it. He continues to respond to it and
to challenge others to do so too because he has survived, with his trust
intact, the psychological threats posed by suffering and death.
The call or invitation (the challenge, really) to join the poet on the
road or in the city does not simply demand that one lose himself in
the confusion of everyday reality—he must do that, of course; but the
real challenge and call demands that one break out of himself, encounter all that is in-the-world, and at the same time transcend it.
Whitman indicates, in Section 42, precisely what hearing and answering the call involves:

> Not words of routine this song of mine,
> But abruptly to question, to leap beyond yet nearer bring.

First, the listener must question his existence and, in effect, reject it
by setting out on the unknown, open road. That radical action indeed
carries him *beyond* the limits and conventions of his previous life; it
may even carry him *beyond* ordinary conceptions of time and space;
nonetheless, his actual direction is *toward* the world. He transcends
himself and the world (leaps beyond), yet that action brings him
closer to himself and to the world. He stands, then, quite truly both
in and out of the game and in and out of himself. As "one of that
centripetal and centrifugal gang," the poet "leap[s] beyond" yet
"nearer bring[s]"—he moves beyond, yet at the same time he moves
toward. Both Whitman's metaphors and my language expose the

inadequacy of a spatial language to describe the experience of transcendence. Logically, it seems to be paradoxical, but existentially it
is not.

By daring to answer a call, by risking himself in the world, and by
hazarding complete loss of his person, Whitman indeed launches
himself into the unknown, and he challenges others to follow him: "I
launch all men and women forward with me into the Unknown." The
poet speaks now with an unwavering confidence that one will discover form or union or plan, so he does not ask himself or anyone to
set out into a void or into a knowingly hostile world. Nevertheless,
danger and possible destruction remain as real possibilities. Mystery
continues as a condition of the open road. And the journey requires
the radical actions of first rejecting the secure life and second of
boldly jumping off "in the midst of the sea."

> Long have you timidly waded holding a plank by the shore,
> Now I will you to be a bold swimmer,
> To jump off in the midst of the sea, rise again, nod to me, shout,
>   and laughingly dash with your hair.

Whitman's song is no routine song. He does *not know* what is on or
at the end of the road, even now, ("I do not know what is untried and
afterward"), but he trusts. He can share the vision and journey, but
he cannot "give" it or teach it, for every man must involve and even
risk his own person:

> Not I, not any one else can travel that road for you,
> You must travel it for yourself.

As the poet traveled his own road, the garments of agony almost
smothered him; surely that possibility exists for any other who opens
himself fully to experience. Confidence indeed prevails, and the
dangers seem passed. But somehow the suffering and death remains,
and so does the possibility for making the usual mistake.

As he begins to explain himself in Section 44, Whitman refers
directly to the two time dimensions in which he exists as a person:
"The clock indicates the moment—but what does eternity indicate?"
He knows chronometric time, accepts it, and lives in it, but he has
suggested before that *he* is the clock, and he says now: "I am an acme
of things accomplish'd, and I an encloser of things to be." So as a
person and a poet, he joins past and future in the present lived
moment and thus sees experience as the *Soul.* The clock becomes a

man, no longer a mechanism. Time becomes human or mythic, rather than non-human. Whitman's images of space likewise dramatize his release from the limits of a realm or a particular place and from chronometric time:

> My feet strike an apex of the apices of the stairs,
> On every step bunches of ages, and larger bunches between the
>   steps,
> All below duly travel'd, and still I mount and mount.
>
> Rise after rise bow the phantoms behind me,
> Afar down I see the huge first Nothing, I know I was even there,
> I waited unseen and always, and slept through the lethargic
>   mist,
> And took my time, and took no hurt from the fetid carbon.

Whitman lives in the continuity of mythic time, yet he lives simultaneously "on this spot," at a particular place in history, as a self-in-the-world. He assuredly does "have the best of time and space"!

Whitman coalesces his relationship to time and space in a single, brilliant image of himself:

> I tramp a perpetual journey, (come listen all!),
> My signs are a rain-proof coat, good shoes, and a staff cut from
>   the woods.

The perpetual journey (a continuing process, not a state) and the raincoat neatly merge the walking trip of the historical man (the *I*) with the mythic journey of the hero (the *Soul*). In that image Whitman captures the intersection of *Soul* and *I*, of myth and history, of spirit and man. At that intersection Whitman discovers the whole man and finds essential existence in the dialogue of that complete person with the world. Thus he *can* say to any man or woman, "Let your soul stand cool and composed before a million universes," as his own soul or essential self does. The self stands before all existence, no longer divided or masked, but revealed. That is, it stands in-the-world, facing and meeting it, and at the same time, it stands over against the world, apart from it. In this situation the "million universes" maintain their integrity and objective reality, but they also become parts of the totality which the poet perceives and encompasses.

Whitman's trust in existence and his confidence that his dialogue with it will succeed become so great that he seems to anticipate a break-through to some ultimate "rendezvous" with "God." "My rendezvous is appointed, it is certain. . . ." The evolutionary patterns that develop in Section 44 and 45 even suggest this, for at the *end* of the process Whitman supposedly will arrive at some ultimate awareness of God. Nonetheless, the context of the poem and the terms of the two sections prevent such a simple explanation; Whitman's relationship to God is as problematic here as anywhere in his poetry. First, it is not likely that he looks forward to a permanent *state* of union with God because he has just insisted "there is no stoppage and never can be stoppage," and he is after all a product of the process and a continued participant in it. Second, he emphasizes a dialogical relationship with the "Lord": he speaks of a *rendezvous* when, in effect, they will meet on equal terms ("on perfect terms"); he calls God the "great Camerado" and "lover." The erotic implications, as well as the dialogue implied in the meeting, seem to reject any dualistic or mystic explanations of this self-spirit relation. Third, Whitman implies, in Section 48, that he sees as much of God as possible in any one present moment; thus, he is not curious about God and does not seem to anticipate an ultimate state of being with God:

> And I say to mankind, Be not curious about God,
> For I who am curious about each am not curious about God,
> (No array of terms can say how much I am at peace about God
>   and about death.)
>
> I hear and behold God in every object, yet understand God not
>   in the least,
> Nor do I understand who there can be more wonderful than
>   myself.
>
> Why should I wish to see God better than this day?
> I see something of God each hour of the twenty-four, and each
>   moment then,
> In the faces of men and women I see God, and in my own face
>   in the glass,
> I find letters from God dropt in the street, and every one is
>   sign'd by God's name,
> And I leave them where they are, for I know that wheresoe'er
>   I go
> Others will punctually come for ever and ever.

Whitman reads letters every day—they are there in the street or in men and women. His call, in other words, comes from existence; and he responds to it through his dialogue with the world. Therefore, Whitman's meeting with "the great Camerado" may well occur *as* he journeys and *as* he engages in his dialogue with the world. If so, his rendezvous with God is appointed for a place in-the-world. Still, the lines imply break-through, in spite of their context, and so Whitman leaves one with indeed faint clues and indirections. The "Lord" remains as problematic in "Song of Myself" for the reader as he no doubt was for Whitman.

From his new perspective Whitman can now return to death and, perhaps, explain it better than at any time before in the poem. In Sections 6 and 7—when he asked questions and guessed about the reality his newly found vision might illuminate—he suggested that "to die is different from what anyone supposed, and luckier," and a few lines later he says that a person "is just as lucky to die," even, as to be born. But the good luck was unconfirmed then, its meaning unclear. When Whitman begins taking on agonies as his *only* garment, death changes; it is not so lucky, for it threatens man with suffering, loss, and obliteration. Near the end of the poem, however, in Section 49, Whitman's transcendent point of view allows him to understand death more fully than he did either at the height of his untested confidence or in the depths of his despair. Whitman readily understands that he will die; he will not escape the "bitter hug of mortality," but that does not alarm him. Because of his *Soul* awareness he can also view death as something other than an end. He comprehends it as part of a natural and mythic cycle, as part of a totality which includes life as well as death. Thus, he can see that death gives forth life: "And as to you Life I reckon you are the leavings of many deaths."

He reinforces his sense of return and rebirth, still in Section 49, as he concentrates on death in a series of striking images. He knows but can say nothing

> Of the turbid pool that lies in the autumn forest,
> Of the moon that descends the steeps of the soughing twilight,
> Toss, sparkles of day and dusk—toss on the black stems that
>   decay in the muck,
> Toss to the moaning gibberish of the dry limbs.

Yet he continues to assert that he "ascends" (that life returns) out of darkness and death. Whitman sees death and life, darkness and day, the moon and the sun as parts of a single, seamless reality—and only in that sense are they the same thing: "the ghastly glimmer is noon-day sunbeams reflected."

Whitman's understanding of death presses on even further, however, although not so clearly and unequivocally. In the last few lines of the section, as in "Out of the Cradle" and "Lilacs," Whitman may be thinking of the death of a man as a personal fulfillment rather than as just a part of some vast, impersonal cycle. As a person, Whitman (or any man) "ascends" out of death ("I ascend from the moon, I ascend from the night") as a complete man because death is a fulfillment or completion of life; it provides the final definition or image of a person. At the same time, Whitman suggests that death brings him to the threshhold of mystery or spirit—he debouches "to the steady and central"—and unless one wants to assume a meaning for the line based on a particular conception, the line provides one of Whitman's *faintest* clues.

The emergence, survival, and transcendence of the confirmed, essential self reaches a climax in Section 50, for there Whitman distills the essence of the whole experience the poem has been dramatizing. He announces that which is in him—the self that has answered the call of existence and now stands realized before a "million universes." Although he claims he does not know what it is, he does know because in the last line of the section he translates the meaning of his discovery. First, he concentrates his transformation into a single image that suggests the physical reactions that accompany the "usual mistake" and the transcendence the poet finally experiences:

Wrench'd and sweaty—calm and cool then my body becomes,
I sleep—I sleep long.

Then he speaks directly to his readers and his comrades who have tramped the road with him on their perpetual journeys:

Do you see O my brothers and sisters?
It is not chaos or death—it is form, union, plan—it is eternal
    life—it is Happiness.

For chaos or death—for torment, doubt, despair, and unbelief—he offers a coherent sense of self and existence and a vision of the totality of experience. He does not offer immortality in any conventional sense, nor does he speak of a vision of unity that dispels all multiplicity and contradiction, or includes them as unreal shadows masking the true reality. For his vision of totality does and must contain multitudes and contradictions. So when Whitman announces:

Do I contradict myself?
Very well then I contradict myself,
(I am large, I contain multitudes.)

he indicates more than a Romantic's confusion, his own diversity, or
even a poet's ironic sense that he is a poet, not a philosopher. He says
directly what "Song of Myself" and many other poems dramatize and
reveal: Whitman accepts the illogicalities and contradictions in reality in order to find that new way—that dialogical way—of dealing
with the multiplicity and crises of existence.

The final merging of the self with the world takes place in the last
section, and with that action the poem reaches its last stage. The poet
presents the action in a series of extraordinary images of physical
merging:

The last scud of day holds back for me,
It flings my likeness after the rest and true as any on the sha-
    dow'd wilds,
It coaxes me to the vapor and the dusk.

I depart as air, I shake my white locks at the runaway sun,
I effuse my flesh in eddies, and drift it in lacy jags.

I bequeath myself to the dirt to grow from the grass I love,
If you want me again look for me under your boot-soles.

Whitman becomes part of the earth, and thus he emphasizes his
oneness with it: he emphasizes the point where the self and world
meet in the sphere of the between. Yet, in another sense, that world
constitutes a reality that is separate from the poet. The dirt, grass,
and sun exist, therefore, not as mere extensions of the poet, but as
separate, concrete objects. Similarly, the poet maintains his separate,
coherent, newly discovered identity even as he becomes the other
(when he effuses his flesh and bequeathes himself to the dirt). He *is*
there, after all, waiting for us as a person, as an "I," and not *as* the
grass or the dirt.

The specific images capture the self-world relationship that has
been developing in the poem, and they reveal the transformation that has taken place in the poet. As a dominant, ego-centric presence—as a monological man, the poet disappears for good at the end
by planting himself to grow from the grass he loves. Instead of presenting the reader with an immensely inflated Romantic hero, the
poet leaves him with a more genuine and complete self—a self living
in-the-world.

Index